RILKE'S DUINO ELEGIES

ROMANO GUARDINI

Rilke's
Duino Elegies

An Interpretation

Translated by
K. G. KNIGHT

1961
HENRY REGNERY COMPANY
CHICAGO

Translator's Note

THE original work from which this translation has been made
was published in 1953 by the Kösel-Verlag of Munich under
the title *Rainer Maria Rilkes Deutung des Daseins, Eine Interpretation der Duineser Elegien*.

Acknowledgements are due to the Hogarth Press for kind
permission to quote the whole of the translation of Rilke's
Duino Elegies by J. B. Leishman and Stephen Spender. Permis-
sion was also given to quote from the *Sonnets to Orpheus* (1936),
Later Poems (1938), *Requiem and other Poems* (1949), Hölderlin,
Selected Poems (1944), all translated by J. B. Leishman, from
Rilke, *Selected Works* (Vol. I, Prose), translated by G. Craig
Houston (1954), and from the *Notebook of Malte Laurids Brigge*,
translated by John Linton (1930).

References to the above editions are given in footnotes.
Quotations from the *Elegies* and from several of Rilke's poems
follow the newly revised text in Rilke, *Selected Works* (Vol. II,
Poetry) by J. B. Leishman, Hogarth Press, 1960. Where possible I have quoted from existing verse translations of Rilke's
poems, but in the case of one fragment I have given my own
rendering. I have also made my own translation of those passages from Rilke's letters which are quoted by Romano Guardini. The reader is, however, also referred to the *Selected Letters
of Rainer Maria Rilke, 1902–1926*, translated by R. F. C. Hull,
published by Macmillan, London, 1947.

CONTENTS

INTRODUCTION ✓

THE task of interpreting the *Duino Elegies* is not an easy one. These poems express the experiences and ideas of perhaps the most sensitive and subtle German poet of modern times. Rainer Maria Rilke's intellectual and spiritual horizon was broad. His life was full of undercurrents, inner tensions and hidden depths. We do not need to read his *Notebook of Malte Laurids Brigge* as autobiography. But Rilke's "Letter to a Young Girl"[1] and his comments to his French translator show clearly the importance of the *Notebook* for a proper understanding of his personality. It is a work which conveys some idea at least of the complexity, and also the constant vulnerability of Rilke's inner life.

This same poet who had things of such importance to say about the end of our own age was also a prophet of things to come. Whereas his *Book of Hours* can readily be understood from the tradition of the past, other works, notably the *Elegies*, refer to the prospects and perils of the future. No interpretation of these prophetic utterances can claim to be final and authoritative.

One other feature of the *Elegies* calls for mention. The experiences which inspired them were not only more profound and subtle than those which generally fall to our lot. To some extent, they were different in kind. Underlying the *Eighth Elegy*, for instance, there is an experience of life which is bound to be unfamiliar to the majority of readers. Rilke's 'Angels' only take on their full meaning if we can conceive of beings who are 'numinous' without being 'absolute'. Rilke's conception of love and death, which he himself regarded as a fundamental part of his message in the *Elegies*,[2] is quite remote from more normal notions of these things. We must also bear in mind the fact that his picture of life was coloured, to a far greater extent than is at first apparent, by his interest in the occult.

Finally, with regard to the content of the *Elegies*, Rilke confidently claims that they contain a message which is profound,

---

[1] See *Selected Letters of Rainer Maria Rilke, 1902–1926*, p. 323 ff.
[2] See Rilke's letter to Witold von Huléwicz of November 13th, 1925.

new and metaphysical or, to be more precise, *religious*. This
message requires careful exposition.

II

Rilke's work is highly relevant to modern Man. It reflects
hopes and fears, experiences of Good and Evil, and inner
searchings which are very much with us today. Hence the task
of interpreting the *Elegies* necessarily involves us in another
task which cannot be dismissed lightly—that of defining our
attitude to their content.

The various attitudes which have already been taken up
towards Rilke's poetry can be shown from a brief glance at the
last three decades. The *Elegies* first appeared in 1922. The
response which they evoked at first was one of sympathetic or
bewildered reserve. Then a small enthusiastic section of readers
began to show an interest in the *Elegies* which went beyond
any merely aesthetic appreciation. Most of Rilke's German
public continued to read chiefly the *Lay of Cornet Christoph Rilke*,
the *Book of Hours* or the *Life of the Virgin Mary*. But the smaller
circle of devotees recognized the *Elegies* and the *Sonnets of
Orpheus* as the work of the real Rilke who also expressed himself
in the *Later Poems*.

This new esteem for Rilke not only grew in proportions. At
times it assumed the character of a religious fervour, similar
to the enthusiasm aroused by the work of Stefan George or
Hölderlin's later Hymns and fragments. It grew to such an
extent that *any* criticism of Rilke was in danger of being ignored
or rejected out of hand.

Then there was another change of mood. Whereas after the
Second World War Rilke's poetry was extolled with almost
partisan extravagance, attention was now also directed to the
negative features of his work and personality. It may be added
that critics of his poetry were never lacking. The followers of
Stefan George, for instance, voiced their criticism with a
severity which can only be explained in religious or semi-
religious terms. They were like the disciples of one master
showing their hostility to another. But even within the ranks
of those who admired Rilke greatly and who devoted intense

study to his works there arose a new critical spirit. Their criticism was not directed only at isolated features of his writing, such as his treatment of words or rhyme, but at his view of existence, his attitude to life and religion, and the whole character of his poetry which was now felt to be ultimately very negative and disturbing.

It is perhaps not surprising that this reaction should have been called forth particularly by the *Duino Elegies* which sprang from depths of the mind which are apparently remote from anything in rational experience. Indeed the reader of the *Elegies* must try to imagine the poet being guided by a 'spirit' which presented him with images and ideas as he wrote. The *Elegies* thus differ in their profundity, and certainly in their content, from other poems which are more commonly inspired by personal or historical experiences. Their vision is like that of a dream in revealing hidden associations which we cannot see, perhaps because we do not want to see them, when we are awake. And if it is true that the poet, when he speaks from his heart, says something which concerns us all, then such poems as the *Elegies* throw some light on the processes and forces which surge up from the dark depths of history.

III

Evidence that the *Duino Elegies* are poems of the kind described above is given in the memoirs of the Princess of Thurn and Taxis and also in the letters which Rilke wrote from Muzot.[1] There was something violent and sudden—something almost dangerous as well—about the way in which Rilke wrote the *Elegies*. The inspiration came to him in a strange fashion while he was living in the castle of Duino on the Adriatic in 1912. Two of the *Elegies*—the first two of the cycle—were completed at that time.

Others, like the opening twelve lines of the final *Elegy*, remained fragmentary.[2] Further fragments followed during Rilke's travels to Toledo, Ronda and Paris, but then his muse fell silent. Knowing that the completion of the *Elegies* was of vital importance, he waited for his inspiration to return, but in vain. Then war broke out and overwhelmed him with its

[1] See *Selected Letters*, p. 352 ff.   [2] See *Selected Letters*, p. 353.

fatality. But he continued to feel frustrated by the first promise of inspiration which had not been fulfilled.

Rilke then decided to lead a strictly solitary life which was made possible by the tenure, and later the purchase, of the little castle of Muzot near Sierre on the Rhone. There, in February 1922, his inspiration returned with an almost elemental violence which compelled him to write again. In the space of a few weeks the whole cycle of ten *Elegies* was completed. Immediately after the last one was written he announced to the Princess of Thurn and Taxis: "All in a few days, it was an indescribable storm, a hurricane of the spirit (as at Duino), every fibre and tissue cracked within me—any thought of food was out of the question, God knows who fed me."[1]

Almost at the same time another work, the *Sonnets to Orpheus*, was taking shape in his mind and trying with equal urgency to find expression. He wrote to Lou Andreas-Salomé that the first twenty-five *Sonnets* had already been written as if "in the prelude to a storm". Thirty others were to follow.

A letter which was written later to Arthur Fischer-Colbrie (Dec. 18th, 1925) tells how Rilke bridged the gap of ten years which had interrupted the writing of the *Elegies*: "Here, where everything assisted me during my strict seclusion of the Winter 1921/22, the joints of my work, fractured in the year Fourteen, were knitted together again—something which I had almost ceased to hope for. The healing process was so gentle and smooth that a few weeks of devotion were sufficient for the whole cycle of the *Elegies* to take shape, as if it had never really been broken off, or had simply been benumbed in its separate fragments. For a man who had felt himself divided to his very depths by the dreadful pressure of those years into a *Then* and a *Now* which was perishing and irreconcilable with the past— for such a man to experience the grace of perceiving how, in the secret depths beneath this open rupture, the continuity of his work and his mind had been restored. . . . . this seems to me to have more than personal significance. For this gives a measure of the inexhaustible stratification of our nature. And how many, who for one reason or another believe themselves to be torn within, might not derive a peculiar consolation from this example of continuity."

[1] Letter of February 11th, 1922. Compare *Selected Letters*, p. 352.

Rilke's letters from Muzot show how close was the relation which he felt to exist between the *Elegies* and the *Sonnets*. To Witold von Huléwicz he wrote: "the *Elegies* and the *Sonnets* constantly support each other—and I count it an infinite grace that I was able to fill both these sails with the same breath: the small rust-coloured sail of the *Sonnets* and the huge white canvas of the *Elegies*."[1] *Sonnets* and *Elegies* differ in their origin, their form and in the mood or ideas which they express. But each work completes and throws light on the other so that together they form a larger whole.

IV

Rilke attached particular importance to the link between the *Elegies* and the *Sonnets*. As is shown by the letters which he wrote soon after their completion he saw himself in the position of a seer or prophet. He was convinced that he was the bearer of a message which had been "dictated" to him from a source which could only be described as 'religious'. He wrote to von Huléwicz: "And am *I* the one who can give the right explanation of the *Elegies*? They pass infinitely far beyond me."

He thus claimed more for his poems than the beauty or profundity of great literature. We might say that he claimed 'authority' for them. He wrote to Xaver von Moos about the *Sonnets*:[2] "To me they are perhaps the most mysterious and, in the way they were revealed and imposed on me, the most enigmatic dictation which I ever endured and achieved. The whole of the first part was written down in one breathless submission between February 2nd and 5th, 1922, without any word being in doubt or in need of alteration. And this at a time when I was already prepared for another great work and already occupied with it. How can one help feeling increased reverence and infinite gratitude for such experiences in one's own life. I myself am just penetrating more and more into the spirit of this missive which the *Sonnets* are proving themselves to be." In a letter which he wrote shortly afterwards to Clara Rilke he stated: "Where an obscurity remains it is of the kind that requires, not enlightenment, but submission."[3]

[1] Letter of November 13th, 1925.   [2] Letter of April 20th, 1923.
[3] Letter of April 23rd, 1923.

Rilke thus demands more from his reader than appreciation of the beauty of his verses or comprehension of great thoughts. His work does not require "enlightenment", but—Rilke emphasizes the distinction—"submission", in other words 'faith'. His own relation to his work is that of a prophet—an inspired vessel filled with the divine voice which speaks through him. He himself had to listen to his own words and "penetrate" them gradually.

This claim which Rilke makes is so far-reaching that the reader is entitled to ask whether or not it is authentic. Usually a claim of this kind is given an aesthetic interpretation as evidence of the poet's inspiration and faith in his own work. We respect his claim and acknowledge the significance of his writings. But this would not have satisfied Rilke at all, for his own meaning was utterly different. This is clear both from the way in which the *Elegies* were composed and from his manner of referring to them. It is especially clear from the deliberate contrast which he drew between the message of the *Elegies* and Christianity.

In view of the far-reaching claims which the poet makes for his work we are not merely justified—we are *obliged* to examine how far they can be substantiated. Such an examination might be made by direct application of the yardstick of religion. We might ask what relation Rilke's message has to man's quest for salvation, what new prospects it opens up to humanity, or how this message stands in relation to human experience as a whole, particularly in Western Europe, and so forth. The present investigation can only follow this course a short distance, for our criteria are primarily philosophical. The question to be answered here is not whether Rilke's message commands respect, but whether his pronouncements are true in themselves: whether his impressive account of life and death, of humanity and personal relations really corresponds to the truth.

An undertaking of this kind may be difficult to understand today. The author has already provoked a certain amount of criticism whenever he left the path of historical or aesthetic appreciation in order to make a philosophical assessment of poetic works—in other words whenever he was concerned with the question of their objective truth. The relativistic spirit of our age is not very tolerant of this approach to poetry. It tries to restrict our enquiry to such questions as *what* the poet really meant, *how* he expressed himself, *which* currents of thought influenced him—but *not* whether what he said was true. In other words it allows us to scrutinize the subjective truth of a literary work—to discover whether or not it is genuine in feeling and pure in expression—but not whether it is objectively true in reflecting the nature of Being.

This neglect of the truth which a work contains may be permissible in the case of poetry which is subjective in character, but *not* when the poet in question seeks to present a coherent picture of the world, and least of all when he has a message to proclaim. If the critical method we have adopted compels us to leave out of account the question of truth, we must not imagine that this is a virtue of the scientific approach. Paradoxically, it arises from a specifically modern sense of insecurity which makes us shrink from dealing with truth in the objective sense and restricts us to subjective experience and interpretation. And this is to misunderstand not only the nature of truth but also the very mission of the poet. For there can be no doubt that a poet's work expresses much more than subjective experience, unless of course he is by nature incapable of progressing beyond his subjectivity. But in that case his very deficiency will affect the character of his work, and this again is a proper subject for philosophical examination.

The problem may be put as follows. A poetic work is more than mere 'expression'—it is a *declaration* and the truth of a declaration is necessarily verifiable. This means that it must not only be sincere and authentic but must also grasp the nature of Being. If a poet says 'It is so', he has committed himself to a declaration and he is entitled to demand our serious attention. But he is also answerable for the truth of his declaration and the reader may test it by this standard.

In former times there was no uncertainty about the proper relation between poetry and reader. The idea would never have occurred to a cultured Greek that it was *not* permissible to question the truth of a poet's statement about human life or the gods. This is after all the established procedure in philosophical, if not in literary, criticism. The view of the Middle Ages was no different. And we can probably say with some confidence that no one today reading a poem naturally and spontaneously would assess its merit according to its aesthetic value alone or by its dependence on sources. The reader is bound to decide for himself that 'this is true' or 'this is false'. The so-called scientific approach, which deals solely with the form or the content of a poetic utterance as a phenomenon, is itself historically determined and open to criticism.

It is necessary to remind ourselves of the fundamental fact that the language of man is a vehicle not merely of subjective expression, but also, and primarily, of objective truth. It involves first and foremost the assertion that 'this is so', and only secondarily the expression 'I *feel* it to be so'. This holds good wherever human language is uttered—and particularly where it assumes the power and fervour of poetry.

THE FIRST ELEGY

Written at the Castle of Duino on the Adriatic in January
1912, about two years after the completion of *The Notebook
of Malte Laurids Brigge* and immediately after *The Life of
the Virgin Mary*

I

THE *Elegy* begins with a direct question:

> Who, if I cried, would hear me among the angelic
> orders? [1-2]

This opening line rings out like the culmination of an inner
struggle or a long meditation. The following account of its
composition is given in the memoirs of Princess Marie von
Thurn und Taxis-Hohenlohe: "Rilke walked up and down,
quite lost in thought, as he was very much concerned with
answering the letter. Then suddenly, in the middle of his
pondering, he stood still, for it seemed to him as though a voice
had called to him amid the raging of the storm: 'Who, if I
cried, would hear me among the angelic orders?' . . . He
stopped to listen. 'What is that?' he whispered under his
breath. . . 'What is that coming?' He took out the notebook
which he always carried with him and wrote down these words
and, immediately afterwards, a few more lines which came to
him."[1] Such was the state of mind in which this sentence was
written.

The atmosphere evoked is one of oppressed loneliness—one
might almost say of desolation. The poet is seeking protection
and companionship, and his first thought is that the Angels
might satisfy his need. Almost immediately, however, he feels
the impossibility of such an idea: None of the Angels would
hear him. They are much too remote and mighty to busy
themselves with him. Indeed—as presently becomes clear—
they are indifferent to him.

[1] Fürstin Marie von Thurn und Taxis-Hohenlohe, *Erinnerungen an Rainer Maria
Rilke*, Copenhagen, 1932, p. 41.

Moreover, even supposing that an Angel *were* prepared to meet him and embrace him in friendship, then the poet, far from finding friendship and protection, would simply be destroyed:

> And even if one of them suddenly
> pressed me against his heart, I should fade in the strength of his
> stronger existence.   [2–4]

The Angel would not destroy the poet deliberately or consciously, as if motivated by anger or contempt. Behaviour of this kind would be out of question for the Angel. Destruction would be rather the result of something intrinsic to the Angel's nature. His very "existence" is too much for man to bear, for the Angel is superior in 'Being'. We may define 'Being' as that quality, entailed by the act of existing, which is proportionate to the 'status' of the thing which exists. For 'Being' is not at all points equal. It means more than the fact that a thing really *exists*, instead of not existing. The higher a thing stands in rank, the more powerful does its 'Being' become. This means that there can be no communion between Angel and Man— and that there could not be any, even if the Angel so wished.

Before proceeding with our interpretation we must say something about this strange figure who is so significant in the *Elegies*—and indeed in all Rilke's poetry—namely, the Angel.

The Angel is first mentioned here at a point where the poet is seeking ultimate reality. And from a religious man—such as Rilke was—one might reasonably expect to hear the name of God. In *The Book of Hours* God's name would certainly be used. But not in the *Elegies*. Indeed, in the *Elegies* God seems to have become remote.[1] God is not repudiated and is actually named

---

[1] In a letter to Ilse Jahr dated Feb. 22nd, 1923, Rilke wrote: "But then Russia revealed herself and bestowed on me the brotherliness and darkness of God in whom alone there is real communion. And this was how I *named* him then—the God who had broken in upon me—and I lived for a long time in the antechamber of his name, on my knees. . . Now you would hardly ever hear me name him, there is an indescribable discretion between us. New expanses now stretch out where formerly there was proximity and penetration—just as in the atom which modern science conceives of as a universe in small. What was comprehensible now escapes us and is transformed. Instead of possession we learn the relationship; and so a namelessness comes into being which has to begin with God again if it is to be perfect and free from pretence. The experience of the sensibility is eclipsed by an infinite joy in everything 'sensible' . . . the attributes are taken away from God, who is now ineffable, and are given back to the Creation, to Love and Death. . ." *Briefe aus Muzot*, 1935, p. 185.

more than once, but he is not a living presence. More precisely, He is not the immediate goal of existence. We shall see later the strange way in which He has vanished from the field of vision. It would be correct to say that God, as an object of religious invocation, has been replaced in the *Elegies* by the Angel.

The angelic figure has an interesting historical development.[1] The Angels of the Old Testament are powerful and awe-inspiring, and, although these qualities are tempered in the New Testament, where Angels become more solicitous and friendly, nevertheless throughout the Bible the Angel retains a superhuman majesty and grandeur. Even in the New Testament the first words spoken by an Angel are "Fear not!"[2] In early Christian art this majestic quality is still there—in mosaics and romanesque painting. It was only after Giotto that the Angel began to lose some of his transcendental power and became sweet, playful and pretty, perhaps by association with child statuary of antiquity. It is true that the Angel recovered some of his lost grandeur in Grünewald's painting and, with certain reservations, in the work of El Greco and Rembrandt, but this did not affect the general diminution of his stature which took place.

The figure of the Angel took on new significance in the poetic work of Hölderlin. His "Angels of the Fatherland", who are heroes of olden times, confront us again as powerful and imposing figures, but they have no connection with the Angels of the Bible.[3] The same process of secularisation continues in the work of Rilke. He was deeply preoccupied with the figure of the Angel, and Angels appear frequently in the *Book of Pictures* as well as in the *New Poems* and *Later Poems*. In the *Elegies* they have an impressive rôle to play. Rilke himself emphasized that his Angel is no longer that of Biblical revelation. In the letter which he wrote from Muzot on Nov. 13th 1925 to Witold von Huléwicz and which is his own authentic commentary on the *Elegies*, he said: "The 'Angel' of the Elegies has nothing to do with the Angel of the Christian Heaven (rather with the angelic figures of Islam)."[4] It is true that

---

[1] See also Guardini, *Der Engel in Dantes Göttlicher Komödie*, p. 33 ff.
[2] *Luke*, I, 13, 30 etc.
[3] E.g. in the elegy "Stuttgart", Stuttgart edition, II, i, p. 89.
[4] *Briefe aus Muzot*, p. 337.

Scriptural images, fragments of Christian legends, and even theological concepts all left their mark on Rilke's imagination, but he intended to create something quite different. Perhaps we may assume that Rilke's Angel represents an attempt to think again in terms of *numina* or gods. The following lines occur among his French poems:[1]

> Si l'on chante un dieu,
> ce dieu vous rend son silence.
> Nul de nous ne s'avance
> que vers un dieu silencieux.
>
> Cet imperceptible échange
> qui nous fait frémir,
> devient l'héritage d'un ange
> sans nous appartenir.

Without defining more precisely the connection here between the Angel and God we may still assume that such a connection does exist. In the *Elegies*, at all events, the Angel is that being to whom religious invocation is addressed and before whom life is assessed and the world runs its course. The Angel appears whenever human life enters a crisis or attains fulfilment or reaches its limit.

The "angelic orders" will be discussed in connection with the *Second Elegy*. Here it is sufficient to say that they are related to the very old theological idea of the hierarchy. This is the pattern to which the world of Angels conforms, though the pattern itself is modified in the process of secularisation which the messengers of God have undergone.

To return to the text: the poet is impelled by his loneliness in the world to ask whether the Angels can offer companionship and protection. But the answer is negative, and the reason is given in that short sentence in line 7 which is also the opening phrase of the *Second Elegy*: "Every Angel is terrible."

Yet is this true? Is the Angel not really beautiful? Admittedly, but—

[1] "Vergers", No. 9, in *Gedichte in französischer Sprache*, 1949, p. 11.

                    For Beauty's nothing
but beginning of Terror we're still just able to bear,
and why we adore it so is because it serenely
disdains to destroy us. Every angel is terrible.   [4–7]

We are here reminded of the psychological phenomenon in
which a stimulus is first felt to be pleasurable, but later, when
it passes a certain level of intensity, becomes painful and ultimately destructive. Thus, according to Rilke, the Angels in
their grandeur are certainly beautiful. But their beauty is simply
the tolerable degree of the quality which they emanate. As soon
as this is intensified the rapture of beauty turns into the terror
of destruction.

Since the Angel is extremely powerful he inspires fear, but
he is neither malignant nor cruel. His purpose is not destructive
and he therefore preserves his distance from humanity. This
does not imply that he is concerned with man's welfare, still
less that he bears man any love. Man simply does not interest
him. The Angel stands above man at an immeasurable height.
Unlike man, he does not belong to this earthly sphere of life;
nor does he, like the dead, belong to the afterlife either. As the
Eighth Elegy makes clear, he moves in the larger universe composed of both these realms. The Angel thus stands for man at
the furthermost limit of experience, illustrating what an earthly
creature is *not*. It is appropriate to quote here a beautiful poem
written in 1913 and called "To the Angel".[1]

            Strong, still light upon the verge of Being,
            burning out into nocturnal space,
            while we spend ourselves in dimly-seeing
            hesitation round about your base.

            Destiny will never let us sally
            from the wandering inner maze below;
            you appear above our bounding valley
            like a glowing cone of alpine snow.

            Downward-dropping lees from your eternal
            happiness are more than we can share:
            pure divider, standing like a vernal
            equinox, between the Here and There.

        [1] *Later Poems*, p. 51; *Selected Works*, II, p. 290.

> Could we hope to cloud your clear sedateness
> with the mixture of our dim distress?—
> You, resplendent with all kinds of greatness,
> we, proficient but in pettiness.

The Angel thus represents the unattainable absolute against
which the finite nature of man is assessed—and also, be it said,
rejected. His position is one of unparticipating detachment.
From this olympian height he "disdains to destroy us".

In the face of this aloofness the only tenable attitude is that
of resigned acceptance:

> And so I repress myself, and swallow the call-note
> of depth-dark sobbing.   [8–9]

The idea of establishing communion with the Angel is not even
attempted; the loneliness becomes still deeper. We notice a
strange phrase in the above lines: "swallow the call-note of
depth-dark sobbing". One might consider this an appropriate
place for the religious act of prayer. Instead, the language of
devotions is replaced by words which belong to life on this
earth, describing the cry of one creature to another. The "call-
note" is part of a "sobbing", an expression of grief which is
shrouded in profound darkness; it is "depth-dark"—yet another
expression of abandonment.

II

There is thus no way which might lead to communion with
the Angel. The question now asked is whether any comparable
approach to other creatures is possible?

> Alas, who is there
> we can make use of? Not angels, not men;
> and even the noticing beasts are aware
> that we don't feel very securely at home
> in this interpreted world.   [9–13]

Here, as elsewhere in the *Elegies*, the verb "make use of" implies more than 'employing' or 'utilizing' as we might 'make
use of' tools or implements.[1] A number of different associations

---

[1] Translator's note: The verb in the original text is *brauchen* which has the two
basic meanings of "use" and "need".

are fused together in this question. In Rilke's sense it means:
With whom can we establish a vital relationship of giving and
receiving, a mutual association in which our need of companionship and protection would be fulfilled?

The answer is: with no one and nothing. Neither with the
Angel, nor with man, nor with the world. That is to say, not
with the "interpreted world", or the world as it is delimited
by our normal categories of thought, our purposes and patterns
of behaviour. In this "world", which we have made into our
environment, "we don't feel very securely at home", for we are
unsure of ourselves. And even the "noticing beasts" realize this.
This theme recurs in the *Fourth Elegy* where the assurance of
the animal is contrasted with our uncertainty; it occurs again
in the *Eighth* where the animal's "openness" differs sharply
from the 'closed' state of imprisonment which is typical of
humanity. The fact that we are not "at home" also implies
that we are unable to "make use of" the animals. Elsewhere,
in some of his finest poems, such as "The Panther", "The
Gazelle" or "The Flamingoes",[1] Rilke evokes that mysterious
self-contained existence of animals and the estrangement which
exists between them and Man.

> There remains, perhaps,
> some tree on a slope, to be looked at day after day,
> there remains for us yesterday's walk and the long-drawn loyalty
> of a habit that liked us and stayed and never gave notice.   [13–16]

The most promising relationship of which we seem capable is
with something encountered at random or by chance, and
where we cannot give the exact whys and wherefores. Where
there is no question of "making use" but where there is still
some kind of connection, however irrational its basis: a relationship which logically could not exist but in fact simply 'is'.

The thing concerned may perhaps be a "tree on a slope"
which we "look at day after day". This line probably refers to
an experience in Rilke's life. Somewhere there was a tree which
made an impression on him and stirred in him a feeling of
intimacy and trust. Later in his life, in Muzot, it could have
been the tall poplar tree which was so dear to him and which
was subsequently cut down by its owner without any real

[1] See *Selected Works*, II, p. 177 f.

reason—an event which seemed to Rilke like a portent. And "yesterday's walk" is still there too, for we have gone along it once and can repeat it today if we wish. Similarly there is "the long-drawn loyalty of a habit"—a habit which we acquired by chance when, like some fickle creature, it took up abode inside us and then would not depart. Characteristically the poem does not say simply that the habit 'remained' but that it "never gave notice". This phrase indicates the deep feeling of homelessness —the sense of not belonging—which underlies Rilke's view of life. He himself was never at home anywhere, nor could he provide anyone else with a home.

Yet perhaps there is after all something which "remains".

> Oh, and there's Night, there's Night, when wind full of cosmic space
> feeds on our faces: for whom would she not remain,
> longed for, mild disenchantress, painfully there
> for the lonely heart to achieve?   [17–20]

The Night remains. There is always a peculiar quality about the night as described in the *Elegies*: sometimes it is a time of magical transformation, sometimes a time of impending danger.[1] Here in the *First Elegy* it is the period of anticipation and disappointment simultaneously. The night returns again and again, but without offering any shelter. On the contrary as we stand by the window the wind blows past us, and it is "full of cosmic space", that is, open on all sides and thus the antithesis of home. Far from protecting us, the wind "feeds on our faces", taking something away from them as it blows past. Thus our homelessness comes to exert an active and erosive effect on us. We cannot help "longing for" the night since this is the time when man goes to rest and returns to the realm of the womb in sleep. But, besides being "mild", the night is also a "disenchantress" since it does not give man the sheltering depth which he might have hoped to find.

Now we might imagine that all this was only true of man as an individual, who standing alone, finds the night "painful"; indeed the very arrangement of the words suggests individual laborious effort: "painfully there for the lonely heart to

---

[1] See the *Seventh Elegy*, third stanza, and the *Third Elegy*.

achieve". But is it really true that the night only confronts us in our loneliness as painful?

> Is she lighter for lovers?
> Alas, with each other, they only conceal their lot!   [20–21]

The night is the same for the lovers too. The mere fact that they are together does not mean that they have found union and shelter in each other. They are really two separate lonelinesses joined together. The illusion of their communion merely prevents either from being aware of the truth.

Again we note a fundamental feature of Rilke's view of life which will be treated more fully in connection with the second stanza: the idea that there is no such thing as a love which enables one human being to find a spiritual home with another —any more than one can make one's home in a given country. We cannot even 'make use of' the person we love.

In the following lines an appeal is made to the personal experience of the reader; Rilke now poses the question which he is convinced must lie behind even the deepest experience of communion:

> Don't you know *yet*?—Fling the emptiness out of your arms
> to broaden the spaces we breathe—maybe that the birds
> will feel the extended air in more fervent flight.   [22–24]

At first these lines make strange reading. Since there is a barrier between one human being and another and even the most passionate embrace is fundamentally devoid of content, the poet now challenges the reader: Make the attempt, he says. Admit that your arms remain empty. Accept their emptiness and fit it into the cosmic space—that same space which enters into our very life when we breathe. Then perhaps the world will be transformed and the space which at present merely exists in it will be vitalised. In other words, by letting your heart receive the emptiness you will endow the space outside with "fervour" or spiritual depth. The very birds, creatures who are at home in space, will feel the change that has taken place around them; their flight—the purest expression of their being —will become "more fervent".

These ideas may seem far-fetched or fanciful. Yet they are part of Rilke's attempt to give a final definition to his view of life. Indeed this *First Elegy* contains most of the dominant themes of his thought. They are concerned with the relationship between the inner and the outer, the spiritual life and physical existence.

There would be nothing particularly novel about the idea that these two spheres are closely related. Nor would it be of great moment if Rilke simply stated that the confrontation of inner and outer was an illusion. But his intention goes beyond this. Rilke asserts that there are external things on the one hand and there is the inner realm of the human mind and spirit on the other; and these two spheres have a duty to each other. As he lives man should take up the 'things' into his soul and thus make them 'inward' or, as the *Ninth Elegy* puts it, "transform" them and make them "invisible". Only when he does this, when the things outside become part of his inner experience, can they achieve their full status. Man, on the other hand, must cease to guard his inner life jealously for himself. He must give it to the world. He can only do this by an act of self-renunciation, by projecting himself into the 'Open'—out of his own separateness and individuality into the whole.[1] In this way his inner self will become a part of external reality. The world will acquire an extra dimension and he will realize his true self, being now freed from the entanglement of the Ego.

So if Man notices that an inner loneliness or void accompanies even his closest intimacy with another person, he may, by accepting this emptiness and giving it back again to the world as a gift of love, endow the outer realm with some of his inner fervour. Rilke intends this, not as a subjective thought or feeling, but as an objective truth. The birds in their flight will feel that the "air" or cosmic space has expanded by acquiring that dimension of breadth which issues from the soul.

Rilke hopes, by giving a vital place to 'things' in our inner experience, to break down the barrier between it and the world. At the same time the world will become more 'spiritual' by man's gift of himself to it. Both processes represent an effort to impose on the world a new shape which is radically different from that of our immediate impressions. This is a world where

[1] Compare the *Eighth Elegy*.

the things outside and the soul within merge into a unity, since external reality is now enriched by an objective inward quality or fervour.[1]

This interplay of the two realms is anticipated in the very nature of the world. The wind at night was described above as "full of cosmic space". Underlying this description is the feeling we have of the night wind as something which comes from afar off and goes far away. Its very blowing brings with it a sense of vast spaces.[2] But Rilke means more than this. He feels not only that the current of air is passing through space, but also that it *contains* space within itself as an inner dimension. Movement, or Time, is a realization of Space, just as Space which has been realized contains Time within itself. A similar relationship is implied by a later passage in our text which states that we "breathe spaces". This means not merely that we inhale air from space, but also that we absorb Space into ourselves as the intrinsic dimension of air in motion. The air in each case—the wind outside and the breath within—holds spacial depth within itself.

There is a more profound and subtle account of this idea in the *Sonnets to Orpheus*:[3]

> Breathing, invisible poem! That great
> world-space, at each inhalation
> exchanged for this human existence. Counter-weight
> of my rhythmical realization. . .
>
> Of all these places in space, how many a one
> has been within me already. Many a wind
> seems like a son. . .

Finally, yet another inner dimension which Rilke attributes to space may be mentioned here. It is religious in character. The following passage is taken from the "Quatrains Valaisans" (No. 32):[4]

---

[1] This is the "deep Being" referred to in the letter to W. v. Huléwicz.
[2] Compare the 'Song of the Sea' in *Requiem*, p. 122:
> primeval breath from sea,
> that only blows
> as for primeval stone
> pure space
> rushing from realms unknown.
[3] *Sonnets to Orpheus*, II, i.
[4] *Gedichte in französischer Sprache*, p. 65.

Quelle déesse, quel dieu
s'est rendu à l'espace,
pour que nous sentions mieux
la clarté de sa face.

Son être dissous
remplit cette pure
vallée du remous
de sa vaste nature.

Il aime, il dort.
Forts du Sésame,
nous entrons dans son corps
et dormons dans son âme.

Here the god, or goddess, is 'dissolved' into space. And for those
who know the Sesame, the magic word which procures entry,
the surrounding space becomes the same as the divine essence.

III

Rilke's thought now takes a new turn. He has said that there
is nothing in existence which we can "make use of" in the sense
of assimilating into the unity of our life. The second section
of the Elegy reverses this relationship:

Yes, the Springs had need of you. Many a star
was waiting for you to perceive it. Many a wave
would rise in the past towards you; or else, perhaps,
as you went by an open window, a violin
would be utterly giving itself. All this was commission.

[25–29]

External reality makes demands on *us*. The demand may come
from the "Springs" in their yearly succession. Or it may come
from "a star". Here Rilke does not mean all stars, but "many
a star", i.e. those which, for one reason or another, attract our
particular attention. These stars demand that we "perceive"
them. The full meaning of this act of "perceiving", this absorption into our innermost heart, is developed in the *Ninth Elegy*.
The demand may come from a "wave" which rises up to us
from the past: some indefinable memory or sense of joy or

fulfilment which suddenly fills our being. Or perhaps we are walking along a street past an open window when someone is playing a violin. This violin presents itself. As it resonates it "gives" itself and seeks to be accepted.

Everyone has known experiences of this kind—experiences which are here defined as a "commission" imposed by the world. Later, in the *Ninth Elegy*, it is called the "urging of the earth" to find entry to the heart in order to become 'inward' and gain another dimension of reality. The meaning of Man's life lies in his response to this urging. . . But, we may well ask at this point, is it not a strange demand that Man should welcome *things* and help them to fullness of Being when we have just been told that he cannot welcome another *person*, and that Love as an I-Thou relationship does not exist? However, in Rilke's world 'things' have in some respects a privileged position over human beings. "My world begins with *things*," he wrote to Ilse Jahr, "and in it even the smallest human being is frighteningly large, indeed almost a monster of size." And again later: "I began with *things* which were the real confidants of my lonely childhood; and for me it was no small achievement to get as far as the animals without anyone else's help."[1] On the other hand the *Ninth Elegy* says expressly that Man, just because he is the most "fleeting" and transitory being, is capable of, and indeed commissioned with, the task of giving things their their essential reality.

All this constitutes a trust or "commission" which continually presents itself. Again and again something in the external world strives to attain full reality through the heart of man.

> But were you equal to it? Were you not still
> distraught by expectancy, as though all were announcing
> some beloved's approach? (As if you could hope
> to house her, with all those great strange thoughts
> going in and out and often staying overnight!)   [30–34]

Unfortunately Man does not perceive his trust; and if he does perceive it he does not collect himself for the purpose of fulfilling it. He is always "distraught by expectancy", always hoping for

---

[1] Letters of Dec. 2nd 1922 and Feb. 22nd 1923.

something for himself. He views every event, not as what it is
in itself, but as though it announced the fulfilment of his desire
—the most intense of all his desires—for the lover.

There is an implicit reproach here: You are only thinking
of yourself. You do not recognize your trust; you only make
demands. But in brackets there is also a parenthetic aside:
Even if this very thing happens and the loved one came, where
would you "house her"? You have no home for her, least of
all where a home should be, inside yourself. On all sides the
doors are open with "great strange thoughts going in and out
and often staying overnight". This is yet another image of
homelessness, but now referring to our inner experience. Not
only is Man homeless in the world but his innermost being is
not a home and therefore cannot shelter anyone.

How then is Man to set about recreating things within himself? Must he not first of all—as was implied above—make a
sacrifice of himself? This question assumes a still more urgent
form in the *Second Elegy*.

IV

What is to be done when a sense of longing stirs within us?
The answer is that we must learn self-renunciation and from
this sacrifice produce something great and worth-while:

> Should you be longing, though, sing the great lovers: the fame
> of all they can feel is far from immortal enough.
> Those—you envied them almost, those forsaken, you found
> so far beyond the requited in loving.   [35–38]

These lines might at first seem to mean that we should renounce
any longing for personal fulfilment, sublimating our desire in
a song on the theme of love—an idea which is familiar to us
from other authors: one of the basic themes in Thomas Mann's
doctrine of art for instance is that to be truly creative one must
make a sacrifice in terms of life. But Rilke does not simply mean
that the work of art is produced by a power which cannot reach
fulfilment in life. He is referring rather to one special kind of
love which should be celebrated in song, namely the love of
those who are "forsaken" and who are found to be much more
"loving" than those whose love was "requited".

For Rilke the true lover is not the one who finds fulfilment;
he is the one who remains unfulfilled but none the less continues
to love.

The great "commission" of those who seek to enter the realm
of true love consists in the praise of these lovers:

> Begin
> ever anew their never-attainable praise.
> Consider: the Hero continues, even his setting
> was a pretext for further existence, an ultimate birth.
> But lovers are taken back by exhausted Nature
> into herself, as though such creative force
> could not be exerted twice.   [38–44]

Since the praise of the lovers can never be "attained" or perfected it must be repeatedly begun afresh. For the lovers stand
at the summit of existence. But beside them stands another
figure—one who dominates the whole of the *Sixth Elegy*—the
Hero. Standing out by his deeds from the current of events the
Hero is preserved in the consciousness of posterity. Possibly the
underlying idea here is of the memorial statue—as history
which has been cast in durable form. Even the "setting" or
fall of the Hero is a step into permanence, for it is precisely in
death that his final shape emerges. This is his "ultimate birth"
—the last of a series of different births—i.e. all those deeds and
events which went to the shaping of his essential form. Now
his form has acquired perfection and reality. The reference to
his "setting" as a "pretext for further existence" means that
the Hero's "setting" was only superficially a 'cessation of
existence' or 'disappearance from view'. In fact it was the shell
from which his 'true Being' emerged.

The lovers, however, are in a different position. Their relationship is something which makes such claims on the vital
natural forces that Nature does not allow them any permanence
of form. She therefore re-absorbs them into herself in order to
use again the energy which went to their making. The same
"creative force" has to be used economically for the next, and
all succeeding pairs of lovers. Love is the most vital "exertion"
or achievement of "Nature". But the energy by which it is
created is, like a rare metal, only available in limited quantities.
When it has served its purpose in one work it is required again

for the next. Fundamentally there is thus not a succession of different love-relationships but only a single one.

It is on this account that the great lovers of history are in need of praise. One particular example is named in the *Elegy*.

> Does Gaspara Stampa
> mean enough to you yet, and that any girl, whose beloved
> has slipped away, might feel, from that far intenser
> example of loving: "Could I but become like her!"?   [44–47]

Gaspara Stampa was an Italian girl who lived in the XVIth century and died at the age of thirty-one. She was deserted by her lover, the Count Collaltino di Collalto, and in her grief wrote a series of poems which Rilke esteemed very highly. Rilke asserted that such lovers as she merited "praise", both for their own sake and for the example which they set, so that others experiencing the same grief might recognize and realize the possibility of rising above their destiny.[1]

To repudiate one's fate after being forsaken in love is, how-ever, only a preliminary stage. The path to greatness in love merely begins when the heart is reconciled to the loss of the beloved and still preserves love for him. Perfection is attained when there is no longer any desire for fulfilment. Here we are close to the essence of Rilke's doctrine of love.

At the end of the *Notebook of Malte Laurids Brigge* Rilke gives an unusual interpretation of the Biblical parable of the Prodigal Son.[2] It begins with the words: "It will be difficult to persuade me that the story of the Prodigal Son is not the legend of one who did not want to be loved." Rilke goes on to describe how as a child the Prodigal was loved by everyone around him, how he found this painful and shaming, and how he finally resolved "never to love, in order not to put anyone in the terrible position of being loved". We must bear in mind here that "love" for Rilke meant primarily the love which seeks to possess another person and to make him serve its own will. A

[1] The Princess of Thurn and Taxis recounts in her memoirs that while writing the early Elegies at Duino in 1912 Rilke was greatly concerned with this problem and wanted "to write something about the 'unhappy lovers'—the 'forsaken' " whose destiny touched him closely. Amongst them he mentioned Gaspara Stampa (*Erinnerungen*, p. 34).

[2] *The Notebook of Malte Laurids Brigge*, trans. John Linton, Hogarth Press 1930, pp. 235 and 238.

different kind of love was later to be revealed to him which he tried to learn. The passage from *Malte* continues: "he had loved and loved again in his solitude, each time with expenditure of his whole nature and with unspeakable fear for the liberty of the other. Slowly he learned to penetrate the beloved object with the rays of his passion, instead of consuming it in them."

Here love has taken on quite a different character, being determined by a "fear for the liberty of the other". This love seeks to "penetrate" its object "with the rays of passion", bringing it into a realm of openness and light where it can be free. And according to Rilke anyone who knows how to love in this sense finds "pure space" revealed to him.

At first all this might seem to be no more than a transition from the selfish love of the instincts to the more spiritualized love of the whole human person. But this would not be an adequate interpretation. It is true that genuine love for a person stands far above mere desire. The person loved is more than an object of selfish possessiveness and stands free in his own right. He becomes the "Thou" confronting and belonging to the "I". But in Rilke's view even the "I-Thou" relationship seems to be abandoned. It would be an oversimplification to repeat the criticism which has often been made of Rilke's view of love, namely that it evades responsibility for the other person and for society. Underlying his ideas on this subject there is something more profound—an experience and a demand which were doubtless connected with his inability to love but were also rooted in a fundamentally religious impulse.

At the beginning of his interpretation of the Parable of the Prodigal there is a passage which refers to youth's innermost secret: "But what he then desired was that inner indifference of spirit, which sometimes, of an early morning in the fields, seized him so unalloyed that he began to run, that he might have neither time nor breath to be more than a transient moment in which the morning becomes conscious of itself."[1] This "inner indifference of spirit" is clearly a religious love which constitutes, not a 'transitive'[2] *act* directed at a certain object, but a state or *condition* with its own significance for the created world around: in Rilke's terminology, the attitude of

---

[1] *Malte Laurids Brigge*, p. 235.   [2] *Malte Laurids Brigge*, p. 233.

C

Openness. In this 'Open' sphere[1] the "morning becomes conscious of itself" and everything created takes on an infinite
wealth of meaning. The same indifference to the object is
required, according to Rilke, in human relationships. The love
which conforms to this demand does not desire the other person,
nor does it scrutinize or judge him; it simply passes straight
through him. This means more than that such love is selfless
and does not trespass on the freedom of the beloved. It also
means more than entering into a purely personal and reciprocal
relationship of "I" and "Thou". Rilke demands that we pass
beyond even this stage, for the supreme importance of the
beloved consists in becoming a gateway to the realm of Openness. The "Thou" gives access to the "unobstructed path to
freedom".[2] Just as we speak of "selflessness" in love we might
here speak of "Thou-lessness", a state which is attained by
transcending, transforming and fulfilling a merely personal
love. When this has been transmuted into the "inner indifference of spirit" then the 'Open' realm is disclosed where all
things attain their fullness. It is through the other person that
this process takes place and this is precisely why the beloved
is of supreme importance.

The response which this love evokes should be of the same
kind: "How he would weep for whole nights with the longing
to be himself shot through with such rays. But a woman loved,
who yields, is still far from being a woman who loves. O nights
without consolation, when his overflowing gifts came back to
him piece-meal, and heavy with transience! How often he
thought then of the troubadours who feared nothing more than
to be granted what they asked", until finally "he no longer had
the hope of meeting the lover who should penetrate him
utterly".[3] Love should thus be returned in the same way as it
is given. It must be selfless for the 'I' as well as for the 'Thou'.
True lovers do not face one another as 'objects' of love. Each
is the occasion for the other's free act of love which leads into
'Openness'.[4]

---

[1] For a more detailed treatment of the concepts "Open" and "Openness" see
the interpretation of the *Eighth Elegy*, p. 211 ff.

[2] *Eighth Elegy*, line 4.   [3] *Malte Laurids Brigge*, p. 238.

[4] Some light is thrown on this train of thought by the letter from Rilke to
Annette Kolb written about the same time as the early Elegies—Jan. 23rd 1912.
Selected Letters of Rainer Maria Rilke (1902–1926), translated by R. F. C. Hull,
London, 1947, p. 200 ff.

The conclusion of the stanza states expressly:

Should not these oldest sufferings be finally growing
fruitfuller for us? Is it not time that, in loving,
we freed ourselves from the loved one, and, quivering, endured:
as the arrow endures the string, to become, in the gathering
    out-leap,
something more than itself? For staying is nowhere.   [48–52]

Our "oldest sufferings" have still not been properly understood
and still less have they been "fruitful". We ought to learn from
them what life's real meaning is. It "is time" for us to learn
this because it is something urgent and decisive in our whole
existence. There is almost a visionary note in the question "Is
it not time?" as if the present time, the *kairos*, were impelling
us to take stock of our situation.

A more detailed explanation of this sense of urgency is given
in the *Ninth Elegy* which expresses the distress which Rilke felt
in the face of the mechanisation of modern life. This always
remained something strange and alien to him. It is apparent
from the *Sonnets to Orpheus*, which are intimately related to the
Elegies, that he made serious efforts to take account of technical
advancement in his view of the world. Indeed, in several of
the *Sonnets* Rilke tried to deal with machines and technical
progress in an affirmative spirit, but without success. The *Ninth
Elegy* expresses his real conviction, namely, that technology
banished those true "images" which give life its meaning and
supplants them with rational and utilitarian forms. This is what
gives urgency to his exhortation in the above lines, that we
should receive *things* into our innermost being. It is time, high
time! Unfortunately, like symbols and things which grow, so
too the experience of great love is being lost in the general
levelling-down. Love, as a sublime "expenditure of the heart",
loses its meaning. It becomes debased and the *grande passion* no
longer exists. It is therefore time now to save what can still be
saved.

And how is this to be done? By "freeing ourselves from the
loved one" in our loving. The sense is clear from what has been
said above: we must learn not to let our love be attached to
the loved one, even though we endow that person with the
highest qualities and values. We must love so as to progress

beyond the beloved into the Openness of Being, reaching the
point where existence becomes conscious of its own pure reality.

This process is fraught with sorrow and peril. Whoever
endures it to the end does so "quivering" in the same way "as
the arrow endures the string". The arrow "endures" the string,
or more precisely the blow dealt by the released string, by
fulfilling its proper function and flying through the air. In
doing so the arrow is not passive but "gathered" and con-
centrated in the action. In its outward leap it becomes more
than it was when merely static and motionless. And we should
follow suit. Quite apart from the great trust imposed on us,
we should do so simply because there is after all nowhere where
we can "stay"—any more than the arrow, as an "arrow", can
stay on the string. It can only "endure" the string and "leap"
outwards.

At first one cannot help feeling bewildered at this strange
interpretation of love. Clearly its psychological roots lie in
Rilke's fundamental inability to establish firm personal relations—not unlike his other inability, mentioned above, to
attach himself to any country as his homeland. This is not the
place to undertake an analysis of these failings. Even if we did
we should probably only reach the conclusion that they
resulted from an inner weakness which caused Rilke himself
great suffering.[1] But perhaps there are no entirely negative
items in the accounts of the soul, for every deficiency points
to something which is potentially positive. Certainly Rilke
gained from this weakness an added sensitiveness to life which
he would otherwise have lacked.

This must not, however, blind us to the fact that Rilke's
view is fundamentally false. To love means to love *someone*.
Love is the most vital impact of one person on another. It is

---

[1] Referring to this in her memoirs Princess Marie von Thurn und Taxis is
clearly aware that she is touching here on Rilke's greatest sorrow: "And in Paris
he had to undergo yet another painful experience. He knew that he could rely
on my deep friendship and spoke freely of this deep wound which pained him so
bitterly. Love—the great Love—which he admired so much in others was something which he felt himself incapable of ever feeling properly. A moment of joy,
inspiration and fiery passion—and then complete disillusionment, revulsion and
flight." *Erinnerungen*, p. 71. See also below, p. 113 f. and M. v. Hattingberg, *Rilke
und Benvenuta*, 1947, esp. pp. 219 ff.

in the relationship of love that the "Thou" comes to life in the loved person, just as the "I" or "Ego" comes to life in the lover, and without this mutual 'I-Thou' relationship there is no love. Although we may recognize and even admire the way in which Rilke turned his inner deficiency to good account, we still cannot escape the conclusion that he lost sight of the essential meaning of love. And with it he also missed something decisive in the meaning of life. For a life which lacks the 'I-Thou' relationship—like a double focal point in the ellipse of existence—is no longer true to itself. An inner vacuity is created which manifests itself in relation to everything else: to things, to destiny and, as will be seen later, to God.

V

Voices, Voices! Hearken, my heart, [53]

The "commission" referred to previously (line 29) is everywhere proclaimed by voices—the voices of things and events. The "commission" is that of transformation through the heart. The heart has to hearken and obey.

The world of Rilke's great poems is fashioned partly by his far-seeing sensitive eye, but even more by his ear. The *Elegies* have the same roots as the *Sonnets to Orpheus* and, in Rilke's words, Orpheus is the "singing god". In Sonnet v of the First Part we read "Once and for all, it's Orpheus when there's song". He is the *numen* of the world heard as sound. Sonnet 1 expresses this with daring boldness:[1]

> A tree ascending there. O pure transcension!
> O Orpheus sings! O tall tree in the ear!
> All noise suspended, yet in that suspension
> what new beginning, beckoning, change, appear!
> Creatures of silence pressing through the clear
> disintricated wood, from lair and nest;
> and neither cunning, it grew manifest,
> had made them breathe so quietly, nor fear,
> but only hearing. . .

The world evoked here contains things which exist simply by virtue of being sung—as structures of sound. A tree rises up;

[1] *Selected Works II*, p. 253.

but the tree is the singing of Orpheus and thus a "tall tree in the ear". The animals which are encountered in this world are made "of silence". Their movements, their behaviour and the stillness and mystery of their nature spring, not from "fear" but "only hearing". With this the image is complete: the orphic world is made up not merely of song, but of the hearkening ear as well—the world which is sung and heard.

The Second Sonnet carries the line of this poetic vision still further:

> And almost maiden-like was what drew near
> from that twin-happiness of song and lyre,
> and shone so clearly through her spring attire,
> and made herself a bed within my ear.

The creature described here is "almost maiden-like"—a mysterious, gentle, ethereal being and a poetic embodiment of the world's orphic character. She takes up her dwelling "within my ear". And then this existence in the ear, as something sung and heard, passes over into an even more mysterious form—that of 'existence in sleep':

> And slept in me sleep that was everything:
> the trees I'd always loved, the unrevealed,
> treadable distances, the trodden field,
> and all my strangest self-discovering.
>
> She slept the world. O singing god, and stayed,
> while you were shaping her, with no desire
> to wake, and only rose to fall asleep?
>
> Where is her death? Oh, shall you find this deep
> unsounded theme before your song expire?
> Sinking to where from me? . . . Almost a maid. . .

Sleep is here conceived of as an intensified form, as it were, of acoustic or orphic experience. An analysis of this relationship would take us a long way. We might, for instance, recall how Hölderlin says of his "God of the Golden Age" in one of the odes that although he had been all-powerful he was not "called by name"; he was "effortless" and yet "greater" than Zeus— the *numen* of the primeval state in which all things were one. And even today, according to Hölderlin, this unity can be felt "in the heart" as "something vital". What was "fashioned" by the later deity, Zeus, then "sets" and passes away, while "shifting Time slumbers in its cradle". According to another variant of the text Time "returns to its cradle" and "disappears" in the timelessness and shapelessness of primeval and unconscious Being. . . Orpheus too is a *numen* of unity; or perhaps it would be more accurate to say 'of the unifying process', of the transition from the Many to the One, of transfiguration. The fifth Sonnet states explicitly that "this is Orpheus" wherever something is in a state of transition. Thus Sleep too belongs to this world. Hölderlin might perhaps have said that it is Orpheus who leads from Jupiter to Saturn.

So the definition of Orpheus is developed still further. First he was the world in its aspect of sound—the "singing god". Now he is the world of change and transformation. He stands at the point of transition from one shape to another. More precisely, he represents the world as it constantly plunges into "deep Being"[1]—out of confinement into the realm of 'openness', out of the separation of forms into unity.

But since this process of union takes place through the heart Orpheus also stands on the frontier between the realm of the heart and that of external things. As will be seen later, he is also encountered at that other decisive transition between the living and the dead. The sixth Sonnet states:

> Does he belong here? No, his spreading
> nature from either domain has sprung.
> Withes would they weave in a cunninger wedding,
> hands to which roots of the willow had clung.

Orpheus then is the guide who leads the way across from the realm of "withes" or "boughs", i.e. the upper world of light, to that of the "roots" in the dark earth. But the boughs and roots referred to here belong to the willow, the tree of grief and mourning, and this same Orpheus had the power to enter the Underworld and return from it. In this profoundly orphic world the heart must "hearken" if it is to learn of that transformation which is its trust.

There is a model for this in the Saints. The heart is therefore counselled to "hearken".

---

[1] See below, pp. 211 f. and 220.

                                                 as only
    saints once hearkened: so, that the giant call
    lifted them off the ground; they, though, impossibles,
    went on kneeling and paid no heed:
    such was their hearkening.   [53–57]

We are here confronted with yet a third form of superior being.
The first was the Lover, the second the Hero. The third is the
Saint. The essential character of the Saint is seen here in the
fact that he "hearkens" while he is kneeling. He listens in piety
and devotion. And what he hears is the "giant call"—this and
nothing else. Precisely what this call means for him is stated a
little later: it is "God's voice", this being the first of three
passages in the *Elegies* where God is mentioned by name.

God is present in the background of the *Elegies* but hardly
breaks through into the text. Whereas Rilke spoke repeatedly
to Him and of Him in the *Book of Hours*, this is no longer so in
the *Elegies*. It is clear from the letter to Ilse Jahr quoted above
how the relationship has altered. Now there is a great "reti-
cence". God has, as it were, shifted his dwelling—whither he
has gone remains to be said. It is the Angel who is now addressed directly, who provides the measure of things and who
gives Man his bearings. The Saints, by contrast, were orientated
straight towards God. They heard his call directly and surrendered themselves to Him.

What now follows, like so many things that Rilke says, can
only be understood aright if we imagine an earlier Christian
experience that has been transposed into secular terms. The
Saints "kneeled" as they listened—i.e. they prayed. And so
forcefully did the call of God strike their innermost being that
it "lifted them off the ground". Here a specific phenomenon
of mystical experience is meant, namely levitation. The person
seized by an ecstasy is raised aloft, but "goes on kneeling" in
the air. If we leave aside here the precise meaning of such
phenomena it remains true that they have been described by
both hagiographers and artists.[1] So here Rilke is not saying
that the Saint who listens to the voice of God is *spiritually* lifted
up, but *physically*, even though he himself is not aware of this,
so completely is he absorbed by the divine. Because the Saint

---

[1] For numerous examples see *Actus Beati Francisci et sociorum eius*, ed. Sabatier
(1902).

experiences something which normally 'cannot be' he is said here to be "impossible".

Here again we come to a point in the *Elegies* where the question of truth must be posed. Why did Rilke write of Christ and Christianity in downright blasphemous tones as if they were not only obsolete but even despicable?[1] Why did he avow an "almost rabid anti-Christian attitude"? Why did he declare in his letter to Witold von Huléwicz, already referred to, that he was "withdrawing more and more passionately from everything Christian"[2]—and still make repeated use of Christian concepts and figures in his poetry? Can words or images or statements which have a specific meaning be taken *merely* symbolically? Can they be divorced from their roots, secularized or made into myths when very many people to-day still believe these same words and images to be strictly true and act in accordance with them?

This question will have to be raised again more than once. To answer it will, however, do no more than disclose the deep ambiguity of Rilke's religious position. It remains a fact that of those works collected together in the volume of *Later Poems*, some of which were inspired at the same period as the *Elegies*, *thirty-five* deal with Biblical themes. While in Duino Rilke also wrote his *Life of Mary*, and of the *New Poems* already published nearly thirty deal with Christian or Biblical themes. This is also true of eight poems in the *Book of Images*. So if the reader takes seriously the various statements in Rilke's letters he cannot help being bewildered by the *Life of Mary* and the *Later Poems*. Is this satisfactory? It may not be of much account to the reader whose interest is purely aesthetic or historical. But if the reader knows something of the meaning and import of Biblical revelation, and especially if he believes in it, then Rilke's way of treating revealed truth must seem very disturbing. We cannot help calling to mind what was said above about Rilke's inability to achieve personal relations.

The Saint, then, is to be a model. Not a model to be imitated directly, for that would be impossible:

[1] Letter from Ronda to Princess Marie von Thurn und Taxis-Hohenlohe of Dec. 17th 1912.   [2] Nov. 13th 1925.

> Not that you could bear God's
> voice, by a long way.   [57-58]

We cannot hear the voice of God in the same way as the Saint.
We could not bear it. Perhaps we may enlarge on this idea in
the sense of the *Elegy* by saying that God's voice would be
"destructive" in quite a different way from that of the Angel.

There is no need of special proof to show that the God spoken
of by Rilke is not the God to whom the "saints" listened. They
were addressed by the Living God of Revelation. They stood
in a direct relationship of prayer to Him, and in His service
they were consumed by the fire of love and sacrifice. They
would have rejected Rilke's God with their whole being. Since
we cannot refer here to all the writings of Suso, Tauler, Ruys-
broeck, Angelo da Foligno (whom Rilke admired so much),
Theresa of Avila and many others who really knew God, let a
sentence from the opening of St. Augustine's *Confessions* be given
instead. Speaking of the recognition and invocation of God he
insists that this must take place under the protection of Revelation. Otherwise it might come about that the supplicant
"invoked another in the place of the one he intended—and
without knowing it" (I.i).

Rilke's 'God' might very possibly be this other, against whom
the Saints would have made every effort to preserve themselves.

> But hark to the suspiration,
> the uninterrupted news that grows out of silence.   [58-59]

What we are meant to hear is the "suspiration". This alludes
to something which is apparent but has no form, something
which we can recognize without being able to identify it.
Probably Rilke means the summons which comes from the
realm of Being—the summons to the heart to embrace things
and transform them. We might equally well say: the summons
of Orpheus.

The words are arresting. Everywhere there is a flow of "news"
which is produced "out of silence". This is the silence of things
which we hear imposing their trust on us, even though they
do not speak; perhaps a silence which lies *behind* the things
themselves—that of original Being.

Then something particular detaches itself from this general "suspiration"—

> Rustling towards you now from those youthfully dead.   [60]

Rilke's concern for the youthful dead is mentioned in the *Memoirs* of the Princess of Thurn and Taxis. She tells us that while at Duino Rilke believed that he sensed the proximity of three members of her family who had died young.[1] Probably a similar experience provided the ground from which sprang memorial poems such as the "Requiem for a Friend".[2]

Rilke was deeply touched by the fate of all those who perished in youth—not just those whom he knew personally—since, in his view, they still belonged to the totality of Being.

> Whenever you entered a church in Rome or in Naples
> were you not always being quietly addressed by their fate?
> Or else an inscription sublimely imposed itself on you,
> as, lately, the tablet in Santa Maria Formosa.   [61–64]

Rilke felt their proximity inside churches—specifically at "Rome and Naples". This is clearly a reference to highly personal experiences.[3] He also mentions his discovery of an inscription which "sublimely imposed itself" on him, so impressed was he by its solemn dignity. Perhaps this refers to the visit which he made with the Princess of Thurn and Taxis[4] to the Church of Santa Maria Formosa. The church stands in a little square in Venice and beside the right side-altar there is a Latin inscription on the wall. The translation is as follows: "While life lasted I lived for others; now, after death, I have not perished, but in cold marble live for myself. I was Hermann Wilhelm. Flanders mourns for me. Adria sighs for me, poverty calls for me. He died on the 16th September 1593."

Perhaps this was the inscription which made such an impression on Rilke—dedicated to a man whom Rilke imagined as young, who lived first for the world, but who now lies alone in the silent chamber of Death, cut off from the confusion of earthly things.

---

[1] *Op. cit.* pp. 44–46. See also the significant references to experiments in automatic writing with a planchette (p. 60 ff. and frequently in his correspondence).
[2] See *Requiem and other Poems*, translated with an Introduction by J. B. Leishman.
[3] *Erinnerungen*, p. 24.
[4] *Erinnerungen*, p. 17 f.

But what kind of "commission" or trust is this?

What they require of me? that I should gently remove
the appearance of suffered injustice, that hinders
a little, at times, their purely-proceeding spirits.   [65–67]

There is an "appearance of suffered injustice" in the life of
one who died young. It is not a real injustice, for in Rilke's
philosophy death is not considered as something fearful. There
remains, however, an "appearance" of such injustice in the
fact that the young person was not able to fulfil himself in life.
This, according to Rilke, is what "hinders" the existence of
the dead. There is a faint echo here, in intellectualized terms,
of the old superstition that the dead have a grudge against
the living.

It is this apparent injustice which prevents the spirits from
"proceeding purely"—words which anticipate an idea to be
developed more fully in the *Fifth Elegy*. Here they simply mean
that something is still not in order and that the person who
sees the tablet is charged with the task of setting it to rights.
In the context of the *Elegy* the implication is that he must take
into his very heart the destiny of the young man who died.
Perhaps we shall not go far wrong in assuming that here, as
with so many of Rilke's ideas, an element of Catholic doctrine
has been translated into secular terms: the belief, namely, that
after death the human soul has need of purification, and that
the dweller on earth is linked with those who have departed
in such a way that he can help them by his faith and love.

VI

The next stanza heightens the sense of the mystery which
surrounds the existence of the dead:

True, it is strange to inhabit the earth no longer,
to use no longer customs scarcely acquired,
not to interpret roses, and other things
that promise so much, in terms of a human future;
to be no longer all that one used to be
in endlessly anxious hands, and to lay aside
even one's proper name like a broken toy.
Strange, not to go on wishing one's wishes. Strange,
to see all that was once relation so loosely fluttering
hither and thither in space.   [68–77]

The opening words—"True, it is strange"—prepare us for a meditation. The dead are those who "no longer inhabit the earth", who no longer belong to the realm of existence as we know it. What can it be like to be as they are? What does it mean "to use no longer customs scarcely acquired"? Those who die young have scarcely had time to "acquire customs" because their stay on earth was short. Apart from this, life itself is essentially "short" because it is transient. And yet, amid this very transience, the spirit goes on living with an intimation of intransience and immortality. So Death always comes too soon, before the dying man has had time to acquire the "customs" of the earth.

The word "customs" in the above passage is equivalent to the *ways* in which man deals with people and things—ways of giving reality to the shapes of earthly life from which the dead are precluded. For instance the dead can no longer use the greeting by which living men communicate with one another; the dead have no further use for the tools or implements by which we assert our mastery over things. Thus, from our point of view the dead stand beyond Time and Space, purpose, society, etc.[1]

The dead no longer "interpret roses, and other things that promise so much, in terms of a human future". The word "customs" here seems to take on a subtler meaning. It now includes the way in which man establishes a link between the things around him and the *meaning* of his own life, namely, in his use of symbols. The specific example given by Rilke is the rose, a flower which in fact has a deep symbolic meaning in his own poetry.[2] The dead stand in the same relation to the

---

[1] Compare also the poem "Soul in Space", *Late Poems*, p. 94, which contains an effective description of the 'lost' condition of the soul when it has just been released from the body.

[2] Cf. *Sonnets to Orpheus*, I. v; II. vi and xxi. See also the "Rose Bowl" in *Requiem*, p. 109 and "Les Roses" in *Gedichte in französischer Sprache*, p. 71 ff. The importance of the rose for Rilke is particularly evident in the epitaph which he composed for his own gravestone in the cemetery at Raron: "Rose, oh pure contradiction, delight of being no one's sleep under so many lids." This epitaph describes the rose as "pure contradiction", i.e. consisting entirely of contradiction. Rilke is referring here to the position of one rose-petal on top of another, like the closed eye-lid over the eye of a sleeper. But whereas in human sleep there is always a person sleeping, here there are only lids closed in sleep, but no one to 'perform' the act of sleeping. Properly speaking one could only say that "there is a sleeping in the rose". This "contradiction" is the mystery of the rose—a deep symbol in Rilke's view of life.

According to Rilke's account of love fulfilment is attained when the lover pro-

rose as to "other things that promise so much in terms of a human future".

The dead person is no longer the same as he was in the care of people who loved him—"in endlessly anxious hands". He must even "lay aside his proper name" which has now become meaningless, like a child's "broken toy". Not merely has he lost his identity with his former self. He is no longer a "someone" at all, in the sense of being a person, for his name, or personality, has been "laid aside". So the dead person is merely a place where the world was experienced—a passing vibration in the cosmic rhythm. The line which follows says the same thing in a different way: the dead person has ceased to have "wishes". At the end of the *Fifth Elegy* the dead are described as "unmurmuring" because they lack sounds and words, or anything which can be put into words. The *Tenth Elegy* describes the existence of the dead as "soundless fate".

To sum up: the dead have cast off "all that was once relation", all the meaningful relationships which existed between things and events on earth. These relationships are now like bonds which no longer have anything to tie, or garments in which there is no longer a body. They "flutter loosely in space" —an effective description of an existence which is utterly different from our own, implying both fulfilment on the one hand and, on the other, deprivation of all those things which are familiar to us on earth.

The sentence which follows now becomes understandable:

> And it's hard, being dead,
> And full of retrieving before one begins to perceive
> a little eternity.   [77–79]

"Being dead is hard". It requires effort for the dead to fulfil their existence. The method must be learnt and it is "full of retrieving". Ideally the condition of death should grow out of this earthly life like a ripe fruit. But this is not so in fact. On

---

jects his love beyond the person, without an object into 'Openness'. In the *Fourth Elegy* (see below, p. 115 ff.) he says that man can only see his life aright when he manages to exclude his own ego and to look at himself simply as a puppet with which an Angel is playing. In the epitaph of the rose sleep is perfect when it simply *is*, i.e. when it is no longer attached to a person. See also the introductory note to the poem "Cimetière" from the "Carnet de Poche": "Est-ce de toutes ses pétales que la rose s'éloigne de nous? Veut-elle être rose-seule, rien-que-rose? Sommeil de personne sous tant de paupières." (*Gedichte in französischer Sprache*, p. 95.) This expresses the same idea.

the contrary a great deal is omitted or neglected on earth which
has to be made up for afterwards. This too must be counted as
part of that "hindrance" referred to at the close of the preceding
stanza.

This idea has an intimate connection with Rilke's own life.
He himself knew the significance of unresolved conflicts in
childhood from personal experience.[1] Psycho-analysis of course
aims precisely at probing out what has not been resolved in a
person's life in order to effect a cure. And it is significant that
Rilke actually had the idea of submitting to analysis, but then—
probably just as well for his poetry—gave the idea up.[2] This
is probably not unrelated to the concept of "retrieving" in the
above context.

In order to adjust himself to his new state the dead person
must first retrieve the unfulfilled and unrealized. Only then
can he "begin to perceive a little eternity". Here once more
we detect the influence of a Catholic idea which was naturally
very familiar to the poet, namely that of purification in the
after-life, though the terms he uses are secularized.[3]

Then, however, as if he had said sufficient about the divisions
between life and death, Rilke again shows that he is primarily
concerned with the unity of the world:

> All of the living, though,
> make the mistake of drawing too sharp distinctions. [79–80]

That is, they "draw too sharp distinctions" between the condition of the living and the dead: between—as is stated later—
this and that "other relation", the Here and the Hereafter.

Both, according to Rilke, belong to the same realm. Both
are of the same Being. In his letter to Huléwicz he wrote:
"*Affirmation of life and of death prove to be* ONE *in the Elegies* . . . . . .
Death is the *side of life* which is turned away from us and which
we cannot illumine: we must seek to achieve the maximum
possible consciousness of our being which is at home in *both
these unlimited spheres* and is *inexhaustibly nourished from both*. . .
The true pattern of life stretches through *both* territories. The
blood with the greatest circulation surges through *both: there is*

---

[1] Lou Andreas-Salomé, *Lebensrückblick*, Copenhagen, 1951, p. 153.
[2] See below, p. 89.
[3] Cf. Guardini, *Von den letzten Dingen*, 1952, p. 28 ff.

neither a Here nor a Beyond, only that great unity in which those
beings who surpass us, the 'Angels', are at home."[1]

The Angels have, by their very nature, that "maximum"
consciousness:

> Angels (it's said) would be often unable to tell
> whether they moved among living or dead. The eternal
> torrent whirls all the ages through either realm
> for ever, and sounds above their voices in both.   [81–84]

These lines in the *Elegy* express the same idea as the letter. The
dead are no less real than the living; the Hereafter is just as
much a part of the universe as life on earth. Indeed the letter
says that "those of the future", the still unborn, have as real
an existence as "those of to-day" and "of yesterday". All share
in the same existence. This is why the Angels, who move through
the whole cosmos, do not differentiate between Now and
Hereafter at all.[2] Here we must not overlook the qualifying
words "it's said" which imply that what follows is true by
repute. As was stated at the beginning of the *Elegy*, no direct
contact with the Angels is possible.

The "eternal torrent" is explained by the reference in the
letter to the "greatest circulation". The universe is a whole.
In it the totality of life flows hither and thither removing all
differences. It "whirls all the ages through either realm for
ever". One image seems here to be superimposed on another.
The first is that of the organism in which the blood flows
through all the limbs—those on earth as well as those in the
Hereafter—so that the living and the dead are joined together

---

[1] *Briefe aus Muzot*, p. 332 f. Italics as in the original where the word "and"
in the first sentence is given additional emphasis. The passion with which Rilke
underlines this Unity between life and death makes still clearer the significance
ascribed to Orpheus. In the same letter he writes: "I am surprised that the *Sonnets
to Orpheus*, which are at least as 'difficult' and filled with the same essence, should
not be of more assistance to you in understanding the *Elegies*. . . They are, as they
cannot help being, of the same 'birth' as the *Elegies*. The fact that they came to
me, without my volition, and associated with the death of a young girl, brings
them still closer to the source of their origin. This association is one more link
with the centre of *that* realm whose depth and influence we share with the dead
and the unborn. We, of the Here and Now, are not for one moment satisfied in
this world of time, nor are we confined within it. Continually we overflow towards those who came before us, to our origins, and to those who will apparently
come after us. In that mighty 'open' realm all people simply *are*—one cannot
say 'simultaneously', for it is precisely the disappearance of time which gives them
their *being*." (p. 333 f.) See also *Sonnet* I. vi, already quoted.

[2] See also p. 115 ff. on the *Fourth Elegy*.

in the same vital current. The second image seems to mean that the "torrent" passes through Here and Hereafter and sweeps along with it the different stages of existence, namely "all ages". Such stages might include firstly those of childhood, youth, maturity and old age; then those of death, including the 'retrieval' of time and the resolution of conflicts; and, finally, the "ages" proper, i.e. the phases of time, Past, Present and Future. Countless different phases of existence would then all be realized within the realm of Being—that "Deep Being" actually mentioned in the letter to Huléwicz.[1] Here again Rilke asserts the idea of a unity which persists beyond all distinctions and divisions.

VII

The foregoing stanzas prepare the ground for the last stage in Rilke's train of thought:

> They've finally no more need of us, the early-departed,
> one's gently weaned from terrestrial things as one mildly
> outgrows the breasts of a mother.   [85–87]

The dead, even the "early departed" who died young, do not really need us. What they have to achieve, they do on their own. Whatever is to befall them will take place of its own accord in their further existence, just like the normal development of the child who "mildly outgrows the breasts of a mother".

We mortals must not therefore imagine that anyone has "need" of us or that we are indispensable to anyone. We are not necessary even to those who might have been expected to need us, namely the dead. On the contrary, we have need of them:

> But we, that have need of
> such mighty secrets, we, for whom sorrow's so often
> source of blessedest progress, could we exist without them?
>   [87–89]

It is we who require those "mighty secrets", those mysteries which are rooted in existence itself. The final *Elegy* has more to say about this.

[1] See below, pp. 212, 220 and 237.

And so the wheel comes full turn. The repeated negative—
in *not*-possessing, *not* having a home, *not* being able to use people
or things—which runs through the *Elegy* is really part of the
mystery of becoming. Out of sorrow springs "blessedest progress". Thus the dominant mood of the *Elegy*, namely grief at
the transience and futility of earthly things, now harmonizes
with a doctrine of 'becoming' through renunciation. The unity
of the two is revealed to us when we understand this secret and
learn from the image of the dead to make "these oldest sufferings of ours yield more fruit".

Finally an example is given of the kind of "blessed progress"
which sorrow can produce:

> Is the story in vain, how once, in the mourning for Linos,
> venturing earliest music pierced barren numbness, and how,
> in the startled space an almost deified youth
> suddenly quitted for ever, emptiness first
> felt the vibration that now lifts us and comforts and helps?
> [90–94]

According to legend there once lived a youth called Linos who
was loved by all on account of his beauty. He died young and
after his death all who had known him were overcome by
"barren numbness". A void was left—the "emptiness" of departure and deprivation. Rilke refers elsewhere, in a note on
his translation of Maurice de Guérin's "Centaure", to the
"legend of those who have departed early". Behind them, he
says, is "the call, the old call searching through Nature—the
Song of Linos in which they are united together but do not
see each other".

This empty space was "startled". Here once more something
external is given a new inner dimension. It is not merely that
there were startled people in the void which Linos left. The
empty space itself was startled by the heart-felt 'inward' quality
of the experience. The "emptiness felt the vibration" which is
called music. And the vibrant sound and song was the Orpheus
of the *Sonnets*—"Once and for all, it's Orpheus, when there's
song". Since then we have had music which "lifts us and
comforts and helps".

THE SECOND ELEGY

Written at Duino, immediately after the First

I

Every Angel is terrible. Still, though, alas!
I invoke you, almost deadly birds of the soul,
knowing about you. [1–3]

THIS Elegy deals with the angelic order, and also with Man
as he is confronted with the Angels. It opens with a cry of
terror. And this cry immediately dispels all those weaker images
which, from the late Middle Ages onwards, have progressively
diminished the stature of the Angels and their power. In our
interpretation of the *First Elegy* we have already described what
happens to the figure of the Angel in Rilke's poetry. As he himself explains in his letter to Witold von Huléwicz, Rilke's Angel
has lost all connection with the angels of the Bible. Indeed his
Angel bears witness to that modern process of secularization
whereby the world cuts itself off from the source of revealed
truth, while trying to preserve the content of such truth in its
own sphere. The Angels of the *Elegies* are large in stature; they
are figures to be taken seriously; but they are no longer the
emissaries of the Living God. They still have inner qualities
which betray their ancestry, but these have been completely
translated into the terms of this world. They are beings whom
one might describe, in simplified terms, as 'gods'.

The words with which the *Second Elegy* opens are almost
identical with those in line 7 of the *First Elegy*. Both passages
convey the remoteness and inaccessibility of the Angels. But
the poet "knows about them" and, since his knowledge is also
a trust, he must speak of them. Indeed he must sing their
praises, "invoking" them and glorifying them at the same time,
whatever the consequences, as he approaches these "almost
deadly birds of the soul". The terror inspired by the Angels
has nothing to do with evil, for evil seems to be quite absent

51

from the *Elegies*. Nor is it connected with the "Horror", the fearful shapeless abyss referred to in the *Third Elegy*. It is rather the feeling described in the *First*: "For Beauty's nothing/but beginning of Terror we're still just able to bear,/and why we adore it so is because it serenely/disdains to destroy us". If the Angel appeared to us from afar off, or veiled, he would seem beautiful; and if he disclosed himself in any way and came closer, then he would simply destroy us. The Angel stands on the threshold of our awareness.

The Angels are the "birds of the soul". The image which we immediately associate with this phrase is that of wings, suggesting that the Angel has a larger realm of existence than we mortals. His movement is superhuman in its perfection as he bestrides all the heights, the depths and the breadths. Perhaps also the traditional idea of the 'soul-bird' comes into our minds, expressing the mysterious volatility of the spirit. However, there is another purpose underlying this metaphor which only becomes explicit in the second stanza: it is the disassociation of the Angel from human form and a redefinition of the angelic nature through new powerful images. Here the image is that of a gigantic bird. But later in the *Elegy* other images are taken from the inanimate world.

The Angels are described as "almost deadly" and these words evoke a picture of mighty bird-like creatures flying through the realm of the spirit and bringing death to Man when they graze his soul. It must be said that we cannot avoid some misgivings at the word "almost" in this line. Why "almost", when the last lines of the stanza refer to the inescapable deadliness of the Angel's approach by "*but a step*"? Is it mere pedantry when this feeling recurs again and again after repeated readings of the passage?

> Where are the days of Tobias,
> when one of the shining-most stood on the simple threshold,
> a little disguised for the journey, no longer appalling,
> (a youth to the youth as he curiously peered outside).   [3–6]

Man cannot withstand the terror of the Angel. Nor could he, even if he increased in strength, knowledge or experience. Only one attitude could resist the power of the angelic being, namely *simplicity*.

Between the beginning and end of the stanza, both of which
deal with the fearfulness of the Angel, there is a reference to
Tobias, to whom the archangel Raphael was sent as a guide.
Out of consideration for human weakness he was "disguised"
and "no longer appalling", though since he was only "a little
disguised" the danger remained. Yet Tobias could withstand
this danger because he was in a state of simplicity. He possessed
that strong yet humble and guileless attitude which alone is
equal to an encounter with the superhuman, a quality which
belonged peculiarly to the 'Beginning' of time.

> Let the archangel perilous now, from behind the stars,
> step but a step down hitherwards: high up-beating,
> our heart would out-beat us. Who are you?   [7–9]

The imagined encounter with the Angel—feared and desired at the same time—is impressive. The archangel, "perilous
now", steps forth from behind the stars, out of the immeasurable expanse of the universe, taking one stride—a single measure of his superhuman movement—"down hitherwards". He
does nothing to man but, simply through the power of his
being, agitates man's life: the human heart is touched in the
centre and frightened into the most violent pulsation, being
shattered in the process. Again we note the different levels of
meaning in Rilke's poetry: the violence of the heart-beat is
brought into relation with the descent of the Angel from on
high. The heart is then driven into an "up-beat", and from
the height attained is dashed down to its death. As it rises in
terror and longing to meet the descending Angel man's heart
"out-beats" himself.

We must still take account of the realm in which the Angel
appears. The Angel is in the first place the "bird of the soul";
then he steps "from behind the stars . . . down hitherwards".
On the one hand he thus belongs to the inner realm which is
revealed to the soul, and which perhaps other souls inhabit too.
On the other hand the Angel also belongs to the realm of outer
space where the stars dwell. Whereas one realm is close to the
human heart, the other belongs to the expanse and brightness
of the larger things of the universe. Yet each of these realms
here assumes a 'numinous' character. The realm of the soul is
not the psychological realm of consciousness but that of spiritual

fervour and transformation. The realm of the stars is not that
of astronomy but rather the mythical heavens where the dead
heroes appear as constellations. This is the mysterious abode
of the Angel and only here can he be encountered.

II

The second stanza is one of the great achievements of visionary writing. Here what was anticipated in the "birds of the
soul" actually takes place: the image of the Angel is now
disassociated from human form and assumes cosmic dimensions.

This stanza can only be fully appreciated if it is seen as the
meeting-place of widely divergent currents of thought.[1] The
first of these is that Christian doctrine according to which the
invisible world, i.e. the world of angels, was created before the
visible world. Thus Augustine said that the word "Heaven"
in the first sentence of the Bible—"In the beginning God
created Heaven and Earth"—meant not merely the Firmament
but the world of angels as well.[2] These angels constitute a
whole world of persons, beings, actions and relationships which
exist purely in the spirit. This is the line of thought suggested
particularly by the opening lines of Rilke's stanza. Secondly
there is the idea of degrees or orders in the spirit world. This
idea occurs in mythological form in hellenistic doctrines of
ascending orders of spirits. It appears again in the New Testament where Paul refers to orders of angels (e.g. *Eph.* i.21; *Col.*
i.16). The same idea took on a new historical significance in
the two works of Dionysius Areopagiticus, *The Celestial Hierarchy* and *The Ecclesiastical Hierarchy*. According to these works
the number of angels is infinite and they are arranged in *orders*
according to their character, their relation to God and the
services which they render to His kingdom. These orders are
described as "choirs" thrice three in number. The choirs also
embrace the idea of a heavenly "hymn of praise" and of an
"eternal dance", in other words those actions or motions which
are the formal representation of a life of eternal fulfilment.[3]

---

[1] It is not, of course, suggested that Rilke knew these particular currents of
thought or was consciously dependent on them. But they run through the whole
history of Western thought.

[2] Augustine, *Confessions*, xii. 9.

[3] Dionysius Areopagiticus, *Concerning the Celestial Hierarchy*, iii, iv, 1–3.

Each of these choirs exists for its own sake, but also for the sake of the others and the Whole. The choirs are linked together in the most varied relationships: they support and permeate one another, they express themselves and are expressed, unfold and comprehend one another.[1] This hierarchical view of the angels is very apparent in the fourth line of Rilke's stanza referring to the "thrones" which correspond to the third choir of the first triad in Dionysius' work.[2] Moreover, all those images which at first seem so strange—"hinges, corridors, stairways"—in fact refer to the same idea of a hierarchy or order, just as the opening lines of the *First Elegy* specifically mention the "angelic orders".

There is, finally, a third line of thought which plays some part here: the Neo-platonic interpretation of the origin, the condition and inner trajectory of existence. According to this the 'particular' is born, by the sheer force of its own self-expression, out of a simple, primordial yet all-embracing 'One' or Whole. From this 'One' there first pours forth, as if in a surging wave, what is simple and comprehensive, retaining its own forms. Then a second surge passes through what now exists and is crystallized into new shapes which are more sharply differentiated, more complicated, and thus poorer in Being. So from the first simple source there emerges a manifold diversity of Being in a pattern of descending orders. The later in time that a thing takes shape and the further it lies from its origin, the *more* differentiated it becomes—the more dense, dark and deficient in Being. However, no sooner does the thing which is born achieve its own shape, than it feels a longing to escape from this shape and strive back towards its own origin. This striving is the *Eros* which prevails throughout creation and, in rational beings, attains awareness of its own mission to return to the source. Thus the whole of existence has the form of departure and return—the "intelligible circle". This concept alone seems to provide the opening of the second stanza with an appropriate background.

> Early successes, favourites of fond Creation,
> ranges, summits, dawn-red ridges
> of all forthbringing, [10–12]

---

[1] *loc. cit.*   [2] *Ibid.*, vii, 1.

The images are strangely contrasted and stem from widely differing spheres; but all alike support the idea of the primordial world.

First there is an image from the workshop: the Angels are "early successes", perfectly fashioned as it were from the fresh power of the Creator. There follows another image drawn from relationships between child and parent or master and servant: the Angels are the "favourites of fond Creation", the darlings of the creative force who are showered with all manner of gifts. Finally there are mountain images: the Angels are "ranges, summits, dawn-red ridges of all forthbringing". We may be reminded here of the hard unspoilt beauty of the mountains in the early morning hours which gives us an inkling of how the world began.

> —pollen of blossoming godhead,
> junctures of light, corridors, stairways, thrones,
> chambers of essence, shields of felicity, tumults
> of stormily-rapturous feeling,   [12–15]

The description "favourites of Creation" was taken from human life. This was then left behind entirely in the image of "ranges" and "ridges": the Angels were likened to mountains. The next image originates from the organic sphere of plant-life: the Angels are "pollen of blossoming godhead". This phenomenon of the blossom producing its fruitful dust is not unlike the Neoplatonic view of the first 'One' pouring itself forth in diversity.

At this point, however, we finally abandon the world of living things altogether, and Rilke audaciously introduces a number of images borrowed from architecture. The Angels are now "junctures of light, corridors, stairways, thrones, chambers of essence" and the full meaning of these words is only disclosed if we keep in mind the underlying picture of the hierarchies: not the larger shapes of the choirs or the relationship between them, but the individual links *within* the choirs, the "junctures" or "corridors" or "stairways" in the gradations of the whole. Now these components are Angels too. An angelic being is a "juncture" between its two neighbours, a "corridor" to those beside it and a "stairway" to those above and below it. Again, they are described as "thrones" or seats of glory. But all these— hinges, corridors, stairways and thrones—are "of light", and light is an age-old symbol, based on our most elemental human experience, standing for the intellect, or more precisely, the spirit or *pneuma*. Then again, the Angels are "chambers of essence": they are not closed forms but extensions, openings, depths and heights which consist of "essence". Here then the Angel has the form of space. We may think of the mighty space between the pillars and under the vaulting of a cathedral, or of the outer space of the universe between the stars.

In the last lines of the stanza the Angels are described as "shields of felicity". Perhaps we may associate this with the words of the Song of Songs which compare the Bride to the "Tower of David" from which a "thousand shields" hang.[1] But possibly this image should be taken together with the one which follows it—the "tumults of stormily-rapturous feeling"— and we recall those baroque paintings in which the Heavens open up and a strange abundance of life breaks forth from the confused shapes and inordinate movement on the canvas. It is perhaps significant that when Rilke was writing this *Elegy* he was near to Venice and the impressive frescoes of Tintoretto. At all events his Angels now become glittering vaults of bliss and whirlwinds of sensation.

> and suddenly, separate,
> *mirrors*: drawing up again their own
> outstreamed beauty into their own faces.   [15–17]

At last, beautifully controlled, this surfeit of images and the storm of seething movements all contract into the calm contour of a single shape: "and suddenly, separate, *mirrors*".

The word "mirrors" is italicized in the original. In Rilke's view of things the mirror has a mysterious meaning.[2] He says of these angelic mirrors that they draw up "their own outstreamed beauty into their own faces". They are apparently alive—perhaps the faces of the Angels themselves. But what do they do? After pouring out their beauty they draw it back

---

[1] *Song of Songs*, iv. 4. The phrase has passed into the Marian liturgy and may have been familiar to Rilke from that source.

[2] See also the *Sonnets to Orpheus*, II, ii and iii; among others "Three Poems from the Cycle: Reflections", *Later Poems*, p. 121, "And so we stand with Mirrors", *ibid.*, p. 123. It is interesting that Dante says of the angels in the *Paradiso* (9, 61), "sono specchi", "they are mirrors".

The mirror motif is connected with that of Narcissus (cf. *Sonnets*, II, iii). There is not space here to give a full account of the significance of mirrors in Rilke's poetry.

again. This is difficult to accept, for a mirror does exactly the opposite: first it draws in and then it reflects. So the image of the mirror must be understood in a special way—in conjunction with that movement of departure and return referred to above. The original 'One' is both a source which pours forth and a home which attracts back. In Neo-platonic terms it "pours forth from its own self" without ever being impoverished, since everything ultimately returns to it. This statement is translated by our image into the realm of light: the "mirror", however, is understood in reverse, so that it first sends out rays of light and then recovers them. It is easy to understand what is intended here if we remember that the mirror image is merged into the image of the human face, and that when the face registers a certain expression of feeling this really springs from the heart, shines forth and later returns to its place of origin. This is how these mighty mirrors must be envisaged, first radiating and then absorbing, rather like gates through which light flows out to the observer and then back from him again.

Rilke's picture of the glory of the Angels reaches a climax in this image. The Angels do not lose their glory when they radiate it. Instead they retrieve it again.[1] This is the secret of their superhuman quality. And this is why, although they are involved in a mighty flux or movement, they remain indestructible.

What follows is a sharp contrast: for our fate as human beings is quite different.

III

For we, when we feel, evaporate; oh, we
breathe ourselves out and away; from ember to ember
yielding a fainter scent. True, someone may tell us:
'You've got in my blood, the room, the Spring's
growing full of you' . . . what's the use? He cannot retain us.
We vanish within and around him. And those that have beauty,
oh, who shall hold them back? Appearance of something
keeps getting up in their faces and going away. Like dew
from the morning grass what's ours exhales from us, like the heat
from a smoking dish.   [18–27]

---

[1] This idea assumes a different form in Rilke's theory of love. According to this, God himself is responsible for "casting their radiance back into themselves again" (see letter to Annette Kolb, Jan. 23rd 1912).

The movement of our lives is an outflowing without return. This is the meaning of the series of strange yet moving images in the above passage.

First there is the image of breath: the whole of life depends on a giving out and drawing in of air. But the essential breath of our Being is only *ex*haled, for the recovery or *in*halation is missing. This is illustrated by the image which follows of the wood embers glowing away. Anyone who has passed through a Southern village in the evening knows the characteristic smell of the open wood fires. First of all the flames burn brightly; then they gradually die down until only the fragrant embers remain; and these too become cool as the sweet smell of the hearth slowly fades away. This image does not mean simply that we are like a burning wood fire which first gives off a strong and then a weaker smell as the flames die down. The burning up and dying down of the fire in the hearth each day represents the pattern of our lives passing away over the days and the years. Again and again the fire is kindled, then goes out and gives off its fragrance, but each time less strongly, until finally everything is consumed and vaporized. Our life may *seem* to have more reality. A friend may confide to us in a moment of intimacy how 'near' he feels to us, so that he senses our presence in everything around—for instance in the "room" or the season of "Spring". This could be a heartfelt expression of affection and if it were justified we might feel safe. But since the very person who says this must, like us, pass away, how can he "retain" us? This is the same difficulty as that of "housing" the beloved, mentioned in the *First Elegy*, since the heart is open on all sides and the "great strange thoughts go in and out". We "vanish within and around him"—in his feelings, in the room which surrounds him and in the Spring which he lives through.

How painful too is the passing away of "those that have beauty". The countenance of a beautiful person, for example, is radiant with no ordinary light; such beauty is not fixed and static like that of a precious stone, but alive and moving. It rises continually, as if in waves, from the heart to the face. The facial expression, and the way in which beauty is revealed in it at a given moment, is an "appearance"[1], an illumination which

---

[1] Translator's note: The German original is *Anschein*, an 'appearance' or, literally, a 'shining upon'.

shines on to the beholder. In radiating from the face, however,
beauty departs and evaporates. This idea recurs in the fifth stanza
which refers to the face which is "hard-worn" by daily life.
From the first stanza of the *First Elegy* we recall that the "wind
full of cosmic space feeds on our faces". Space, the very realm
of existence, removes layer after layer of man's vital reality.

The picture now changes again, and the next example is
not a face radiating beauty, but a meadow lying in the fresh
morning air with the dew evaporating from the grass and the
blossom. This is succeeded by a steaming dish, left standing on
the table and losing its heat, aroma and taste.

All these images which come in quick succession say the
same thing in different ways: Human life is transient. The
images also have a certain consistency of colour and tone.
Those which refer to the Angels have power and radiance
while their spaciousness suggests the height and expanse of the
universe. The images which deal with Man, on the other hand,
are earthy, warm with the warmth of our life, and bring home
to us the transience of things.

> O smile, whither? O upward gaze:
> new, warm, vanishing wave of the heart—alas,
> but we *are* all that. Does the cosmic space
> we dissolve into taste of us, then? Do the angels really
> only catch up what is theirs, what has streamed from them, or
>   at times,
> as though through an oversight, is a little of our
> essence in it as well? Is there just so much of us
> mixed with their features as that vague look in the faces
> of pregnant women? Unmarked by them in the whirl of their
> coming back to themselves. (How should they remark it?)
>   [27–36]

The painful question now presents itself: Where do all these
things go which pass away from us? The smile, the glance, the
surge of inner feeling? And immediately comes the answer,
like a primitive cry of fear: "Alas, but we *are* all that". All
these things are not mere external appearances; they are
reality—*our* reality. When we "dissolve into cosmic space",
when our soul departs, does it stay there? Have we any significance in that vast expanse?[1] Do the Angels at least feel that

---

[1] See above, p. 25 ff., on the *First Elegy* and the *Sonnet* quoted on p. 27.

they have retrieved whatever streamed out of them in the powerful recoil of their life? Does some part of us perhaps—"at times, as though through an oversight"—pass into them, even if it were something indefinite, as vague as that enigmatic expression sometimes seen on the faces of pregnant women? Might we not in this way, unobtrusively and indirectly, have a small share somehow in the angelic existence which the *First Elegy* renounced? We do not know. But even if it were so they would not notice it. Rilke's tentative suggestion of this possibility is swept away in the powerful image which follows describing the second motion of the Angels—the "whirl of their coming back to themselves"—like that of a geyser sucking back the water which it has thrust out.

The last two lines show again how far Rilke's Angels are removed from the figures of the Bible. They are indifferent to Man. They are mighty beings who exist in their own lofty heights and are quite indifferent to earthly life. It might seem that the Old Testament angels are no different. But it is only in their power that they are similar. For the rest they stand in the service of God and help to further the divine plan within the larger framework of history. The angels of the New Testament are much warmer and nearer to man as an individual. For instance, the little children in *Matthew* (xviii, 10) have their own guardian angels in Heaven who "behold the face of the Father". The Angels of the *Elegies* are a long way from this. They are not concerned about Man. We might say of them what Hölderlin says of the gods: they have no human feelings. Indeed they have even less than Hölderlin's gods. The hymn to "The Rhine" contains the following lines:[1]

> Immortality more than enough
> Have the gods of their own, and if one
> Celestial need remain,
> That need is for heroes and men
> And what else may be mortal; for, since
> Of themselves the most-blessed feel nothing,
> Needs must,—if such daring thought
> May be uttered,—performing his part
> In their name, feel for them another:
> They need him . . . . .

[1] Friedrich Hölderlin, *Selected Poems*, translated by J. B. Leishman, London, 1944, p. 111.

Rilke's Angels do not have even this "need", i.e. a share in the feelings of the men who love them. In relation to human beings they are even more olympian than Hölderlin's gods. Their feelings can only embrace the universe *per se*, as a generalized whole which is beyond the grasp of us mortals. The scale of their feeling is thus, as the *Ninth Elegy* states, superhuman: "in the cosmos where he more feelingly feels you're only a novice" [53–55].

There is a poem which dates from the same period as the early *Elegies* where this idea is even more clearly expressed:[1]

> Angels, angels, penetrating space
> with their sempiternity of feeling.
> Our whitest-heatedness would seem congealing
> to angels, glowingly pervading space.
>
> While we, accustomed to our hard conditions
> fail to reach or fail to understand,
> they blissfully pursue their intuitions
> through their unobstructed land.

Here the Angel is likened to a bright star whose fire consists entirely of feeling as it courses through outer space.

The foregoing shows clearly how complex is Rilke's view of the Angel. It derives from various sources. There is the Biblical angel, from whom, however, Rilke's Angel differs in not being the messenger of God concerned with human salvation. He owes to the gods of antiquity a certain universal and olympian character, enabling him to survey earthly things with sublime indifference. On the other hand, like Hölderlin's gods, he derives from Christian tradition an inner quality of feeling which is rarely associated with mythical beings. Rilke's Angels *are* capable of feelings, but the compass of their feeling is cosmic, not earthly.

One final question presents itself. In his letter to Huléwicz, Rilke tried to relate his own angelic beings with those of Islam, appropriately enough, since these too are composite figures. He clearly intended to give his Angels a numinous character. But it would be interesting to know whether they have in fact ever inspired any sort of religious feeling among Rilke's readers.

---

[1] *Later Poems*, p. 172.

Or whether the feeling which they arouse is not simply aesthetic,
or perhaps that ambiguous mixture of feeling, aesthetic and
religious, so characteristic of the religiosity of modern times.

IV

Lovers, indeed, if only they could, might utter
strange things in the midnight air. For it seems that everything's
trying to hide us. Look, the trees exist; the houses
we live in still stand where they were. We only
pass everything by like a transposition of air.
And all combines to suppress us, partly, perhaps,
as shame, and partly as inexpressible hope.   [37–43]

Where, then, does Man stand in all this? This question,
which we ordinary mortals cannot answer, is now put to the
lovers, since they in their love lead an existence of rare intensity.
They are therefore more keenly aware of what is essentially
human in our life: "in the midnight air", in the enchantment
of the nocturnal silence, they could "utter strange things". The
phrase reminds us of the oracular words of the prophetess in
Hölderlin's hymn "Germania" whose prophecy is not intended
for the ears of the many. The lovers, then, ought to be able to
throw light on man's problematical state if anyone can. Unfortunately they cannot speak, so absorbed are they in their
own experience.

But if the lovers remain inarticulate, everything else is even
more so! If the riddle of Man cannot find clear explanation
through them, how can our nature, diffused as it is on all sides,
become manifest in "trees" and "houses"? The problem now
becomes more specific. For whereas the third stanza said that
we "evaporate" into the world, here "it seems that everything's
trying to hide us". Whatever departs from us is lost, not simply
because of its evanescence, but because the world does not *wish*
it to be seen.

The trees "exist". As the *First Elegy* said, when we take our
usual walk and pass by the same spot, the same tree always
stands on the slope "to be looked at day after day". But from
yesterday to today *we* have changed. The house in which we
live remains the same, but our life flows away inside it. Different
things stand all around us, but we "pass everything by like a

transposition of air". Far from being stable or fixed in any
sense we are in constant flux, like a sigh or a breath—except
that our breath is never recovered, as it is with the Angels, but
simply departs outwards. Indeed, as is suggested in the fifth
stanza, it is questionable who, if anyone, is breathing our
breath at all!

Whatever flows out from us is concealed by *things*. They have
a tacit understanding to "suppress us", for they regard us
"partly, perhaps, as shame, and partly as inexpressible hope".
The whole paradox of Man's situation is that he is necessary
to the world and yet at the same time presents a problem. And
his problematic nature is manifest precisely at the summits of
human experience, e.g. in love. Clearly the lovers are all and
everything to each other. But to the bystanders are they not
often incomprehensible, or sometimes even ludicrous? In a
heightened form they show a characteristic shared by other
human beings—that of being "the shame" and also the "inexpressible hope" of the world. Mountains and trees and
animals are sufficient in themselves and are justified as such.
Man, on the other hand, is confused and brings confusion into
the world. Like the indictment in the *Eighth Elegy*, these lines
contain an echo of the doctrine of man's Fall. This is why all
Nature is ashamed of Man and repudiates him, while still
looking on him with a kind of ultimate hope because he has
within him great potentialities. It is interesting to compare the
message of the *Ninth Elegy* concerning the "transforming" power
of the human heart and the "command" of the Earth. Here
again there is an echo of Christian doctrine which has been
secularized and is now felt to be no more than an intangible
'Perhaps'—the doctrine of regeneration in the heart of the
believer (*Rom.* viii, 18–25).

V

Lovers, to you, each satisfied in the other,
I turn with my question about us. You grasp yourselves. Have
   you proofs?
Look, with me it may happen at times that my hands
grow aware of each other, or else that my hard-worn face
seeks refuge within them. That gives me a little
sensation. But who, just for that, could presume to exist? [44–49]

The fifth stanza again takes up the question which was addressed to the lovers, but no longer as if expecting an answer from them; rather to convince them that the answer which they would like to give is false. Each lover assumes a unique significance for the other as a point of stability. And those same things which flow away from ordinary mortals seem with *them* to be passed over from one lover to the other—held fast, as it were, in the I-Thou relationship. The lovers become mutual guarantors of permanence, and transience now seems so far overcome that they can even afford to speak of "eternity" (line 60). But are they not mistaken? Everyone imagines that he can sense the reality of the other person by touching him. But has anyone "*proofs*" that this is so?

Like a wise and experienced man talking to the foolish and ignorant, so the poet addresses the lovers in order to correct their error: "Look, with me it may happen. . . ." Sometimes when he folds his hands one hand becomes aware of the other. Or he may lay his "hard-worn" tired face in his hands because it yearns for shelter; and his face then feels their protection, just as the hands feel the face within them. But all this is just "a little sensation". Can we infer from this that we really exist? Dare we make the claim to be permanent and to endure?

It is remarkable how Rilke here sums up his sense of transience in a fleeting gesture. Yet the passage is disturbing, because it seems to convey something else besides transience— something that is perhaps almost destructive. Involuntarily we recall the *Notebook of Malte Laurids Brigge* which contains so many of these marginal experiences.

We have already referred to that radical uncertainty in Rilke's attitude to the human personality. The same uncertainty is, however, apparent long before he comes to deal with human beings, in his very way of looking at the act of 'be-ing'. His own 'be-ing' has not a determinate quality which can be directly experienced. On the contrary it flows like a liquid or blows like the wind. For Rilke the act of 'be-ing' cannot be "presumed" or taken for granted (1. 49); it can only be approached obliquely. Real Being—i.e. the "infinite", "pure" and "deep Being" of the *Eighth Elegy*—must be sought in the world's hidden 'inner' realm. This realm is reached by that 'inward' process which finds its objective expression in the

E

word. But the word must be earned or "won", as the *Ninth Elegy* puts it. Also it must be "pure", i.e. spoken in such a way as to describe things as they "hoped intensely to be" (*Elegy* IX. 30; 35). It is in the poem that the word achieves fulfilment of this kind, for here pure Being is given definite form. And this is how the poet himself penetrates the realm of Being as he speaks; for his words are precisely the fulfilment of that trust which the Earth and existence impose on him.[1] This relationship is very delicately expressed in one of the *Sonnets to Orpheus*:[2]

> Breathing, invisible poem! That great
> world-space, at each inhalation
> exchanged for this human existence. Counter-weight
> of my rhythmical realisation.

In the 'inward' process the external and internal merge together and true Being is achieved. In this case it is the Being of a person who 'realizes' rhythmical fulfilment by breathing, and the physical recovery of the breath itself becomes an artistic form—a "poem". By 'internalizing' the reality which lies outside him man can 'poeticize' it into real Being. But how ethereal this conception of Being seems when illustrated in a process such as this!

> You, though, that go on growing
> in the other's rapture till, overwhelmed, he implores
> 'No more'; you that under each other's hands
> grow more abundant like vintage years;
> swooning at times, just because the other
> has so expanded: I ask you about us.   [50-55]

Mortal man in all his transience was the subject of the third stanza. The fifth deals with the lovers whose experience seems to prove the contrary. The lovers discover each other, and each *in* the other discovers himself. Far from diminishing or passing away each lover seems to "expand" or grow in stature through the beloved—so much indeed that he is almost overwhelmed by his partner's superiority. This is the meaning of the image of the "vintage years" when grapes are so abundant that the vintner does not know where to store them. The feeling of the lovers exceeds all measure.

Here there seems to be no disappearance of the Self but

[1] *Ninth Elegy*, 67-70.   [2] *Sonnet* II, i.

rather an increase; for each partner in love becomes more in
the other's eyes than he was—and therefore in his own eyes
as well. How can this be? "I ask you about us". What can the
lovers answer to this?

> I know
> why you so blissfully touch: because the caress withholds,
> because it does not vanish, the place that you
> so tenderly cover; because you perceive thereunder
> pure duration. Until your embraces almost
> promise eternity. Yet, when you've once withstood
> the startled first encounter, the window-longing,
> and that first walk, just once, through the garden together;
> Lovers, are you the same? When you lift yourselves
> up to each other's lips—drink unto drink:
> oh, how strangely the drinker eludes his part!   [55–65]

The lovers are "blissful" because in their mutual tenderness
they have such a confident awareness of each other. So they
imagine that they have passed beyond transience to the point
of permanence. "The caress withholds" or endures. The em-
bracing hand feels that the body of the beloved "does not
vanish" where it is covered. Indeed, the hands seem to have
the power of counteracting physical transience. The lover feels
so strongly that the "place" on the body is still there during
and after a caress that he overcomes all feeling of imperma-
nence. He imagines that his hand is covering "pure duration",
real "Being" in which there is no Before or After, no Becoming
or passing away.[1]

Although their embraces "almost promise eternity" the lovers
are wrong. At first their feelings are so deeply stirred that they

---

[1] In his letter to the Princess of Dec. 16th 1913, Rilke says: "I am also
concerned about this phrase describing the lovers which is very dear to me."
There follow lines 55–59 of the *Elegy* and then: "This is intended quite literally
to mean that the place where the lover lays his hand is exempted thereby from
the process of passing away—the ageing and anything which involves the decay
of our essential nature—and that this place simply *endures* and has *Being* under
his hand. It should be possible to make this comprehensible just as literally in
Italian, for the meaning is lost in any paraphrase. Is that not so? And I am
particularly attached to these lines, having had such pleasure in forming them".
Apart from its relevance here the passage in the letter shows clearly the kind of
interpretation which a Rilke text demands. We have to begin with the most concrete sense of the words and then, without losing this, penetrate more and more
deeply into the underlying layers of meaning. In the case of the *Elegies* this depth
of meaning is considerable and a more searching analysis would be rewarding.
But this would lead us into problems of ontology which lie outside the compass
of our interpretation.

cannot perceive their error. Yet when once the first anticipation
and the first "encounter"—the "first walk, just once, through
the garden together"—are over, will not everything be different
again? At first the lovers simply accepted their existence as a
matter of course, or so it seemed. But is that still so? Will the
same unquestioned sense of security continue? When they
embrace one another and the mouth of one becomes both glass
and drink to the other, is there anyone there who is drinking?
Do they not see that an action is taking place without an
'actor'? Again we may feel that this is a dangerous line of
thought to pursue. Yet there *are* evil moments in life when
things become shadowy and unreal. A man's own self may
become unreal and he may wonder whether he is more than a
phantom. We cannot simply dismiss this feeling as imaginary
or morbid. Certainly it is not exactly 'healthy', but it has a
certain meaning as well. It is a marginal experience where a
phenomenon of normal life emerges in an extreme form. In
this way Rilke comes to grips with a problematical side of
existence which would otherwise remain inaccessible.

The above passage is one of several in which the human
person seems to dissolve into unreality. Rilke calls the mouth-
to-mouth relationship of the lovers "drink unto drink" and
comments—"how strangely the drinker eludes his part". In
the action of the kiss only the object is present—the mouth of
the other. The subject, one's own mouth, "eludes" or escapes
the action. Once more there is an action without a performer,
an object without a subject and the disturbing eclipse of the
human personality.[1]

VI

What then is the answer to the question of Man's situation?
It is not given in the form of a real reply at all. Man hovers
in significance between "shame" and "inexpressible hope". It
is impossible to define more precisely where he stands, whither
his personality goes after death or what his meaning is for the
world.

At the same time we must not lose sight of that "commission"
or trust imposed on Man which consists in giving a meaning

[1] Compare the poem "World was in the Face of the Beloved", *Selected Works*,
II, p. 348.

to the Earth through his inner life. The ambiguity of Man's status and this trust are complementary, for together they express his whole problematical nature. Although men are the "most fleeting of all" beings (*Elegy* IX. 12), they are presented with their "commission" despite the evanescence of their Being. And perhaps not merely *despite* but *because* of it. This is the link between the "shame" and the "inexpressible hope" mentioned above. We may detect here, in the impassioned tone of his words, a hint of Rilke's peculiar existential need—especially if we keep in mind what was said previously about his view of the human personality and Being.

> On Attic stelæ, did not the circumspection
> of human gesture amaze you? Were not love and farewell
> so lightly laid upon shoulders, they seemed to be made
> of other stuff than with us?   [66–69]

Man is a shadowy indefinite creature, though normally he is not aware of this. He may imagine that because of his capacity to learn and strive and accomplish various things his life is substantial and well-defined. Yet in earlier periods of history men had a clearer sense of their own condition.

Again and again on Greek tombs the picture of departure or leave-taking appears. We may see a young woman going away as her husband bids her farewell; or friends separate, feeling for the last time all that they have meant to each other. But the gesture expressing their love or leave-taking is always guarded, full of a "circumspection" which "amazes" us. The "human gesture" lays "love and farewell lightly upon the shoulders" of those who remain behind. It is as if their loving farewell were different in quality from ours—as if these people were not, like us, weighed down and oppressed by it. But that sort of gesture was the right one. For we are, after all, fleeting beings and unable to bear such a great burden. Like *things*, we "live on departure" (*Elegy* IX. 62). Every gesture or movement addressed to another human being should therefore be restrained like those on the tombs.[1]

---

[1] "I think it was in Naples, in front of some ancient headstones, that it suddenly struck me that I ought never to make less restrained gestures to other people than those depicted here. And I really think that I have come to the point where I can express all the tumult of my heart, without loss or disaster, simply by laying my hand gently on a person's shoulder." From a letter to Lou Andreas-Salomé of Jan. 10th 1912, i.e. at the same time as the *Second Elegy* was being written.

                                        Oh, think of the hands,
how they rest without pressure, though power is there in the
    torsos.
The wisdom of those self-masters was this: hitherto it's us;
ours is to touch one another like this; the gods
may press more strongly upon us. But that is the gods' affair.

                                                    [69–73]

The hands rest without force, "without pressure", on the
touched body. But the reason is not that these men were feeble,
for "power is there in the torsos". The word 'torso' is used here
in the original Italian sense, meaning the rump of the body,
the main support of the human form. These men were strong
and trained in many exercises, but they were also "self-masters".
They possessed the ancient virtue of *sophrosyne* which means
knowledge and self-control, perspicacity and moderation at
the same time. The meaning of their gestures was—"*ours* is to
touch one another like *this*". On the other hand these men also
had an awareness of beings who stand above Man, who are
fashioned differently and have other tasks and privileges, namely
the gods. Men may only "touch" one another and will remain
whole and unharmed. But the gods "may press more strongly
upon us". The implication here is perhaps that the Angel could
act in like fashion, though then the outcome would be the same
as if he "stepped hitherwards" "from behind the stars"—Man
would be destroyed. "But that is the gods' affair". They have
a different *sophrosyne* which tells them how to act.

   It is significant how the gods suddenly emerge here out of
Rilke's innermost experience, and how gods and Angels merge
into one another quite naturally, as if their identity could be
taken for granted. Rilke's Angels are really the gods of this
world. God is certainly mentioned in the *Elegies*, but if one
collects all the references to Him and considers them against
the larger pattern of Rilke's work it is clear that the Living
God of revelation has disappeared. What the word still means
for Rilke is explained in the *Eighth Elegy*.

        If only we too could discover some pure, contained,
        narrow, human, own little strip of corn-land
        in between river and rock.   [74–76]

Here too there is a kind of answer to the question which was originally put. It takes the shape of a wish which—it is impossible to say how—*can* be fulfilled. It emerges here as if in a dream, as a yearning for something which is tangible and concrete but which also symbolizes the depth of existence. Amid all the transience of the world we still aspire to self-awareness and self-control. And despite our clouded vision we still try to find something "pure" and "human", something which may indeed be "narrow", unpretentious, "contained" or limited, but which really belongs to us. All this is summed up in the vivid image of our "own little strip of corn-land in between river and rock". Probably Rilke once saw this narrow strip of fertile earth, hemmed in on one side by the river and on the other by the rising cliff wall. What is "ours" may be equally modest—a space left between rushing water and hard rock—if we ever find it at all.

> For our own heart still transcends us
> even as theirs did. And we can no longer gaze
> after it now into pacifying image, or godlike
> body, wherein it achieves a grander restraint.   [76–79]

We have to accept our lot in a similar way, for truth is only found in such acceptance. "Our heart" too will "transcend" us as it did others. As long as men live they will hanker after the boundless and the infinite. The same idea is explored more fully in the *Ninth Elegy*. Our yearning always exceeds our capacity, though according to the ethos proclaimed here this should not be so. Pascal's profound *pensée* was that "l'homme passe infiniment l'homme". Rilke, the modern man, or rather the man of transition, exhorts us to accept our limitations and to content ourselves with the "narrow strip of corn-land" where our existence can take root.

This attitude of acceptance was easier for the Greeks—in so far as it really *was* their attitude. When their hearts overreached themselves they were calmed by the sublime sight of the temples in their towns, by the thoughts of their philosophers or the verses of their poets. These things "pacified" their infinite longing which they subdued and turned into *sophrosyne*. Or else they projected it into those "godlike" bodies, the divine shapes which stood above men without being infinite. Their deities did not entice men into limitless realms but helped them to "restrain" themselves and to accept their allotted sphere. But that is not for us. We must follow the path of renunciation towards whatever lies between running water and arid stones. We must discover "our" land without the help of images and take up our stand there.

THE THIRD ELEGY

Begun 1912 at Duino; completed 1912 in Paris

I

One thing to sing the beloved, another, alas!
that hidden guilty river-god of the blood.   [1-2]

THE individual sentences of the *Third Elegy* can be more easily interpreted if we first examine the ground over which the *Elegy* moves as a whole. This is defined clearly in the opening two lines.

The central figure is the youth or "lover" who is introduced in the third line. It is his fate with which the *Elegy* deals. He himself does not act. On the contrary, he is acted *upon* and striven *for*. In this drama of existence man is the object of dispute between contending forces.

The first of these forces is embodied in a figure who is mentioned at the very beginning—the "beloved" who later becomes simply the "girl". She incorporates that power which works on man from above and is described variously as "pure", "intimate", "feeling" and "gentle". The determining factor in her nature is Light—"the purest star".

The girl is opposed by a power which works from below. The latter cannot be described in human terms but only by reference to mythology. It is a *numen*—the "river-god of the blood". A little later he is called the "Neptune within our blood". He represents the power of the instinct—the instinct which has not been absorbed by the integrating power of the personality—the dark, powerful, elemental and impersonal force within us.

These are the two forces which contend for the possession of the youth.

In the second stanza there is another antithesis. The central figure is the same as before but now appears as a child. The child is lying in bed at evening time and is filled with fear as the two opposing forces fight for his possession.

One of these forces is again embodied in human shape—this time as the "mother". She and the girl are similar, and the *Elegy* specifically mentions the mother's "slender form". We might say that she *is* the girl all over again, but now in the shape of a mother watching her child. These two figures stand in the same relation to each other as Demeter and Persephone —the former as Mother, the latter as *kore* or daughter.[1] Both are manifestations of a kindly, beneficent power in the shape of woman.

The mother who can soothe the child and equip him for life is opposed by a hostile power. This power is expressed in all the strange uncanny things which surround the child, e.g. the darkness of the room or the movement of the curtain. This is what Rilke calls the "surging abyss".

Together the two women represent that benevolent power which tries to endow man with a clear ordered existence of his own. They are opposed by the infinite torrent of life, the burden of the unconscious and the legacy of past generations—those powers, in others words, which engulf the individual in spite of himself.

The *Elegy* thus deals with that same primitive tension, described in myth, between the upper and the lower, the light and the dark, the heights of Heaven and the depths of the earth.

But Rilke's way of presenting this antithesis is all his own. The representative of the lofty heights in the *Elegy* is not Zeus, the powerful ruler, nor Apollo, the unconquerable god. It is neither male nor, strictly speaking, a numen at all, but a female being who is transfigured by the "purest star". And the depths are not represented by Gaia, the earth goddess, either in the guise of dark Hecate or as life-giving Demeter. They are depicted in the shape of that restless fluid element—the image of primeval chaos itself—Neptune, or Poseidon, who is both male and a *numen*.

Two forces are at work in the youth's life: the gentle force of light and goodness giving him protection and loving care;

[1] See C. G. Jung and K. Kerenyi, *Einführung in das Wesen der Mythologie*, Part 3, *Kore*, Copenhagen, 1941, p. 145 ff.

and the contrary force of darkness and violence. Of these forces the latter seems from the outset to be the stronger.

II

The tragic note can be detected in the very first lines. The *Elegy* as a whole deals with Eros and his different forms; and it is soon evident that the lower Eros which springs from the blood is mightier than the higher Eros of the spirit.

Rilke pronounces the word "Alas!" over Eros and calls him "guilty". Now this word "guilty" betrays something very significant about the whole antithesis. For here what is really a *contrast*—i.e. a tension between complementary realms of being such as the upper and the inner, the day and the night, infinite possibility and formal restriction, etc.—is equated with a *contradiction* such as exists between good and evil, purity and guilt, light as the ordering power and darkness as the force of rebellion and error. The former are genuine poles of existence, for both are real, creative and full of opportunities for good and evil. The latter, by contrast, challenge us to make a decision, for one term of a contradiction *should* be, whilst the other should *not*. But as soon as a contradiction is identified with a contrast— as "guilt" is here equated with the "night" and the "surging abyss"—both of its terms are sanctioned and the need for a decision is obscured.

Our interpretation—as was stressed in the Introduction— does not aim simply at exposition of the 'thought-content of the *Elegy*' or of 'Rilke's idea'. Over and above the definition of his idea we must try to examine the truth of the idea as well, and here it must be affirmed that Rilke's construction is false and disastrous—just as false and disastrous as that dualism which, in its gnostic form, pervades the whole of Western thought. It is because of this dualism that the essential character of Evil is obscured. For Evil cannot be the fruitful counterpole of Good but must be considered as Good's negation. And so we must not seek any unifying polarity or tension between these terms; we must look for the 'either-or' of the contradiction. The latter cannot be fitted into the form of a synthesis—on the contrary it calls for a decision. But this decision is not made in the *Elegy*, any more than, if I am correct, it is made at all

in Rilke's poetry. This seems to be so, at least if we assume that
the term 'Evil', as something which should not be, is relevant
to his work at all. Rilke's attitude here is closely connected with
his way of presenting and resolving the problem of the human
personality. For personality is intimately bound up with the
call to decision.

The next few lines add something new to the above antithesis:

> Him she discerns from afar, her lover, what does he know
> of that Lord of Pleasure, who often, out of his lonely heart,
> before she'd soothed him, often as though she didn't exist,
> streaming from, oh, what unknowable depths, would uplift
> his god-head, uprousing the night to infinite uproar?   [3-7]

The girl in the *Elegy* is surrounded by a bright aura of light.
Later she is said to have communion with the stars, the higher
world, or, in psychological terms, the world of consciousness
and freedom. And it is to her that the youth belongs, in so far
as he too moves in brightness and light. This is the sense of
the words "Him she discerns from afar".

But the sequence of thought is still incomplete. For there is
something else about her lover which she does *not* know, namely
the realm of the unconscious which is hidden even to himself.[1]
Out of this realm, which we cannot know directly, the dark
forces of the *physis* or the instincts work their way up. These
forces, previously called the "river-god of the blood", are now
represented by the "Lord of Pleasure".[2]

The Lord of Pleasure now asserts himself in the youth. Rilke's
powerful description transports the reader straight into the
situation. It is night-time, when the tumult of vitality takes
possession of us more easily. The youth is described as "lonely",
for although the girl he loves is not there to "soothe" him, still
he feels the bond which connects them. Then, however, the

---

[1] The fact that she too, like the mother a little later, possesses an unconscious—
a plane of existence which does not belong to the realm of the "star"—is omitted
for the sake of the antithesis.

[2] Here Rilke's equation of 'contrast' and 'contradiction' is even more evident.
Light and darkness, the conscious and the unconscious are vital levels of existence.
At both levels there is the possibility of contradiction between Good and Evil.
The Light contains some Evil and the Darkness some Good. But here the un-
conscious, the depth and the darkness are all considered together as "Pleasure",
Evil or "Guilt". The logical and bewildering consequence of this is that Evil
becomes an element of being and is thus legitimized.

inner storm becomes so powerful that it is almost "as though she didn't exist". His loneliness now becomes complete. He is not just physically alone, but in what he now feels there is no possibility of sharing or communion at all. His passion is no longer attached to anything human: it is neither shaped by the personality, nor transmuted by the heart into fervour, nor is it the responsibility of the mind. His passion becomes simply a blind force, arising out of a strange realm and "streaming" from "unknowable depths". It is like a numen which emerges from an inaccessible world and, once arrived, cannot be understood by the *logos* but can only be endured by the *pathos*. But the ensuing tumult and "infinite uproar" transcend the capacity of the individual and therefore have a disintegrating effect on the personality.

In a mythological view of the world every facet of real experience is felt to be divine: all impulses—of whatever kind, even the "guilty" ones—are made into *numina*. Yet even Plato objected to this association of divinity with the concept of evil or wrongness.[1] Strictly speaking, the word 'divine' should only be applied to something which not merely exists but is also 'worthy' of its existence.

We can hardly fail to be impressed by Rilke's description of the young man's experience as he lies alone in his room. The integrated world which he had shaped for himself is engulfed all at once by an impersonal, elemental wave which rises up in spite of him. What precipitates the sudden change is the "night". And here the "night" of the room merges unobtrusively into the night of the ocean—that part of Nature which is the symbol of chaos.

The transition takes place in the next few lines:

> Oh, the Neptune within our blood, oh, his terrible trident!
> Oh, the gloomy blast of his breast from the twisted shell!
> Hark, how the night grows fluted and hollowed.   [8–10]

The "river-god" has now become the god of the ocean. The "river" was the torrent of the blood, and it is perhaps not pedantic to assume that "river" here was associated with the channel or veins of the body. But now there are no longer any channels directing the current; there is simply a flood or an

---

[1] E.g. in the *Euthyphro*.

ocean of the "blood" in all its unbridled power. From this
ocean emerges Neptune who is addressed with religious awe
and acclamation.

The final sentence "Hark, how the night grows fluted and
hollowed" continues the sense of the preceding line, "Oh, the
gloomy blast of his breast from the twisted shell". Here again
we notice the way in which Rilke projects an image and gives
it an extended meaning. It is Neptune who blows on the shell,
and Neptune's image here includes the triton who stirs up the
storm by blowing on his conch-horn, for every triton is a kind
of individualized sea-god. As we read, we feel the hollowness
of his breast as it is transferred into the hollow of the shell; and
this in turn is projected into the whole of nature at night—"the
night grows fluted and hollowed"—like the shell. So the breath
from Neptune's breast turns into the breath of the world, i.e.
the wind. . . Then, however, the sense of the image is reversed.
The depths which have released the storm are transformed
into a dark void which draws things in to itself. The second
element of passion now asserts itself—the hungering, consuming
urge which is the opposite of the first overflowing and outward-
thrusting impetus.

What link can there be between this Eros and that of the
'beloved'? How can they be united?

> You stars,
> is it not from you that the lover's delight in the loved one's
> face arises? Does not his intimate insight
> into her purest face come from the purest star?   [10–13]

This "delight" of the lover has no connection with the "river-
god of the blood" or the "Lord of Pleasure". The "delight in
the loved one's face" is joy. It includes desire too, but not that
crude unspiritual desire which springs from incomprehensible
depths. This desire marks a progression towards Truth[1] and
is linked to the stars from whence true perception comes—"the
intimate insight into her purest face". These words sum up all
the beauty and tenderness and nobility of life: the "insight"

---

[1] The same idea plays an important part in the doctrine of love expounded
by Augustine, Dante, Pascal and also recurs in the philosophy of Scheler.

means both the act of looking into a person's eyes and the recognition of the inner human depths; the "intimacy" means a kind of inward perception of the heart; and the "purity" in the face of the beloved is not merely moral but refers also to a larger metaphysical purity—that of the "purest star".

The original antithesis is now complete.

III

The second stanza refers to different planes or levels of human existence. One level is immediately evident to our eyes: the one which we see and on which we act and live. Beneath this level, however, there is another which is inaccessible and unknown, but which has real effects on everything we see and touch.

> It wasn't you, alas! it wasn't his mother
> that bent his brows into such an expectant arch.
> Not to meet yours, girl feeling him, not to meet yours
> did his lips begin to assume that more fruitful curve. [14–17]

The life of the "youth" is apparently the direct product of certain determining causes and experiences. There is, for instance, the encounter with the girl and also—something which is developed more fully later—his relation to his mother and all that this implies. The life of the youth seems to be complete in itself without any need for further explanation. But is this really so? Can a person's experience be accounted for in terms of the causes which operate directly on him. Are there not other hidden forces at work below the surface? When the youth meets the girl "his brows" are "bent into an expectant arch" and the experience of love begins which will later bloom and ripen in fulfilment. But can this be accounted for simply in terms of the other person? Was the girl, who could "feel him" in her heart, or the mother, with her tender care, strong enough to create this powerful tension, or to make the youth's "lips assume that fruitful curve" of a smile?

The passage is ominous and full of foreboding: the initial "alas!" of the first stanza recurs at the beginning of the second.

The same question is now put more vehemently:

> Do you really suppose your gentle approach could have so
> convulsed him, you, that wander like wind at dawn?   [18–19]

The encounter with the girl has "convulsed" the youth—but
is her delicate nature sufficient to explain the extent of this
convulsion?

One might reply that the Eros has its own logic which is
different from that of the material world. The intensity of the
youth's experience springs from the tension between the sexes
which has its own dynamic, for this tension may be produced
by something apparently incommensurable with it, such as
gentleness or delicacy. But, the poet asks, does this not show
that there are tensions more abysmal than those which are set
up between people? The question seems the more pertinent
when we read the beautiful description of the girl whose
approach is "gentle" as the wafting of the "wind at dawn".

The poet gives his own answer:

> You terrified his heart, indeed; but more ancient terrors
> rushed into him in that instant of shattering touch.   [20–21]

The fear which the youth feels is the tremendous impact of
Eros. It is more than could be aroused simply by the encounter
with the girl, for "more ancient terrors rushed into him". Thus,
beneath what could be directly apprehended, another hidden
realm has been disclosed.

This realm is, however, not described in terms of space as
lying "below", but temporally as "more ancient"—belonging
to the past and yet subsisting into the present. It not only
stretches *downwards* into abysmal depths of the present time but
also *backwards* into an earlier period.

Do you imagine, the poet asks the girl, that you have this
effect on the youth unaided, and that he exists only in relation
to yourself?

> Call him . . . you can't quite call him away from sombre
> consorting.   [22]

If things were as you imagine, then you would certainly be able
to summon him to you once and for all. He would be entirely
yours in a love undarkened by any shadow. But this is not so.
If you use your perception carefully you will see that a part

of your lover does not respond to your bidding but stays behind, imprisoned in another sphere.

Once more the image of this other realm is expanded—not just spacially in the abyss, not just temporally into the past, but in the mysterious pattern of behaviour and action which is here suggested by the "sombre consorting".

The youth may well wish to enter wholly into the bright relationship of love, but can he succeed?

> He certainly wants to, he does escape; disburdenedly settles
> into your intimate heart, takes up and begins himself there.
> Did he ever begin himself, though?   [23–25]

One of the fundamental features of human love is very finely observed here. Love implies the possibility of "escaping". The word "escape" here means on the one hand the liberation of the imprisoned self both from inner toils and from the power of the external world; on the other hand it also means growth and development into personal individuality. When this takes place a load falls from the lover's back; he is "disburdened" and acquires a new refuge in the "intimate heart" of the loved one.

He "takes up and begins himself there". Previously he was not 'self-possessed' at all since he belonged elsewhere. Now he "takes" himself in hand, as it were. Formerly he was no more than an element in the stream of life; now he begins an individual life of his own. One of the mysteries of the human personality is that it only awakens to a real life of its own when it has left the self for the sake of someone else. Man cannot really say "I" until he has said "Thou".

But is this what has happened? Has the youth succeeded? Has he been able to complete this first stage of individual growth?

IV

Now the second theme, which was only touched on before, becomes dominant. The mother emerges in place of the girl. Instead of the awakening of the personality through love we have the beginning of individual life in birth. The link between the two is in the idea of "beginning". Love is just such a begin-

F

ning, for it brings about the emergence of personal consciousness. But love presupposes another beginning which preceded
it, namely the generation of life itself.

> Mother you made him small, it was you that began him;
> for you he was new,   [26-27]

We must bear in mind Rilke's tendency to give words a fresh
intensity by reducing them to their elementary meaning.
"Mother, you made him small" does not mean primarily "first
he was large and then you made him small" but rather "you
created him as a small being". It is true that what is said later
(line 55 ff.) might suggest another reading, namely that the
mother brought him out of the limitless expanse of a larger
life into the "small", i.e. the closely confined, shape of an
individual. Here, at all events, it means the same as the words
which follow—"It was you that began him". Again this is an
odd turn of phrase—to "begin" a person as one might begin
to weave a garment! It means 'You made him begin to exist'
or 'You began the influence on the new-born babe which others
will continue later', when he is fashioned into a man by his
teachers, friends, colleagues and opponents in life.

The words which follow add yet another nuance of meaning.
You *thought* he was "small" and had just begun to exist. The
sentence says "for you he was new": for you, who bore him
into this world, he was a creature newly made for life—strange
and mysterious in not having existed before but in being present
now—whereas in fact he was very old!

It was this feeling that prompted the maternal tenderness,
striving to protect the newly-born creature from the alien
world which was already established in possession of life. And
how did she do it?

> you arched over those new eyes
> the friendly world, averting the one that was strange.   [27–28]

The mother bends over the child—over his "new eyes" which
have only just begun to see and are unpractised in perception,
so that the world seems strange to them. Her face, on the other
hand, is the familiar "friendly world", for only a short time
ago he was a part of her. This friendly world of the mother
dispels the "strange" world of things not yet understood.

Just as the girl has here become the mother, so the youth
has turned into the child. The atmosphere too has changed.
There is a sheltering intimacy between mother and child. This
child, we should add, is the poet himself. As often happens in
the *Elegies*, Rilke's own childhood emerges in the poem:

> Where, oh, where, are the years when you barred the way
> for him, with your slender form, to the surging abyss? [29-30]

As is clearly shown in the letters to Lou Andreas-Salomé and
the Princess of Thurn and Taxis, Rilke was acutely sensitive
to the strange and fearful elements of life. As a man he had to
struggle with them. In retrospect the years of childhood seemed
blissful for that was a time when life's problems could be solved
more simply. The terror of the "surging abyss" was already
there, but it was easily overcome when the mother interposed
her "slender form to bar the way".

This protection of the child from strange, unfamiliar things
was necessary if only because there was so much to be warded
off.

> You hid so much from him then; made the nightly suspected room
> harmless, and out of your heart full of refuge
> mingled more human space with that night-space of his.
> Not in the darkness, no, but within your far nearer presence
> you placed the light, and it shone as though out of friendship.
>
> [31-35]

In the child's world things have an altogether different character from that of the grown-up. The inner and the outer, people
and things, reality and dream, reason and mystery merge into
one another. They may do this in a benevolent friendly way,
in which case the child experiences that marvellous harmony
in life which has become inaccessible to the grown-up. The
Fifth Elegy refers precisely to this. But the things surrounding
the child may seem eery or threatening and then the child
suffers anxieties from which the grown-up is protected. When
darkness falls the room becomes "nightly suspected", ambiguous and dangerous. As soon as the mother enters, however,
summoned perhaps by a frightened cry, everything becomes
"harmless".

The sentence which follows is most apt. The mother's heart is "full of refuge", that is full of the shelter that her strength and protective care can give. But this is to give the words too rational and literal a sense. "Refuge" here means rather a quality that fills the heart. Again a connection with the girl is apparent, for her heart too is such that the youth can find in it a shelter and a home. What happens then, when the mother offers the refuge of her protecting heart? In two senses of the word the child lives in *space*: he dwells in the physical space of his "room" and he is also surrounded by his "night-space"—the abode of dark, mysterious forces which have power over us. For the child the night is the space where his fears originate. And it is into this strange space that the mother pours out the warmth of her heart, mingling "more human space" with it. We may recall what the *First Elegy* said about the different dimensions of space and the possibility of project-ing something from the heart into what is primarily physical space by an act of love. The same thing happens here. The non-human space of the night receives a human element from the mother's heart and everything is then transformed.

She brings a night-light and sets it on the table. The little light consoles the child, not only because it illumines the physical darkness, but because she herself is present in the light. The light does not stand "in the darkness" of the room but becomes the centre of her "nearer presence", her own sphere of gentle and protective tenderness. It shines "as though out of friendship"—as though it too were alive and caring for the child.

The mother puts right all those things which are accepted by grown-ups as normal but which frighten small children:

Nowhere a creak you could not explain with a smile,
as though you had long known *when* the floor would behave
   itself thus . . .
and he listened to you and was soothed.   [36–38]

A floor-board creaks and the child asks fearfully—What was that? But the mother "explains with a smile" that the floor was tired and wanted to stretch. The answer and the smile dispel all fear, for the mother knew exactly "*when* the floor would behave itself thus", when it would make a noise and what it wants. The child sighs with relief and falls asleep. Again we are reminded of the girl by the word "soothe" describing the mother's effect on the child.[1]

Indeed the child's fears of the "strange world" *around* him are the same as the "older" fears which grown-ups feel *within*. The things which the latter sense inside themselves or beneath the surface seem to surround the child. The child does not separate animate and inanimate, personal experience and the world outside.

The following lines give a hint of the shape of the Future which lies behind the childish Present:

> So much it availed,
> gently, your rising: his tall cloaked destiny stepped
> behind the wardrobe then, and his restless future,
> that easily got out of place, conformed to the folds of the
> curtain. [38–41]

The mother can do everything. Her strength and her vocation are also evoked in Rilke's "Uncompleted Elegy" which contains the following lines:[2]

> For who can fail to see that the guardian hands
> lie, while trying to defend it,—themselves in danger? Who
> *may* then?
> 'I!'
> —What I?
> 'I, mother, I *may*. I was fore-world.
> Earth has confided to me what she does with the seed
> to keep it intact. Those intimate evenings! We rained,
> earth and I, softly and Aprilly, into the womb.
> O male, who shall make you believe in the pregnant concord
> we felt together? For you no annunciation
> of cosmic peace concluded round something growing!
> (Maternal magnanimity! Call of the comforters!) Yet,
> what you've described is peril itself, the entire
> pure perilousness of the world:—and thus it turns to protection,
> soon as you feel it completely. The fervour of childhood
> stands like a centre within it: *out*-fearing it, fearless.

[1] See line 5.   [2] *Selected Works*, II, p. 326.

But anxiety!—Learnt all at once in that disconnexion
formed by us, by insolid humanity: draughtily
jerks itself in through the cracks: glides up from behind,
over its play, to the child, and hisses
dissension into its blood,—

This poem has great depth of meaning and would warrant a careful interpretation. But that cannot be attempted here. The *Elegy* differs from it in dealing, not with the legendary loneliness and grandeur of maternity, but with one particular mother as she watches and tends her child by the bedside. Yet even she has some of the transcending greatness of a mother-figure. For she only needs to stand up with her face full of kindly assurance, and then all the big disturbing things are put in their place. We must add that the lines which follow are probably not concerned merely with a child who is afraid of the creaking floor, but with a boy who fears the threats of the future. Rilke was very conscious of these. Until late in life he did not know where he really belonged or what career he should take up.[1] Only someone who has experienced this irresolution and uncertainty himself can know how fearful was Rilke's sense of 'not belonging' anywhere. This feeling looms up indistinctly, and therefore all the more disturbingly, behind the shapes in the room. But even here the mother comes to his aid. A moment ago "his destiny" stood there, "tall", that is threatening, and "cloaked" or hidden. Then, perhaps after sitting by the side of the child's bed, the mother stands up and the "destiny steps behind the wardrobe". It disappears, as a ghost vanishes when someone comes with the power of exorcism. He was still there of course, for destiny cannot be banished for good. But at least he was no longer in the foreground. It was now possible to behave as though he did not exist. A few moments previously the "restless", i.e. disturbing, future was "out of place", but as soon as the mother stood up it "conformed to the folds of the curtain". Here a whole complex process is rendered in a few words. The disturbing element of the "future" steps forth from the folds of the curtain—the future and the curtain are related in being shrouded and swaying—and then goes back to its place again. Although it is still there in the folds the child can now at least go to sleep.

[1] See Carl Sieber, *René Rilke*, p. 92 ff.

V

The second stanza closes on a note of tranquillity—a provisional tranquillity, it is true, for destiny and the future remain. But for the moment their threat has been dispelled.

> And he himself as he lay there in such relief,
> dissolving, under his drowsy eyelids, the sweetness
> of your light shaping into the sleep he had tasted,   [42–44]

The banishing of the child's fear is well described—how his inner peace comes from his mother, indeed, how she herself is a part of this peace. The depth of his tranquillity is evoked by the words "as he lay there in such relief". These lines are a kind of prelude to the sharply contrasting passage which follows and describes what goes on below the surface. For the moment, however, the child can enjoy the soothing moment before sleep. He is filled with the vision of his mother whom he still sees "under his drowsy eyelids". So she enters into that first sleep which he has already begun to "taste". Again her "light shaping" reminds us of her kinship with the girl.

Yet already the peace of sleep is disrupted. The child in bed

> *seemed* to be under protection . . .   [45]

But he only "seemed" so, for the mother's protection reaches no further than the consciousness. The inner world is quite different.

> *Within*, though: who could avert,
> divert, the floods of origin flowing within him?   [45–46]

Once more the dark hidden world emerges from which he had escaped. This time it takes the form, already foreshadowed in the second stanza, of "floods of origin", i.e. the legacy of his own pre-past.

This in itself has no meaning, for the past is past and only has any reality in its effects. But here Rilke is asserting something more than this. According to the *Elegy* the past consists not only of earlier events and causes, but of elements which

are actually present in the life of here and now. The human
personality seems, it is true, to exist here and now in its own
right—just as father and mother apparently used to exist with
their own personalities, and *their* parents before them. All
seemingly led self-enclosed lives in private worlds of their own.
But only seemingly. For below the surface all our forbears are
joined together, in much the same way as a plant may appear
above the earth as several growths or clusters, whilst the roots
form a single mass underneath. This idea is now transferred to
the sphere of time. Below the realm of consciousness, in the
unconscious, time is indivisible. There all the generations,
which here appeared to succeed one another, are to be found
together. The conscious cannot penetrate so far down—nor
can those aids which come to us from the brighter realm above,
not even a mother's love.[1]

Not even the individual's natural assertiveness, not all the
vigilance with which he defends himself against the destructive
element, can reach down to these depths.

> Alas! there *was* no caution within that sleeper: sleeping,
> yes, but dreaming, yes, but feverish: what he embarked on!
> He, so new, so timorous,   [47–49]

The boy is an individual. But as he has only just attained individuality he is described as "new". Having just achieved
self-hood he is still "timorous" of anything that might call his
'self' into question. This at least is true on the plane of consciousness. But beneath the surface things are different. And
when he falls asleep he quits the upper realm of light for a
place where there is no more caution and where he abandons
himself completely. It is true that he is sleeping. But sleep does
not mean the interruption of his whole life. If the conscious life
ceases, the unconscious life goes on—and with renewed vigour,
especially when it shows itself in his dreams, or fevers, or the
involuntary excitations of his instincts through which his
tensions are expressed.

So this apparently self-sufficient human creature leaves behind the world of consciousness where he shunned everything

---

[1] There is a similarity here with Rilke's idea of the "deep Being" of the world
where past, present and future become the same thing. See his letter to W. V.
Huléwicz below, pp. 211 and 220.

which might threaten him. And in that lower realm he changes
his behaviour altogether. There he willingly "embarks".

What follows is like a magical transformation. The earlier
themes of self-possession and individual growth—themes which
were touched on when the youth was said to "take up and
begin himself"—are now abandoned. The individual loses his
identity and becomes only an element in a larger whole.

> how he got tangled
> in ever-encroaching creepers of inner event,
> twisted to primitive patterns, to throttling growths, to bestial
> preying forms!   [49-52]

Human life is now left behind as images from a non-human
world begin to obtrude. Like Philomena or Daphne in the
mythical metamorphoses, the human being is transported into
the world of plants and beasts. But even this world does not
consist of clearly differentiated creatures, trees or animals. It
is composed of a tanglewood, a luxuriant primeval forest, where
it is impossible to know whether a plant is a parasite or grows
from the earth, or whether we are looking at a liana or a
serpent, a flower or an insect. We see merely "encroaching
creepers", "throttling growths" and "bestial preying forms".
The only "patterns" here are primitive ones resulting from the
very profusion of growth—lines in whose structure the individual is merely an element to be swallowed up.

Worst of all, the dreamer, although repelled by all this, still
desires it!

> How he gave himself up to it! Loved. [52]

He surrenders himself. He *loves* it . . . Here again we cannot
avoid a fundamental question: can we—*ought* we to refer here
to "love" at all? If love has already been mentioned in connection with the "pure face" of the girl, the "heart full of
refuge" of the mother, the "purest star" and the "intimate
insight" which sprang from it—then can this be called love?
Probably there is an influence here from Freudian psychology
with which Rilke was familiar, especially after his friendship
with Lou Andreas-Salomé. According to Freud all forms of

desire and sacrifice—from the physical to the spiritual—are simply different forms of the *libido*, or sexual urge. This is a biological materialism which one might expect to be quite alien to Rilke's nature. And, indeed, he wrote to Lou Andreas-Salomé in the following terms:[1] "You will understand that the idea comes to me now and again of having myself analysed. It is true that what I know of Freud's writings is repugnant to me and, in parts, hair-raising. But the idea running through his work has certain genuine and convincing sides to it. . . As I wrote to you before, I feel great misgivings about this clearing-out process in my case and, my nature being what it is, could hardly expect anything good from it. The result of this process is something like a disinfected soul, a monstrosity—alive, but corrected in red like the pages of a school exercise-book." Nevertheless, the theories of Freud, which first opened up the hidden depths of the human mind and countered the thin concepts of the psychology of the conscious with others of quite different calibre, clearly exerted an influence on Rilke. Indeed, so strong was this influence that in this *Elegy* he could ignore the difference between Sexus and Eros, instinct and love of a person, summarizing them together under the single heading 'Love'. Of course it would be wrong to overlook the fact that even the most platonic attachment includes a certain instinctive urge which may be a weakening factor. But if one accepts the word 'love' as it is used in the *Elegy*, one is bound to ignore the most obvious experiences of human life as well as the testimony of philosophy and poetry.

The fact that Rilke does use the word in this way is closely linked to that other feature of the *Elegies* which gives the reader so much cause for concern, namely the disintegration of human personality. A biological materialist may well identify the spiritual essence of love—the encounter of the 'I' with the 'Thou'—so closely with the impersonal physical impulse that he can classify both under the heading 'Love'. But this should have been impossible for Rilke. If he was nevertheless capable of doing this then there must be a special reason for it, which seems to lie in his theory of love. This theory is so ethereal that it transcends not only all sensual desire but the very I-Thou relationship itself. And in the process it ignores what stands at

[1] Letter of Jan. 20th 1912.

the very centre of our existence, namely the human person. If Rilke had only grasped the idea of the 'person' with his or her unqualified demands, then this might have made impossible the use of "loved" in the above context—particularly since this poem deals with the problematical relations between impulse and personality.

What was said above may equally well be put the other way round. Only if one's sense of human personality is as weak as Rilke's clearly was can one postulate this theory of love which he regarded as the essential message of the *Elegies*. The idea that the "instinct" is "guilty" in itself (see line 2) serves to justify his prescription that true love must be dissociated from the Thou and should pass straight across to the realm of pure 'openness'. There is a latent dualism here which, as the history of gnosticism shows, is liable at any time to turn into its opposite and legitimize both instinct and intellect. It may be a strange paradox, but it is an essential law of existence, that what ultimately does justice to the instincts and makes physical purity possible is precisely the dignity of the human person.

The *Elegy* continues:

> Loved his interior world, his interior jungle,
> that primal forest within, on whose mute overthrownness,
> light-green, his heart stood. [53–55]

The views expressed above must not prevent us from recognizing the grandiose quality of Rilke's images—the "jungle" and the "primal forest" inside the sleeping youth.

The forest was described a little earlier in the poem as full of "throttling growths". Now its other side appears—that of death and decay. The giant trees have fallen down—a "mute overthrownness" and on one of the trunks his "heart" stands, light-green. We have all at one time or another seen a dead tree lying in a dark wood with something growing on top of it, perhaps a tiny plant which had taken root, or a leafy shoot of the tree itself which was still alive. Here a ray of light comes to rest on the little leaf and makes it a brilliant green. This is "his heart"—an image, seen as in a dream, which arouses delight and deep fear at the same time.

> Loved. Left it, continued
> out through his own roots into violent beginning
> where his tiny birth was already outlived.   [55-57]

Again the word 'love' occurs, for the third time in four lines!
As in line 52 it is given the maximum possible emphasis by
being set apart to form a sentence of its own.

Now, however, the dreamer leaves "it"—his inner world—
and "continues out through his own roots". He journeys back
along the links in the chain of his own evolution towards the
"violent beginning" of the past. This 'past' is still accessible
since here the superficial distinctions between Now and Then,
between Being and Having-Been, are no longer valid. The past
is there and yet not there, gone and yet still with us, so that
such defining qualities of human personality as character or
honour lose their meaning.

Down there "his tiny birth was already outlived". There,
where 'formerly' and 'now' and 'later' are all confused and
undifferentiated, *Someone* was born. But even before his life
started the "violent beginning" had already "out-lived" and
survived him. The primal vitality in all its might covers up the
beginning of any individual life and engulfs it in timelessness—
an obscure counterpart to what we call Eternity.

The journey continues:

> Descended,
> lovingly, into the older blood, the ravines
> where Frightfulness lurked, still gorged with his fathers. And every
> terror knew him, winked, was as though it were waiting.
> Yes, Horror smiled at him. . .   [57-61]

The traveller descends from one level in the blood to the other,
back in time from one generation to the next. The territory
which he has penetrated reveals its true character more and
more clearly. The "blood" turns into a world of its own—a
subterranean landscape. This is not merely psychological—any
more than the "purest star" was astronomical. Like it, the
subterranean landscape lies in that mysterious realm of the
"Other". It is the Underworld, Hades, the seat of Chaos and
the Dead. There are "ravines" here, where the mountains
draw together to hem life in. This is the home of Frightfulness,
a nameless monster, "still gorged with his fathers". He has

devoured them. He is the primeval dragon who brings forth life and also consumes it. He "winks" with weary recognition, sure of his own invulnerability, as though "waiting". Finally this gruesome account reaches its climax in the words: "Horror smiled at him".

Again we cannot help asking whether this way of using words can be reconciled with a responsible attitude towards language as a vehicle of truth. Can one apply the word "smile", previously used of the mother, to this cold monstrosity? Our very task as human beings is surely to find a firm foundation amid the turmoil of life—to discriminate true values in the midst of confusion. If this is so, truth must be distinguished from falsehood, the good from the bad and the noble from the paltry, and words which are appropriate to the one must be withheld from the other. Here, however, Rilke portrays the weird and confused character of dark threatening forces without distinguishing them adequately from their opposites. The word "love" is applied elsewhere to the girl and the word "smile" to the face of both her and the mother. If the selfsame words are permissible in connection with these monsters this means that there must be evil in good and horror in beauty. Indeed good *is* evil and the horrible is beautiful. Goodness becomes simply one element of a primeval reality whose other element is evil. In that case *both* are equally valid and there is no point in struggling to choose between them.

But the supreme struggle in life depends on a choice between the opposites Either and Or. If we evade this choice by regarding good and evil simply as poles of existence or as elements which are present in all phenomena, then the challenge to make a decision loses all its force. Life is reduced to a horrible confusion.

The foregoing is confirmed by the lines which follow:

> Seldom
> did you, Mother, smile so tenderly. How could he help
> loving what smiled at him? Long before you
> he loved it, for even while you bore him
> it was there, dissolved in the water that lightens the seed.
>
> [61–65]

Can the poet really be fully aware of what he is saying in these words? How can he attribute to Horror such a quality as "tenderness", which springs straight from the goodness of the heart? He even gives this tenderness priority over that of the mother![1]

So the youth's love for the cold amphibia of the depths is deeper, and of longer standing, than his love for his mother's pure face. This 'love' is a primal urge of man, stemming from his pre-natal life—the same sphere of primordial being where the fear lurks which obliterates the human personality. Such are the roots from which it grows in our earthly life—in the womb of the mother bearing her child, in the "water that lightens the seed" surrounding the embryo. Here Rilke's original idea has apparently taken on an independent life of its own: it is no longer under his control and, as happens sometimes in the work of Nietzsche, it runs its own compulsive course.

VI

The *Elegy* now returns to its opening theme. The preceding lines were addressed to the mother. The following sentence, unless it is intended simply as a transition, is spoken to the girl once more:

> Look, we don't love like flowers, with only a single
> season behind us; immemorial sap
> mounts in our arms when we love.   [66–68]

The new use of the word "love", now in a botanical sense, after it has just referred to "Horror", does not call for further discussion here, although it throws light on Rilke's attitude to the problem of human personality. Apart from this, however, the image has to be seen in perspective, otherwise it is merely confusing. Properly speaking, flowers do *not* love "with only a single season behind"—any more or less than Man does in the *Elegy*. For, like him, they owe their life to a seed which in turn sprang from another seed which came before it. The same could thus be said of the flower as is said above of Man. But every image in the *Elegies* is used to bring out a particular

---

[1] Unless, of course, these lines should be taken as reflecting on the complex relationship of Rilke with his mother and the influence of her problematical personality on his own view of life. But an investigation of this problem would lead us beyond the limits of this work.

similarity and sometimes even a minor detail serves to give a
certain emphasis or colour to the whole. Here what is meant
is that the flower only lives a short span, and in this time it
"loves", i.e. blossoms and bears fruit. With the flower everything is compressed into a few weeks or months of life. With
us things are different, for "immemorial sap mounts in our
arms when we love". Two images are fused here and behind
the shape of a man we see that of a tree whose "arms" are
branches. What flows in us is "immemorial sap", the quint-
essence of something that took place long ago.

> Oh, maid,
> *this*: that we've loved, *within* us, not one, still to come, but all
> the innumerable fermentation; not just a single child,
> but the fathers, resting like mountain-ruins
> within our depths;—but the dry river-bed
> of former mothers;—yes, and the whole of that
> soundless landscape under its cloudy or
> cloudless destiny;—*this* got the start of you, maid.   [68–75]

Again a vision of horror is evoked, similar to that of the third
stanza, except that here it is tempered and more restrained.
By this the girl is to learn that the lover—her partner in this
deep personal relationship—has already loved "within himself". Then, however, he did not love the girl, but something
obscure inside; not a particular creature, the "one still to
come" as the offspring of love, but the "innumerable fermentation", the chaos which existed before time began.

"Not just a single child, but the fathers". Here the order of
love is turned upside down in a most perverse fashion. The
emotion which properly belongs to the child is transferred to
the "fathers" who "rest like mountain-ruins within our depths"
—dead, stiff and broken. This profoundly unnatural feeling
inevitably alienates the girl whose innermost wish is to be a
mother. But again it is reiterated that the youth does not love
the child who will enter into the bloom of life, but rather "the
dry river-bed of former mothers". Each mother was once the
"river-bed" of a stream of life which passed over it and now
they are all dead and dried-up. These are the real objects of
the young man's love. The same point is then given final
emphasis: he does not love the coming world which should

spring from true love itself, but "the whole of that soundless landscape" down in the depths—the past that now lies "under its cloudy or cloudless destiny". This landscape of the past, like any other landscape, has a sky—in this case the sky of its presiding "destiny" or fate which may have been "cloudy" and dark, or "cloudless", bright and sunny. But in any case it is now past and dead.

All this "got the start of you, maid". When she met the youth she imagined that his love for her was the beginning of something new; in reality something very old was at work drawing his love towards itself. According to the last stanza the girl herself was responsible for summoning up this ancient power:

> And you yourself, how can you tell,—you have conjured up
> prehistoric time in your lover.   [76–77]

This links up with what was said at the beginning of the second stanza; the girl has certainly found her lover and awakened his affection for her, but, beyond this, she has stirred up his hidden depths as well.

This is the situation she has to deal with now. When her lover approaches her and shows his feelings or intentions he is not there alone. Beings from the past are stirring in him too.

>   What feelings
> whelmed up from beings gone by! What women
> hated you in him! What sinister men
> you roused in his youthful veins! Dead children
> were trying to reach you. . .   [77–81]

Everything is eery and confused here. The feelings do not arise spontaneously but "whelm up". The creatures which clamour for expression have "gone by"; they have no clear-cut form for they have dissolved into lemurine shapes.

"Women" come and are filled with jealousy for the girl. "Men" rise up, sinister and full of evil intent. "Dead children" want to reach you, seeking life and yearning to be born anew. Thus the lower sphere strives towards the higher in order to re-establish itself there, but only inspires dread and creates havoc.

What then shall the girl do? She must use the power which she has and which was praised so warmly in the early stanzas of the *Elegy*:

                              Oh, gently, gently
show him daily an honest, confident task done,—guide him
close to the garden, give him preponderance
over his nights. . . . . .
                        Withhold him. . . . . .   [81–85]

In the daytime she should do an "honest confident task"—those
good homely services which woman performs in the house and
by which she preserves life. She should also "guide him close
to the garden". The garden is of course an ancient and well-
known symbol: it is the sphere where nature and man meet
together in harmony. In the garden man leaves the confines
of the house without losing himself in the boundless expanse
of nature; and nature, for her part, can come close to man
without being simply exploited by him. So the garden is a
symbol of peace and of flourishing, enclosed beauty. This is
where the girl should lead the youth.

And at night she should bring him that fulfilment which,
being rooted in order, stills his longings while guarding him
from the chaos of excess. She will then be a 'counterbalance'
to the powers which might lure him to destruction. She will
"withhold" him—help him to preserve his integrity and his
identity as an individual. We may perhaps call to mind here
the "starry nights" in the *Seventh Elegy*. For the girl's sphere is that
of the "purest star" and it is her task to reveal this to her lover.

So the *Third Elegy* closes on a note of hope, similar to that
which concluded the *Second*. There it was the "little strip of
cornland in between river and rock" where something "pure,
contained and human" could be realized amidst the inhospi-
tality of the world. Here it is the power of the individual human
heart which, despite its fragility, may succeed in warding off
the forces of darkness by its sheer goodness.

THE FOURTH ELEGY

Written at Munich during the First World War,
November 22nd–23rd 1915

I

IN the *Fourth Elegy*, as in several of the others, the opening line plunges the reader straight into the ideas and feelings which dominate the whole poem:[1]

> O Trees of life, what are your signs of winter? [1]

The poet sees the trees standing stiff and leafless. Like the rest of nature they are affected by the time of year. This immediately prompts the thought that we human beings are like Nature: our nature too has its own trees, its mountains and seas and animals. Moreover *our* nature has its seasons as well, and in each season certain things must happen if life is to remain whole and develop. The question then arises: *When* does a season begin in our lives? When is it Winter for *our* trees? Do we even notice when a season is at hand?
The answer is 'No':

> We're not at one. We've no instinctive knowledge,
> like migratory birds. Outstript and late,
> we force ourselves on winds and find no welcome
> from ponds where we alight. [2–5]

The second image is also taken from external nature—the "migratory birds". The departure of the birds when Winter draws near provides a link with the preceding image. The birds know when to begin their outward passage, for they receive due assurance from their "instincts". The same rhythm prevails in their natural environment and in the prompting of their instincts—in biological necessity and real behaviour. Their whole life is "at one".

---

[1] The directness of this opening question is even more marked in the original which means literally: "O Trees of life, *when wintry?*"

98

Our life is not. There is no harmony between our behaviour as individuals and the seasons of our lives. Had the first image been completed it would have continued as follows: the trees in our life may already show signs of Winter, but we go astray by looking for fruit on them as if it were still Autumn. The second image says something similar. We behave like sick birds of passage whose instincts do not work properly. They fly "outstript and late"—outstript by the season and too late to make a safe arrival. They must therefore venture forth in contrary winds—i.e. "force" themselves on winds which do not want them—and when they pause for rest they settle on ponds which are frozen and give them no welcome. Here the general image of the migrant bird is narrowed down, referring now to specific breeds like wild geese which settle on water. This is precisely what we do. When we act we are outstript by the world in which we live: our actions come too late and are "forced" or imposed on the world in such a way as to create confusion and conflict.

> We comprehend
> flowering and fading simultaneously.
> And somewhere lions still roam, all unaware,
> while yet their splendour lasts, of any weakness.　　[5–8]

Here a new image is introduced—a flower. "We comprehend flowering and fading simultaneously". The different stages of our growth do not follow one another in a correct natural sequence; they are intermingled so that we are conscious of one stage at the same time as another. Hence our feelings of confusion and insecurity.

Yet another image: There are lions who rejoice in their own strength. There are "still" such lions, as if they had survived from an earlier, more glorious period of time—like the great cathedrals of the *Seventh Elegy*. "Somewhere" they roam. The very imprecision of this line gives the figure of the lion a power-ful and mysterious quality. While they are still in their strength and "their splendour lasts" they are "unaware of any weak-ness". Either they are in the full bloom of their strength and they feel simply strong, or else they fall sick and die, and this is all they know.

Here Rilke's characteristic use of metaphors becomes clear. His images succeed one another rapidly—no fewer than four in the eight lines of the first stanza. None of them is fully developed, but each is calculated to illustrate a certain feature of our life. This is, of course, the purpose of any image. But if we compare Rilke's images with those of, say, Homer or Dante the difference is clear. Events and people in their works are described in detail with tireless interest. Rilke depicts only the little that matters. His images are like colours with which an artist paints a broad surface here, a spot there and perhaps somewhere else adds a nuance to the whole. The third image in the above passage—that of the flowers—is like a tiny point of colour in the right place.

II

The lines which follow go more deeply into the realm of inner experience. Indeed, the first sentence is like the definition of a psychological truth:

> We, though, while we're intent upon one thing,
> can feel the cost and conquest of another.   [9–10]

Here Rilke explains what he means by "not at one". No sooner do we become "intent" on one thing than we feel the "cost and conquest of another". This feeling rises up within us in spite of ourselves. When we relax, we still feel that soon we shall have to return to work. When we experience joy a sense of pain is never long absent—either sorrow in anticipating the end of our happiness, or the memory of some past grief. It can therefore be rightly said that:

> The Next's our enemy.   [11]

The "next" thing to happen or the thing that is "next" in the sense of having affinity with us is "our enemy". Even those things which concern us most directly and which should be most familiar to us still awaken our mistrust or hostility.

In order to illustrate his point Rilke now turns—as he always does at decisive points in the *Elegies*—to the human experience of love.

> Aren't lovers always
> coming to precipices in each other,—
> lovers, that looked for spaces, hunting, home?   [11–13]

The lovers too know the meaning of hostility. Each lover feels
near to, and at one with, the beloved. So he seeks in his partner
for "spaces, hunting", and "home". Here "spaces" means the
discovery of ever new feelings, the exploration of all the realms
in the heart. The "hunting" is the constant quest for the other
person. Once the unknown lands have been found and the
wild game hunted down they become one's own. Love also
means "home", i.e. shelter without danger, a place of rest
where there is no fear of sudden ambush.

So it seems. But how are things in fact? The lover is always
reaching "precipices" in the other person. He finds himself
suddenly confronted by a sheer drop instead of the flat road
which seemed to lie before him. The "precipice" may mean
here a confinement of the open spaces, an obstacle to the freedom of the hunt, or a threat to the sheltering home.

Counting up the images which have occurred up to this
point, we arrive at the surprising total of nine in thirteen lines!
Yet all these images blend into one another. Each one is like
a sound or a colour which contributes to the sense of the whole.

The following sentence fuses together an abstract psychological idea and its concrete embodiment:

> Then, for the sudden sketchwork of a moment,
> a ground of contrast's painfully prepared,
> to make us see it. For they're very clear
> with us,   [14–17]

The "moment" here means the *present* moment and its significance as revealed to us through our feelings and consciousness.
The image which Rilke uses—a different one again!—is the
"sketchwork". Events are now likened to the strokes of a brush
held in a painter's hand. So that the brush-strokes may be clear
the artist must paint a "ground" or background of colour to
set them off. This colour is the "contrast"—in real life the
opposite of what we feel at any given time. If we preserve the
example already used above we might say that we have to be
aware of how hard tomorrow's work will be in order to enjoy
our peaceful relaxation now. This preparation is "painful".
The word hovers between two associations: it is painful for the
man who holds the brush, since he must take care to find the
right colour contrast for his sketchwork. And it is painful for

us, too, in the sense that all our efforts to gain experience and understanding of life bring pain and suffering.

Here we may note the implications of this passage. Who in fact holds the brush in real life? Who is it who sketches in each moment as we experience it and who prepares the background so that we can recognize clearly what has been drawn? The answer is strangely uncertain and yet penetrating at the same time. The *Elegy* says that the 'ground *is* prepared' and that "*they're* very clear with us". Perhaps a parallel may be drawn here with the novels of Franz Kafka. There too no names are given. We are not even told that the judge or the clerk in the story actually did anything but that "in the castle *they*" ordained such and such; it "was decreed" in this or that way; something happened in "a certain room". So it might be said that a motive force is at work in Kafka's novels which has receded into anonymity. This hidden force is not weakened by its anonymity; perhaps rather the contrary, since it is intangible and unassailable. We do not know whether it has a human aspect or can be spoken to in human terms. All we know is that it is inaccessible. Clearly this power is intended to be God —the God of the Old Testament—but, one might add, a God who is not believed in and yet is known to be present.[1] Possibly this parallel brings us nearer to Rilke's manner of speaking in the *Elegy*. The impersonal "they" refers to the prime mover in existence—'Destiny'—but, as in the novels of Kafka, this concept transcends any closer definition.

The sentence "they're very clear with us" means on the one hand that the supreme authority who holds the brush is concerned to give an edge to our experience. In addition it seems to refer to a specific situation, namely that of the 1914–1918 War, in the second year of which this *Elegy* was written. In this sense Rilke's words take on a profoundly bitter tone, as if he were saying: 'Certainly they don't leave us in any doubt'; they are ready to use the most extreme measures to make things clear. All the bloodshed, the destruction and sufferings serve to make us appreciate the full meaning of happiness in our life, work and growth.

[1] A religious phenomenon which has a sociological parallel in the modern state. The 'state' today penetrates our life more and more, but less and less does it provoke the question of 'who?' or 'why?'

> we that don't know our feeling's shape
> but only that which forms it from outside.   [17-18]

"Shape" means the contour of a thing. It can be regarded as
having two aspects, one facing inwards and the other out. Here
"shape" in its first aspect is meant—the form or contour which
expresses a thing's inner character. According to Rilke it is
impossible to form any picture of such a shape. Our experience
only reaches our consciousness from without, namely through
our proximity to whatever is alien or hostile to us.

Again the same phenomenon often noted before: the weakness attaching to the human personality. In fact it is simply
not true that we are only conditioned from outside. Even as
we live our lives and feel our feelings we are constantly re-
forming ourselves anew from within, i.e. setting ourselves
limits and thus determining our own contours or characteristic
"shape".

III

Now Rilke's train of thought takes a new and surprising
turn:

> Who's not sat tense before his own heart's curtain?   [19]

This describes the situation of someone sitting in the theatre
in front of a curtain which is closed before the performance
begins. This new metaphor is now sustained and developed
throughout the long second and third stanzas. The retention
of a single theatrical image is all the more effective after the
Elegy's impressionistic beginning. It is not at first clear how a
transition is effected from the earlier images to the theatre.
Perhaps the words "from outside" in line 18 provide an answer.
What goes on in our hearts is not apparent from inside but
shaped from without; let us then accept this as a fact and
examine ourselves objectively from outside. Our heart will be
the stage and we shall witness the spectacle of our inner life.

> Up it would go: the scenery was Parting.
> Easy to understand. The well-known garden,
> swaying a little.   [20–22]

Now something happens which we see every time we go to the
theatre. The curtain "goes up" and the play begins. The

scenery is "Parting"—the stock scenery of our existence. "We
live our lives, for ever taking leave", as the last line of the
Eighth Elegy says. Something is always coming to a close. The
idea is fundamental to Rilke's attitude to life. We cannot have
or hold anything, nor can we be permanently joined to anyone.
This fact is taken for granted as "easy to understand".

The stage on which the action takes place is the "well-
known garden", i.e. as it appears again and again on the
average stage. As was stated above, the garden has a symbolical
meaning: it is the place where Man and Nature meet and is
almost as necessary to life as a house. It is even more necessary
for a parting or leave-taking, since the house is definitely
'inside' and connotes 'dwelling' whereas the garden is essentially 'outside' and reminds us of departure. Incidentally we are
reminded that the whole performance which we shall see is of
rather a low order. This is indicated by the description of the
scenery as "swaying" because it is cheap and insecure.

> Then appeared the dancer.
> Not *him*! Enough! However light he foots it,
> he's just disguised, and turns into a bourgeois
> and passes through the kitchen to his dwelling. [22–25]

This is a dance in mime, not a drama. The dancer enters
straight away and begins his performance. Then the spectator
exclaims "Not *him*!" The pronoun is italicized for emphasis and
clearly means: 'That dancer in front of us is not the man we
expected—not the right one for this situation.' The short
vehement sentence, without a verb, expresses an impatience
which is heightened by the single word "Enough!" which
follows. The performance in front of our eyes is so pathetic that
it is dismissed with an impatient gesture of contempt.

And this contempt is not without foundation: for the man
on the stage is merely trying to imitate a dancer. He pretends
that he has the dancer's essential quality—the ability to move
lightly, to 'transform' himself with apparent effortlessness, from
one pose to the next, though in fact this can only be achieved
by constant effort and training.[1] We may describe the true
dancer in Rilke's own terms as having perfected his 'orphic'
talent for transformation into an art form. But this dancer is
not of the right calibre.

[1] Compare the *Fifth Elegy* on the training of acrobats.

The peculiarity of the actor lies in his being a man with a life of his own, but who acts the lives of others. This accounts for a strange ambiguity in his character: he can never project himself completely into the role of the *other* person because he himself is *someone*. And if he were able to assume the role completely he would betray himself and lose his own identity. Although the second point is not made in the *Elegy* the first one is, because here we obviously have to do with a bad actor, a "bourgeois" who nervously keeps a heavy grip on himself and nowhere really manages to achieve the proper transformation. He is "just disguised" as a dancer and immediately recognizable for what he really is. He will only be properly himself later, when he has removed his make-up, put on ordinary clothes and "passes through the kitchen to his dwelling". The image is very evocative. Normally one enters a house through the hall rather than the kitchen. But the whole commonplace mediocrity of the man has to be suggested. So the first place he visits is the kitchen where there is a smell of food. He enters the dwelling here, perhaps looking into the pots and pans on the way, before going on to the living-room—the very embodiment of the complacent bourgeois with his crude appetites, and poles apart from the artistry of the real dancer.

The whole passage may, of course, be given a different and more fundamental meaning. Every actor is a man of flesh and blood and therefore a bad artist. In spite of the effortless movements which he simulates in his art and in his life he will always remain basically a "bourgeois" and therefore ultimately incapable of true artistry.

The spectator's impatience now breaks loose. For he wants to see something flawless: either complete reality or pure form—"mask". Here, however, there is half of each. There is no full-blooded man producing an effect from within himself, but a small man disguised to create a big effect. Neither is there a genuine *mask* here with the power of pure form. This is not, as the doll is described a little later, "appearance", but a mask which is "half-filled" by the man within.

> I will not have these half-filled masks! No, no,
> rather the doll. That's full. I'll force myself
> to bear the husk, the wire, and even that face
> of sheer appearance.   [26–29]

The true spectator demands true acting and purely expressive form. But this is only found in the doll or marionette. We may have read Heinrich von Kleist's dialogue on the puppet-theatre and have perhaps felt the fascination of the marionette figure ourselves: the strange quality of a movement which is undisturbed by any organic hindrance, psychological inhibitions or intellectual doubts—simply form in motion and nothing else. The puppet is not, like the human actor, "half-filled". It is quite "full" or, one might equally well say, quite 'empty', because it is wholly itself and consists entirely of pure form. This is what is required by the spectator—at least by the spectator who is himself 'full' of, i.e. given over completely to, the performance.

We cannot help feeling a sense of something uncanny here. For when we look at the dancing puppet it is often just a short step from delight in the puppet's movements to that eery feeling produced by something unnatural which might be associated with the magical and demonic—in this case a figure which is alive and moving but without body or soul. A slight shift in our perspective might make us see something from which we would like to flee. But Rilke says "I'll force myself to bear the husk, the wire", i.e. the dead things which can take on such a ghostly life. He will even accept the "face of sheer appearance" —a strangely periphrastic way of describing what a mask is.

Here again we notice a feature of Rilke's thought which recurs more than once in the *Elegies*. There is a curious link between this "face of sheer appearance" because there is no one looking out from behind it, and the "rose" with a thousand sleeping eyelids but no one to 'sleep the sleep', and the "love" which has neither lover nor beloved. We shall see later how this line of thought is consistently pursued.

Here it is the "doll" which the spectator desires, for he will only be satisfied by the 'pure' phenomenon. But the performance will make demands on him. To "bear" it will require courage and effort, as is indicated by the resolute words which follow:

> Here! I'm in my seat.   [29]

At this point we realize who the spectator sitting in front of the stage really is. It is the poet himself. And, as will become

clear, he is not there merely in his capacity as poet; he is there
with his whole being.

Perhaps we may ask ourselves whether this part of the *Elegy*
is not a little contrived or exaggerated. If we admit the uncanny
quality which emanates from the stage and the doll or marionette—is it really so overpowering that we have to summon up
all this courage to withstand it? But if these *are* our feelings
then we have lost the thread of the poem. The stage and the
events which take place on it are so vividly described that we may
easily forget what *sort* of stage this is and what kind of performance is being played. In fact it is still the stage of our heart.
And, as the next lines show, the pantomime which passes over
this stage is our own life.

At first we saw only a simple theatrical stage. But the stage
becomes stranger and stranger:

> Even if the lights go out, even if I'm told
> 'There's nothing more',—even if greyish draughts
> of emptiness come drifting from the stage,—   [30–32]

The play is at an end and it is some time before we notice the
strange thing that has happened. The curtain remains up. The
stage has become empty and the lights go out. The spectator
sits alone in his seat amid the deserted stalls and he is "told"—
anonymously and mysteriously *it is told to him by someone!*—that
"There's nothing more". This "nothing" is, as it were, objectivized in the "emptiness" which is wafted down in the draughts
from the stage. The emptiness which pours *from* human experience into outer space was described in the *First Elegy*. Here the
direction is reversed. The emptiness comes from outside, from
a stage where nothing is going on, and then pours down in
draughts to *enter* the feelings of the spectator.

It is significant that the draughts are called "greyish". We
might have expected another adjective here such as "cold",
since air is not visible and cannot really be grey. But this refers
to our inner soul or spirit and its colour, or 'colourlessness'
which is that of dust. The word is defined unequivocally at the
end of the *Elegy* in the description of the child's "death from

grey bread that gets hard". The greyish colour is Death.¹ The physical quality of colour is thus transferred from objective reality to our inner experience.

> even if of all my silent forbears none
> sits by me any longer, not a woman,
> not even the boy with the brown squinting eyes:
> I'll still remain. For one can always watch.   [33-36]

These others who had previously sat beside him were no ordinary spectators such as we usually meet in the theatre. They are the essential co-spectators who form part of his very life. They include in the first place all his "silent forbears". His ancestors were not simply annihilated in death, nor did they break all connection with the living, but entered that hidden realm of existence from which they could emerge again. The lonely poet can feel that they are even more close to him than the living and a little later he gives a striking description of their proximity. For the moment, however, they have departed and he does not feel their presence. "Not a woman" is there any longer. Here we may recall certain experiences of Rilke's, one of which is related in the memoirs of the Princess of Thurn and Taxis. While he was in Duino Rilke believed for a long

---

¹ See also the poem "Death" in *Selected Works*, II, p. 316. As the Princess of Thurn and Taxis relates in her memoirs, it grew out of a kind of vision which Rilke had in 1915 at about the same time as he was writing the *Fourth Elegy*:

> There, a blue draught for somebody to drain,
> stands Death, in a large cup without a saucer.
> A rather odd position for a cup:
> stands on the back of a hand. And still quite plain
> and visible along the smooth glazed slope
> the place where the handle snapped. Dusty. And 'Hope'
> inscribed in letters half washed down the sink.

> The drinker predetermined for the drink
> spelt them at breakfast in some distant past.

> What kind of creatures these are, that at last
> have to be poisoned off, it's hard to think.

The mood conveyed by the "greyness" in the *Elegy* is heightened here by the words "blue draught", "dusty", "snapped" and "poison" until it reaches a climax of fearful despair. But then, after a few lines of verse, and one of dots, a triumphant change of spirit takes place:

> O falling star,
> seen from a bridge once in a foreign land:—
> remembering you, to stand!

These lines were also inspired by a specific experience, namely the sight of a falling meteor which Rilke witnessed at Toledo.

time that he could feel the presence of three women who had died and who belonged to the family circle.

The *Elegy* then mentions one person separately: "the boy with the brown squinting eyes". "Not even" he sits there any longer, suggesting that he at least might have been expected to remain. The boy referred to was in fact Rilke's cousin Egon, the second son of his eldest uncle on his father's side. The same boy, who died young, also appears in the *Notebook of Malte Laurids Brigge* as the little Erik Brahe, a child who was in touch with the hidden depths of existence.[1] Rilke said that he belonged to "his most unforgettable memories".[2]

All these people have departed. The poet is now quite alone and it is clear what has happened: Death, the destroyer and depriver of all things, has taken his toll.

In spite of his eery isolation the poet says nevertheless: "I'll still remain. For one can always watch."

If life is transient, and if a man can neither place reliance on things nor establish firm relationships with people, there are still several ways of "standing", as the poem "Death" puts it, or of getting a 'footing' in life. He will probably seek a final meaningful point in life which will support him. He may do this in the manner of the stoics by abandoning to Fate everything that is dispensable, while at the same time energetically mustering his inner resources of strength. Any idea of this sort would have been far from Rilke's mind, for his sense of having inner resources was not sufficiently strong. On the other hand a man might make an effort to struggle with his fate, either triumphing or perishing in the attempt but still achieving a kind of self-fulfilment. But this would not have been in keeping with Rilke's nature either. In the *Elegy* he explores a third way. Here man becomes a spectator. He does not live but observes, and what he observes is himself. This explains how everything else becomes strangely detached and remote from him.

[1] This is said by Rilke himself, in a passage from a letter quoted by Carl Sieber in *René Rilke*, 1932, p. 59 f.

[2] *Loc. cit.* The passage in the letter continues: "Much of the child about him, and the sadness and helplessness of being a child are embodied for me in his form, in the neckruff which he wore, the little neck, the chin and those beautiful brown eyes which were only disfigured by a squint."

IV

Now one of those characteristic shifts in the inner movement of the *Elegy* takes place which always announce something new:

> Am I not right?   [37]

The poet here demands confirmation that he has chosen the correct course. As soon becomes clear, his words are addressed to his father who must therefore presumably have reappeared to him:

> You, to whom life would taste
> so bitter, Father, when you tasted mine,
> that turbid first infusion of my Must,
> you kept on tasting as I kept on growing,
> and, still arrested by the after-taste
> of such queer future, tried my clouded gaze,—
> you, who so often, since you died, my Father,
> have been afraid within my inmost hope,
> surrendering realms of that serenity
> the dead are lords of for my bit of fate,—
> am I not right?   [37–47]

Some details of the above passage are not easy to understand, though the general meaning is clear enough. Any son might address his father in this way if he shared his inner confidence. But our understanding of the passage is assisted if we take into account one or two biographical facts as well. The elder Rilke, the poet's father, was an officer who had to give up all hope of promotion and then took employment with a private railway company. He always had the feeling of being *déclassé* and therefore put all his hopes in his son. Understandably enough, he tried to give him the career which he himself had missed. This is what produced the grotesque tragedy that Rilke, who was as unsoldierly as any man could be, was sent first to the Military School at St. Pölten and later to the Military Academy at Mährisch-Weisskirchen to become a professional soldier. These plans for Rilke's career ended in complete failure and brought painful disillusionment to his father.

To what extent his father really found the taste of life "bitter" on account of his son, I cannot judge. Certainly he cannot have known him very well if he was capable of settling on such an impossible career for his son, and this in itself does not suggest any great unselfishness. But certainly he loved his son in his own fashion, and it is equally true that he was worried about him. For young René, after the attempts to train him first for a military and then for a commercial career had both failed, did not seem to fit into life at all well. So the way in which Rilke addresses his father here is understandable: "You, to whom life would taste so bitter . . . when you tasted mine, that turbid first infusion of my Must . . . . as I kept on growing."

The father finds a bitter flavour in his own life when he "tastes" the life of his son, the "turbid first infusion of his Must". The son's life is thus likened to a kind of tea whose first infusion is turbid. The "Must", the inevitability of life, represents Destiny. When the father tastes this he senses the direction which his son's life will take as he grows up. He "keeps on" tasting it, and after he has swallowed the 'sample' of his son's future he is "arrested by the aftertaste" as he dwells on the prospects for the future. Although the passage is tortuous, not to say contrived in places, it still remains most effective largely due to the way in which the future is considered as past, and yet present as an aftertaste at the same time. The passage is made still more complicated by the description of the future which the father tastes as "queer" or strange. This is another example of Rilke's sense of the distance separating one person from another.

Another image which makes a brief appearance deserves note. While the father was "arrested by the after-taste" he looked into his son's eyes, and "tried" his gaze. But the son's eyes were "clouded" like windows through which people outside cannot look *in* and the person inside cannot look *out*. The "clouded gaze" of the son means the same as the earlier "turbidity" of the "Must", namely the distress of the boy or youth who does not know where he belongs.

The son's appeal to the father becomes still more insistent until it finally reveals a deep bond running beneath their separation. When the father died he entered another sphere, the "other relation" mentioned in the *Ninth Elegy*.[1] And yet, even there he still remained on earth in the person of his son.

[1] *Ninth Elegy*, line 21.

Indeed, now he was more deeply involved in his son's life than
before and continued to be "afraid" for him. This is where the
centre of the relation between the two seems to lie, in the fear
and concern felt by the father for the son, and also in the fact
that this concern of the father arouses in the son feelings of
sympathy, gratitude and perhaps irritation. When the son is
hopeful, the father is "within" this hope and feels "afraid".
The son therefore feels: 'My father has no real confidence in
me, otherwise he would not be afraid'. This oppresses him and
perhaps irritates him too. On the other hand he also says to
himself: 'How poor my father was, that he could no longer
hope for anything for himself, and could not place hopes in
me either. And that is still the case. He still cannot trust me.
He still has not released me to pursue my own course.' The
concern felt by the father is so deep that he is ready to sacrifice
the "serenity" of the dead for the sake of the son. This "serenity"
is itself so large that it embraces whole "realms". The father
cannot let this serenity ripen because he is for ever tied to the
son's "bit of fate".

What inconsolable tragedy there is in these lines! How moving are these concluding words "my bit of fate". This phrase
too belongs to a larger context of meaning which has been
mentioned several times already. The weight of destiny does
not vary according to what happens to a person but according
to what he *is*. The more vigorous and unequivocal he is as a
person, the more "fate" he has. Then even everyday experiences are sufficient to give him a great destiny. But if a man's
inner centre is weak, his life can be filled with the mightiest,
most stirring events and still his destiny will be 'small'. Whose
life could have been more richly filled than Rilke's? He was
a poet, probably the greatest German poet since Mörike. He
was in touch with countless people, some of them very distinguished and others of exceptional vitality. He was offered love
from all sides. He travelled in Europe from one beautiful place
to the next. Places were open to him which others were only
allowed to see from outside. And yet he had this feeling of "my
bit of fate". This is the thought which echoes through the
Ninth Elegy after the introductory words "Why *have* to be human
and, shunning Destiny, long for Destiny?"[1] This is what Rilke

[1] *Ninth Elegy*, lines 4–6.

in fact did: he shunned Destiny. To put it more strongly, he was incapable of Destiny, because Destiny depends on the ability to love, to enter into a real bond with another person, and yet to "long for Destiny" at the same time.

He asks his father "Am I not right?" But right in what? Rilke means in seeking a meaning for life, *not* in stoical self-sufficiency, *nor* in the suffering and overcoming of Fate, but in being a spectator.

The question goes on:

> And you, am I not right,—
> you that would love me for that small beginning
> of love for you I always turned away from,
> because the space within your faces changed,
> even while I loved it, into cosmic space
> where you no longer were. . . ,   [47–52]

The same question is now put to those who loved him and, as we have said, there were many such. They loved him "for that small beginning of love" for them "which he always turned away from". They loved him more than he loved them. And their love endured whereas his soon ceased. We have to pay close attention to the wording here. His love not only ceased, but he "turned away from it". It did not break in a struggle but was so weak that he always evaded it. We cannot help feeling that the words betray an inner failing. And how significant it is that the same passage should contain Rilke's definition of the essence of love! When he loved another person he really loved "the space within your faces"—not the other person at all but the 'spacial' quality in him. But what meaning, we ask, could this possibly have for the other person? For the poet *this* space passed over into "cosmic space" and merged into the "Open realm", but what happened to the other person who thought he was loved? Previously he had somehow been part of the "space within his face". But in this cosmic space he is no longer present.

The passage can, of course, be given another interpretation. Rilke may have meant: 'I have sought cosmic space everywhere; my love was always on its way to a place where there was no object. If I chanced upon one of you and loved you, that was only in the course of my journey towards "the Open".' But

H

this would be an artificial explanation. In fact the whole tone of the passage betrays a hidden sense of guilt together with a feeling of helplessness. The poet is well aware of the impact he had on others by being what he was. Even his theory of love makes no difference to this. The factual background against which our interpretation must be read is in the memoirs of the Princess of Thurn and Taxis quoted above.[1]

Let us return to the *Elegy*. The poet is asking those who loved him to confirm that he is "right" to sit as a spectator in front of the world and to observe his own existence from outside. Is he right to demand the completion and fulfilment of the play—that fulfilment in which real events and live people would be replaced by the performance of marionettes?

This is the second point in the *Elegies* which refers to Rilke's private life and his parents. The second stanza of the *Third Elegy* described the child's fears and the consolation which he received from his mother. The *Fourth Elegy* deals with the fear of the boy or young man and the reactions of the father. The *Elegy* does not say that the father ever consoled the son or helped to clarify his mind or give him guidance. But if we read this passage carefully we shall see that it says less about his *own* distress than about the father's. For the father can only fret and worry without giving any help. This surely is Rilke's meaning, unless we read into the poem a subtle reproach to the father, making *him* responsible for the son's anguish. In that case the fear of the father would really have been a will to dominate in disguise.

V

The poet has asked his father and those whose love he did not return: "Am I not right?"

> when I feel like it,
> to wait before the puppet stage,—no, rather
> gaze so intensely on it that at last
> a counterpoising angel has to come
> and play a part there, snatching up the husks? [52–56]

He "waits" before the stage—and this time it is the "puppet stage", the marionette theatre in all its purity. He now wishes

[1] See p. 36.

to become wholly absorbed in the spectacle: to fulfil the role
of spectator so completely that an "angel has to come and play
a part there" to "counterpoise" his gaze. The angel "snatching
up the husks" provides the only fitting spectacle for the true
spectator. The human string-puller is not satisfactory. He
would be as inadequate here as the human actor, or, we may
add, as the ordinary spectator who cannot "gaze intensely"
with complete surrender but only gives half his attention. The
latter allows himself and his personal interests to interfere with
his appreciation: he is not merely a seeing eye, but an eye
mixed with a will and a heart. In his own way he is just as
"half-filled" as the ordinary player in his acting. But as soon
as the 'pure' seeing eye is focussed on to the stage, the 'pure'
player should be there too, i.e. the marionette, which in turn
must be directed by the 'pure' string-puller.

This means the Angel, who, as we learnt in the *First* and
Second Elegies, is not harnessed to earthly events but spans the
whole cosmos. He is not concerned with the individual in this
world. He has that sublime indifference described at the
beginning of the *First Elegy*. That god-like olympian quality
which is characteristic of Rilke's Angels and which distinguishes
them so sharply from the angels of the Bible, emerges here once
again. It is because they "serenely disdain to destroy us", and
because they cannot "hear" us, that one of them can play his
part and "snatch up the husks" in perfect freedom. But what
indifference he must have for this thing in his hands—this
"husk" and the "face of sheer appearance".

In the *Elegy* this is followed by a deep satisfaction and a sense
of having reached ultimate reality:

>   Angel and doll! Then there's at last a play.   [57]

Now the relationship is complete: On the stage is the puppet,
the perfect vehicle of expression; directing it is the Angel, the
completely detached performer; in front of the stage is the
spectator who does nothing at all but observe.

But, we may ask, what does all this really mean? Where is
this leading? Do we still remember what the stage and the
puppet really are? We are watching a performance by the
"heart" of the spectator! And since the *Elegies* are visionary
poems and intended to impart wisdom, this is not merely the

expression of the poet's experience. It represents the heart of everyone who hears the message.

The human heart has now become something which performs and is observed—*only* performs and is observed—nothing more. According to the *Elegies* our life finds its ultimate meaning when it has become a pure drama, a mere mime, when everything we mean by the words 'living', 'willing', 'responsibility', 'seeing eye to eye', 'consideration', 'I and Thou', and 'sacrifice' has been abolished. When life means no more than a play which is directed with supreme equanimity by the Angel.[1] We ourselves are the onlookers at this play, in so far as we are only 'eyes', without a will to live or to realize ourselves, but quite content for the play to be put on and observed.[2]

> Then there unites what we continually
> part by our mere existence.   [58–59]

The sentence is monstrous. By "our mere existence" we prevent the sense of our existence from taking shape! By our reality as persons we disturb the pure play of forms!

We see here how deadly serious Rilke is in repeating that same assumption which underlies his conception of love: The 'self' is a disruptive agent. And not merely when it is selfish, self-asserting and self-affirming, but just the 'self' as such—the human personality. Personality does not, according to Rilke, belong to true existence at all but must be overcome in the act of perfect loving, i.e. in the projection of love into a sphere where there is no object. Here he is not talking about love but about the act of observation and once more he makes a similar demand. But must there not be an object if observation is to take place—namely the thing we observe? To some extent this is true, for what we observe is "appearance", something visible. But it must be something visible and nothing more—without substance, without a living interior and without personality—

---

[1] Perhaps we should say 'with supreme irony'; for if the powerful angelic being knows of man's claim to live his own life, and *also* knows that he, the Angel, is directing him as a doll, how can his relation to man be other than ironical?

[2] If we accept the logical conclusion of this, namely, that of the inherent 'irony' of existence, then we must continue the argument as follows: our life finds its ultimate meaning when man is prepared to *accept* this irony. In this lies his superiority and his (negative) participation in the olympian life of the Angels. There are links here with the philosophy of Thomas Mann in the *Magic Mountain, Doctor Faustus* and Goethe's soliloquies in the novel *Lotte in Weimar*.

mask and doll! And the observer himself must be no more than
a pure spectator: an eye without anyone looking through it—
just as beneath the "lids" of the rose there was a thousandfold
sleep which no one 'slept'.

Now the unity is there, the unity of existence between Angel,
puppet and spectator.

> Then at last
> emerges from our seasons here the cycle
> of the whole process.   [59–61]

This is a new image, inserted without warning into the larger
image which runs through the two long stanzas of the *Elegy*.
We cannot dwell on its full significance here, but must simply
accept it as sketched into the whole in order to reinforce the
idea of unity. The image is linked in meaning with the earlier
description of our seasons as out of joint. These must be joined
together again in order to give shape to "the cycle of the whole
process", i.e. the unity of the life-process. This is only possible
if our Ego is eliminated and if we allow the larger flux of things
to pass through us.[1]

The *Elegy* expressly states:

> Over and above us,
> then, there's the angel playing.   [61–62]

The structure of this image may make it difficult to grasp.
Previously the spectator sat facing the stage on which his life
was being played. The Angel who pulled the strings was above
the stage. Now the Angel is "over and above us". But these
words do not apply literally to the realm of space; their essential
meaning is that the Angel acts beyond and apart from my
personal willing and feeling. For the Angel I do not exist as a
'self' at all. On the contrary he takes me as his puppet and
plays my life for me—a vision with all the power of a myth but
fearful in its implications.

We must take Rilke just as seriously as he himself wanted to
be taken. We should not be doing this if we simply said: 'he
had such and such an idea', 'these influences operated on him',
or 'his ideas developed in such and such a way'. Nor would it

---

[1] Compare the "eternal torrent" in the *First Elegy* which "whirls all the ages
through either realm for ever, and sounds above their voices in both" (lines 82–84).

be enough if we dealt with his ideas as stimuli or with the aesthetic aspect of their formulation. No. Rilke makes certain declarations. He asserts and proclaims that life is like this or like that. But if a declaration has any meaning at all it must claim to be true. And if we are to take it seriously we must ask 'Is this so?' Only in this way can we be truly scientific, if science in the broadest sense of the word is what it should be, namely the quest for complete truth. In dealing with this question here we are bound to assert that human existence is *not* as Rilke describes it. He has erased from it what should form the central core—the human person and all that goes with it: human destiny, love and responsibility.

Some of the *Later Poems* seem to progress beyond this view of life. On June 8th 1914 Rilke wrote under great inner stress to Lou Andreas-Salomé: "If I have pleaded several times in recent years that certain of my attempts to get a more human and natural footing in life had failed because the people concerned did not understand me, and had done violence, injustice and injury to me one after the other, and had so made me lose self-control—now, after these months of suffering I stand judged in quite a different sense: because this time I have to realize that no one can help me, no one; and even if someone came with the most upright and open heart and could give proof of his credentials to the stars and could bear with me, however stiff and difficult I made myself, and if he preserved a pure undeviating attitude to me, even if I broke his ray of love ten times over with the dull denseness of my submarine world, I should still, as I now know, find a means of exposing him in all the fullness of his inexhaustible help, and of shutting him up in a realm of airless lovelessness, so that his helpfulness, not finding an outlet, would get over-ripe within itself and would perish, withered and horrible." What the letter expresses is clear enough: awareness of being unable to receive love because one can only do so if one *wants* to receive it and if one gives love in return.

On June 9th another page followed which refers in a post-script to an essay by Rilke which had appeared in the *Weisse Blätter*. This essay deals with the phenomenon of the doll; in fact it is a kind of final settling of accounts with this "creature without occupation" which was so "abysmally devoid of fantasy, that our imagination became inexhaustible in dealing with it". He continues—"I wish I could remember if we inveighed against it, flew into a passion and let the monster know that our patience was at an end? If, standing in front of it and trembling with rage, we did not demand to know, item by item, what actual use it was making of our warmth and what had become of all these riches. It was silent then, not out of superiority; it was silent because that was its constant mode of evasion, because it was made of useless and entirely irresponsible material."[1]

This doll has quite negative characteristics. It has no imagination whereas "the marionette has only imagination". By this Rilke perhaps means the marionette's pure flexibility, i.e. its capacity to enter a dramatic role completely. The doll is "precisely so much less than a thing as the marionette is more". This probably means that the thing is self-contained and self-determined, whereas the doll is only material for the fantasy of a child, a "half-object". The letter which Rilke sent to Lou Andreas-Salomé on June 20th closes with the words: "But is it not fearful that one could unwittingly write such a thing down, dealing with a really personal experience on the pretext that this was a memoir about dolls; and that one should then lay aside one's pen to undergo the ghostly experience again to the full, as never before! Until each morning one's mouth was dry from the oakum one was stuffed with—like a husk the whole way through." The whole of this passage, especially the last sentence quoted from the letter, suggests that Rilke felt the puppet to be a symbol of his own existence and that he was ready to reject it.

In the *Elegy* the doll and the marionette are combined. The "husk", which is a deprecatory word in the letter, is accepted, and a figure that is "appearance" takes shape and becomes in the hands of the Angel a symbol of existence as a spectacle to be observed.

The letter of June 20th 1914, quoted above, begins with the words: "Lou, my dear, here is a strange poem which I wrote this morning and which I am sending you straight away, because I have involuntarily called it 'Turning', since it represents the turning which must come if I am to live, and you

[1] See *Selected Works*, I, p. 46 f.

will understand how it is meant." The text of part of the poem
is as follows:[1]

> Long his looking prevailed.
> Stars collapsed on their knees
> under his wrestling gaze.
> And when he knelt as he looked
> his instancy's perfume
> made an immortal tired
> till it smilingly slept
> . . . .
> . . . .
> Looking, since when?
> How long fervently fasting,
> beseeching in depth of his glance?
> When, waiting, he lived in foreign lands: the inn's
> distracted, alienated room
> morosely around him; in the mirror he always avoided
> once more the room,
> and then from his harrowing bed,
> the room again:—
> airy councils were held,
> inapprehensible councils,
> about his still, through the painfully cumbered body,
> still perceptible heart:
> councils unoverheard
> judged that he had not love.
> (Further consecrations withheld.)
>
> For, indeed, there comes in time a limit to looking:
> the looked and looked-at world
> longs to bear fruit in love.
> Work of sight is achieved,
> now for some heart-work
> on all those pictures, those prisoned creatures within you.
> You conquered them; but do not know them as yet.

A similar mood pervades another poem written about the same
time—"Introspective Woodland-pool".[2] This describes someone who is lying unable to sleep and in whose thoughts two
images are struggling for mastery: one is the picture of a still

---

[1] See *Later Poems*, p. 61 f., or the revised version in *Selected Works*, II, p. 305.
[2] *Later Poems*, p. 59 f.

"woodland pool" in all its tranquillity and the other that of a
raging sea.[1] It continues:

> Who knows his more prevailing tendency:
> composure? Terror? Faces? Voices? Reading?—
> All nothing more than sheets round some unheeding
> childhood, sleeping peacefully
> through this distracted life as in a bed.
> Let calm possess me, or let storm assail!
> Shudderingly I bow my head,
> for I know that *love* would turn the scale.
>
> Who's equal to what love should be?
> When, passionately concentrating,
> I failed to find the link relating
> things all unlike, I'd gaze incessantly;
> if what I gazed for would not yield,
> I'd gaze more deeply, gazing while I kneeled,
> until I'd drawn it into me.
> . . . .
> O, the world's soul will never be united
> with mine, till what appears outside me,
> as though it always meant to be inside me,
> delightedly alights in me!

In these poems the attitude of mere 'observation' is felt to be
wrong and this is expressed in one passage of "Turning" which
is almost an echo of the XIIIth Chapter of *Corinthians*: "Airy
councils were held. . . . about his . . . . heart. . . . [and] judged that
he had not love".[2] This judgment on his self is the same as
Rilke's condemnation of the doll which had served as a symbol
of his own 'half-existence'.

The two poems clearly illustrate transitional stages in the
development of Rilke's ideas. They represent a reaction, prompted by recognition of the claims of love, *against* the attitude of
pure 'observation', for the latter is closely linked with his other
idea of 'love without an object'. Between the writing of the
essay on the doll and the *Elegy* the figures of doll and marionette
became fused. Lines 26–29 of the *Elegy* transfer the reproaches
of 'halfness' from the doll, i.e. from his own self, to the actor

---

[1] Compare the setting of the *Third Elegy*.
[2] After listing the charismata, the great gifts of grace, Paul says "If I have all
these things but have not love then I am nothing" (*Cor.* 1; xiii, 1–3).

who cannot provide the counterpart to pure 'observation' by being "all outside". The poet then resolves to overcome his revulsion for the "husk" and "oakum" of the puppet, to accept them, while he himself becomes wholly a spectator. The *Elegies* which were written at Muzot, especially the *Eighth* and the *Ninth*, show that the above poems reflect late phases of Rilke's struggle within himself as he found his way to a final definition of the meaning of life. There are, however, no traces of this in the *Fourth Elegy*.

VI

Let us return to the text. If our existence were not out of joint it would consist of pure play, "outside" appearance and "gazing observation". In fact, however, everything is a "half-filled mask", only we do not recognize it as such because we are so caught up in the falsity of things that this has become our normal condition.

At times, it is true, life does take on a vital essential quality. Then we become aware of the inadequacy of normal existence:

> Look, the dying,—
> surely they must suspect how full of pretext
> is all that we accomplish here, where nothing
> is what it really is.   [62-65]

The moment of death is a time such as this, when the real quality of existence breaks through—just as it does when we love, or as the *Second Elegy* says more specifically, when we *begin* to love. The dying too are released from the bondage of growing and passing away; they are freed from the purposes we set ourselves in life and the conventions which hem us in. They become, in Rilke's sense, "open". In the *Eighth Elegy* he says "nearing death, one perceives death no longer, and stares ahead —perhaps with large brute gaze" (lines 22-23). Perhaps at death's door man reaches the point where the animal always is, where he is at one with himself and can enter that 'open' realm of Being which he sees ahead of him. In this condition the dying should be able to realize, or at least to "suspect how full of pretext is all that we accomplish here". This use of the word "pretext" is unusual. Normally we say that a person has a pretext for doing something if his action is implausible or if he uses a subterfuge. Here it means that everything we do constitutes a 'pre-text', in the original sense of the word, a disguise woven in front of reality. We are reminded of the "mask" mentioned earlier, but now used in a bad sense as a camouflage. Everything we do is masked in this way. We could only act truly or 'without pretext' in one of two conditions: if we were guided by superior powers *or* if we shared the vital integrated state of animals—for in neither case would the self be involved as a disturbing factor. Instead of this, however, our lives are ruled by artificiality and convention.

This idea is now pursued a stage further. Besides the animal and the dying, a third form of existence exemplifies the integration which can be achieved by the exclusion of the self. This is the life of the child.

> O hours of childhood,
> hours when behind the figures there was more
> than the mere past, and when what lay before us
> was not the future! [65–68]

The condition of childhood comes before the process of division which adulthood brings. The child is at one with himself, because its self is still unawakened. It simply lives.

This explains how the child can accept things for what they are. The grown-up, by contrast, feels that events and things are artificial because he himself is caught up in artificiality. The word "figures" is significant in the above lines and suggests something of the formal quality of the marionette. Properly considered every thing and every event is a 'figure' or meaningful shape. A 'figure' should reveal the hidden 'essences' of things —like the true marionette which is pervious to the essential nature of the world. But the figures in our lives are so limited by time and transience that they cannot show the eternal reality behind the present, but only memories of the past and fears or hopes for the future. For the child this dwelling in the past and in the future—like the inadequate aims and conventions of our daily life—still has no meaning. The child is not concerned with either past or future, but only with the present, just as he is interested in movement and play but not in social customs or intentions. This is why the "figures" can speak to him. They reveal the essence of things.

Admittedly, this condition does not last, for the child grows up:

> True, we were growing and sometimes
> made haste to be grown up, half for the sake
> of those who'd nothing left but their grown-upness. [68–70]

The "growing" means transition to the adult state, a process which only one half of the child can resist. Its other half accepts the change, indeed speeds it on. In spite of the wisdom inherent in its earlier condition it finally yields to the grown-ups; though it may feel the senselessness of it all, the child complies with their stupid wish to make it adult. So it too becomes one of those who have "nothing left but their grown-upness", i.e. whose childhood has already passed and whose adulthood will soon pass away likewise.

But if the grown-ups only leave the child in peace he again reverts to his true condition:

> Yet, when alone, we entertained ourselves
> with everlastingness: there we would stand,
> within the gap left between world and toy,
> upon a spot which, from the first beginning,
> had been established for a pure event.   [71–75]

As soon as the child can be alone he again moves in his proper sphere, which is not that of transience, but that of permanence or, in Rilke's particular sense of the word, "Being". The child is "entertained with everlastingness". This is a fitting description of that combination of ease and intentness which is peculiar to children as long as adults do not intervene in their lives. Then they experience what the *Eighth Elegy* calls "that pure unsuperintended element one breathes, endlessly knows, and never craves" (17–19).

The child's experience and that of the grown-up are both parts of human life and yet fundamentally quite different. The child's element is pure Being—simple unpondered reality; it has the same vital quality as human breath; it is complete in itself and free from acquisitiveness. Adult life is the opposite of this in every way: illusory, transient, filled with constant calculation and hankering after possession—and for this very reason it continually runs off its proper course. The existence of the child is perfect, like that of the animal, like that of the lover at the beginning of his love and like that of the person who is close to death.

And now the *Elegy* defines the child's life in terms of the *place* where it finds realization. This is in "the gap left between world and toy".

Here the word "world" is used in a derogatory sense—as it is later in the *Eighth Elegy*. It means the whole set of day to day conventions and objectives as well as the temporal pattern of past and future from which real existence is absent. At opposite poles to the world stands the "toy". This word still bears a certain imprint from what was said earlier about dolls and marionettes, for the child's favourite toy is a doll. But now even more emphasis is laid on the fact that the toy in itself is nothing and only becomes something in the fantasy. It is created anew in the child's imagination every moment. A child may ignore the most beautiful object of art in favour of some dirty old thing without face or limbs, provided that this allows his imagination free play. Between the "world" of grown-ups, which becomes absurd due to their sheer self-assertiveness, and the "toy", which is nothing in itself but can become everything in the imagination—this is where the child stands, already quite fulfilled, without set objectives and selfless in the simplicity of its being.

This is his place, "which from the first beginning, had been established for a pure event". These words, like the word "they" in the second stanza, suggest some higher creative agency or agent, veiled in anonymity. The "pure event" is the life of childhood.

The theme of the child's existence is impressively developed in Rilke's "Uncompleted Elegy".[1] The opening lines of this poem serve to clarify the shape of that hidden 'establishing' power which is suggested in line 75 of the *Elegy*. It is "Heaven".[2] Childhood, however, is not merely the first phase of life which quickly passes away, but a fundamental stratum of existence which exerts lasting effects.

[1] *Selected Works*, II, p. 326. See above, p. 85.
[2] *Translator's Note*: Literally "the Heavenly ones".

Don't let the fact that Childhood has been, that nameless
bond between Heaven and us, be revoked by fate.
Even the prisoner, gloomily dying in a dungeon,
it has sat by and secretly nursed to the end, with its timeless
hold on the heart. For the sufferer,
when he staringly understands, and his room has ceased to reply,
because, like all the other possessions around him,
feverish, fellow-suffering, it's curable,—even for him
Childhood avails. For purely
its cordial bed blooms among nature's decay.

Not that it's harmless. The petting and prettyfying error
that be-aprons it and be-frills only deceived for a time.
It's no more certain than we and never more shielded;
no god can counterbalance its weight. Defenceless
as we ourselves, defenceless as beasts in winter.
More defenceless—no hiding places.

The section of the poem which refers to the child's mother
has already been quoted. Here let us simply note once again
those lines, following the passage which exposes the 'legend' of
infancy, which deal with the defencelessness of the child. First
we are told that the defencelessness of "something growing",
in the womb or in infancy, is "the entire pure perilousness of
the world". This is intended to sum up the character of our
finite existence which is always, by nature, exposed to peril.
The poem continues:

> —and thus it turns to protection,
> soon as you feel it completely. The fervour of childhood
> stands like a centre within it: *out*-fearing it, fearless.

The essential feature of our finite world is vulnerability. But
then the threatening peril "turns to protection". For if this
defencelessness is completely accepted and if all guarantees and
precautions are renounced, then a refuge can be found. In the
same way a peaceful haven may open up to the sufferer if he
stops resisting his pain and gives himself over completely to it.
    The "out-fearing" of a danger which has been wholly
accepted thus turns into fearlessness. The child's life, naturally
filled with "fervour", now appears as the centre of the world.
This, however, is only because the final and decisive factor is
the "nameless bond between Heaven and us".

The link between this passage and the conclusion of the
Elegy should now be clear:

Who'll show a child just as it is?   [76]

We can appreciate the sense of wonder underlying these words:
the feeling that the child is an archetype. The figure of the child
grows enormously in stature here. Who is capable of showing
it "as it is"?

                                   Who'll place it
within its constellation, with the measure
of distance in its hand?   [76–78]

This is the process of transfiguration into myth—to place a
mortal in a constellation. The "who" referred to is not a human
being but that mythologizing power which elevates to the stars
those who have been heroes in their mortal lives. The heroes
pass from earth to Heaven, out of a contingent temporal state
into one which is eternal and normative. In the myths the stars
are not shining orbs viewed from the perspective of the earth
but celestial figures which regulate human life.

Rilke means that there ought to be a stellar figure called the
"Child". One of the *Sonnets to Orpheus* suggests something
similar:[1] "Look at the sky. Is there no 'Horse-man' reckoned
among the constellations?" And the *Tenth Elegy* gives a whole
list of imaginary constellations which *should* exist:

                                           There,
look: the *Rider*, the *Staff*, and that fuller constellation
they call *Fruitgarland*. Then, further, towards the Pole:
Cradle, Way, The Burning Book, Doll, Window.
But up in the southern sky, pure as within the palm
of a consecrated hand, the clearly-resplendent *M*,
standing for Mothers. . . . .   [89–95]

In the same way the child should become a constellation and
should bear the "measure of distance" in its hand. This measure would define the distance separating him from the "world"
where life is dominated by conventions and shrewd calculations.
It would also show the distance between the child and the toy
round which his fantasy plays. This attempt to convey through
an image something which is really inexpressible is not unlike
the reference in the *Fifth Elegy* to the "ineffable spot where the

                    [1] *Sonnets to Orpheus*, I, xi.

pure too-little incomprehensibly changes, veering into that
empty too-much" and "where the many-digited sum solves
into zero".

There are kindred ideas in the "Uncompleted Elegy" already
quoted.[1] The penultimate stanza contains the following lines:

> O doll,
> farthest figure,—as stars upon distance
> train to be worlds, you make the child into a star.
> Is cosmic space too small for it? Space out of feelings
> you stoundingly stretch between you, intensified space.

In the final stanza, admittedly, a different note makes itself
heard:

> But all at once it occurs . . . What? When?—Unnameable,
>   rupture—
> What?—Betrayal . . . filled with the half of existence,
> the doll will have no more, disowns, doesn't recognise.
> Stares with refusing eyes, lies down, doesn't know; no longer
> even a thing—look, how things
> are ashamed of it . . .

In this poem the same negative character is attributed to the
doll as in the essay quoted above. In the *Elegy* the repugnance
for the doll has been overcome.

The lines which follow attempt to bring out the uniqueness
of the child's existence at a particular point in its life, namely
that of death:

> Who'll make its death
> from grey bread, that grows hard,—   [78–79]

A curious image. Perhaps it should be interpreted to mean:
"Who" or what power could depict the death of a child? It
would have to take bread to do so—*grey* bread, reminding us
of the *greyish* draught blowing across from the stage and bringing down emptiness with it[2]—and knead a figure from it. First
the figure is shaped from the soft living bread and is itself alive.
Then, however, imperceptibly it becomes hard and dies.
    The sense of these lines is that for a child there is no intrinsic
division between life and death: these two aspects of existence

---

[1] See *Selected Works*, II, p. 327.   [2] See lines 31–32.

are still one for the child and not, as for the adult, separated by fear. As one of Rilke's poems says, "trustful Nature" in her transformations is the "friend of Death" whom she "intertwines a hundred times". We may leave aside the question of how far this is true. Anyone who has seen a child die would probably not use an image of this kind and Rilke's attempt to turn the grim reality of death into an orphic transformation will be treated more fully later. Here, however, his meaning is that the child does not have death "in front" of it, but "behind" it, like the "animal" in the *Eighth Elegy*. Death is behind the child as it glides forward from the not yet realized into the real.

This provides a clue to the meaning of the next image:

> or leave it there,
> within the round mouth, like the seeded core
> of a nice apple? . . . . . .   [79–81]

This is another strange, almost grotesque image; but there is a particular purpose in the contrast between this and the "constellation" a few lines previously. Who "leaves" the child's death "there, within the round mouth"? Who causes this little creature to hold death in its mouth "like the seeded core of a nice apple"? The child has eaten a beautiful apple and finally pushed the core into its mouth. This fills the mouth and makes the lips round. But if for any reason the child tries to swallow the core it may suffocate: then the fullness of life is followed all of a sudden by death. The eating of the fruit, which is itself full of life and contains future life in its seeds, turns into death.[1]

---

[1] The significance which Rilke saw in fruit may be shown from one of his *Sonnets to Orpheus* (I, xiii, in *Selected Works*, II, p. 259):

> Banana, rounded apple, russet pear,
> gooseberry . . . Does not all this convey
> life and death into your mouth? . . It's there! . . .
> Read it on a child's face any day,
>
> when it tastes them. What infinity!
> Can't you feel inside your mouth a growing
> mysteriousness, and, where words were, a flowing
> of suddenly released discovery?

Here something which is only expressed briefly in the *Elegy* is developed at length, namely, the mysterious quality of the fruit which contains both an end and a beginning: it is the end of the tree on which it has grown and the beginning of the new tree which should spring from it; it is capable of giving life or stifling it. Its taste mysteriously epitomizes our existence. Again we notice Rilke's effort to make one sphere extend into another. The taste of the fruit contains everything. *Sonnet XV* goes still further and translates the fruit and its taste into movement and dance.

I

There is another interpretation, though it is perhaps less convincing. Death is contained in the mouth of the child—the
function of which is to sustain life by taking in food—like the
core of the apple. In this case the little head of the child itself
becomes the apple with the core, i.e. Death, inside.

The image of the apple is followed by an ellipsis such as
Rilke always uses when he wishes to suggest something inexpressible. This brief pause gives time to ponder the mystery
more deeply. The poet deliberates, and then:

>   Minds of murderers
>   can easily be fathomed.   [81–82]

It is not by chance that a dark shape intrudes at this point
where the *Elegy* touches on the mystery of death. For the
murderer always remains a riddle to us. How *can* one man take
the life of another? Life is, after all, the one thing which we
can really call our own and everything else we have is contained in it. Yet, compared to the mystery of a child, the mind
of a murderer can "easily be fathomed". We may perhaps
complete the thought by saying that we only need to feel once
what hatred, cruelty, stupidity or fear really are, and we know
the things that go to the making of a murderer.

>   This, though: death,
>   the whole of death, before life's start, to hold it
>   so gently and so free from all resentment,
>   transcends description.   [82–85]

That is the real mystery, the inexpressible thing about this
phase of existence which we have all passed through: that the
child should already have death—"the whole of death"—
within itself and yet live happily on; that the child should "hold
it so gently", without being poisoned or upset by it, and "free
from all resentment". Death and Life are united in the child,
just as the realms of the dead and the living are one in the
universe. This is what "transcends description".

THE FIFTH ELEGY

Completed at Muzot, February 14th 1922

I

In its content the *Fifth Elegy* is very closely related to the *Fourth* which was written in 1915 at Munich. This may be taken as evidence of the way in which the later *Elegies* joined perfectly on to the earlier ones, as Rilke said so thankfully in his letters. It will therefore be just as well here to review again briefly those sections of the *Fourth Elegy* which are relevant to the *Fifth*.

The *Fourth Elegy* began by contrasting man's inner divided-ness with the assurance of the animal. The realization that the pattern of human feeling is not shaped from within but received from "outside"—i.e. through environment or conventions—led to an attempt to observe man as an external object. For this purpose Rilke used the image of an actor playing his part on the stage. The actor certainly showed himself to be more integrated than man in real life, but he was still only "half" integrated, consisting as he did of a mixture of man and mask. This led to the last step, the invocation of the marionette, for the marionette was wholly itself—pure movement. And, we may add, whilst the actor was guided by someone as 'half' as himself, namely the producer, the marionette required the perfect master, the Angel.

Then the *Elegy* returned to Man and considered whether there were not perhaps some forms of human life which are equally 'genuine' and 'whole'. In which man *as* man is no less genuine than the animal *as* animal. According to the *Fourth Elegy* such forms of life do indeed exist, but only for a short passing time. To this category belongs the dying man who is already so deeply involved in death that he has nothing more in front of him but simply looks straight ahead. As the *Eighth Elegy* tells us later, the lover also belongs here, at least when his love is just beginning. The final example is the child who

131

has not yet been forced into the conventions of the grown-up world but lives wholly in the present, linked with the realm of pure Being. The child's existence is rooted in that central point, impossible to grasp intellectually, which lies between the normal *man*, who belongs wholly to the "world", and the *toy* which is nothing in itself but can become everything in the imagination of a child. This condition, however, only lasts a short time, for the child is growing and is therefore soon led into the spurious world of grown-ups.

The images of the *Fourth Elegy* form a dialectical pattern giving brief glimpses of the true and the genuine between the false and the spurious. This pattern is further extended in the *Fifth Elegy*.

This *Elegy* is dedicated to Frau Hertha Koenig, whose guest Rilke had been in 1915. Hanging in his room was Picasso's famous picture, *Les Saltimbanques*, "The Acrobats". This picture probably underlies the descriptive portions of the *Elegy*, although a comparison of the two would not help our understanding of the poem.

On the other hand there is a revealing note by Rilke, dated "Quatorze Juillet 1907" which refers to "Père Rollin and his troupe", i.e. troupe of acrobats which "took up its pitch in front of the Luxembourg towards the Panthéon".[1]

II

The *Fifth Elegy* begins *in medias res*, as if a conversation were already in progress:

> But tell me, who *are* they, these travellers,   [1]

The "but" is part of a reply to something which has already been said. One might be tempted to connect it with some of the ideas expressed in the *Fourth Elegy*. If what was said there about the reality and unreality of existence is true, what can be the significance of these "travellers"? In what relation to the rest of humanity do they stand—these jugglers, acrobats and tight-rope walkers, these restless people who go from one

---

[1] See below, p. 146.

place to the other with their pointless and yet strangely attractive arts. How do they stand with respect to the actor, and marionette or the toy. Or to the child and other forms of integrated life? In what way *are* they (the italics are Rilke's)? What is their position in the realm of Being?

As soon as they start to perform their turns they no longer stand there as the individual persons they really are. This is evident from the lack of respect with which 'respectable' members of society regard them. Are they actors then? Apparently not, for they do not present a story or action, but simply execute movements which are graceful, difficult and often dangerous. So they must resemble the dancer, but not the dancer of the *Fourth Elegy* who plays a part in a pantomime and is therefore close to the dramatic actor; rather the pure dancer who only carries out expressive movements. On the other hand, they differ from him too because their performance lacks the essential character of true art. It is directed at our more deeply seated instincts—at everything we call 'sensation'. It is intended to excite, to astonish, to bewilder and even, on occasion, to appeal to our sensuality or cruelty.

Who are these acrobats then, and where do they stand among the other figures we have encountered? Where is their place among the different forms of reality and illusion?

The acrobats express very clearly the fugitive, transient character of man. They do this in the first place by their very way of life. It is not by chance that they are called *travelling* players, for they are the migrants, the homeless ones, who wander from place to place without any permanent dwelling, always remaining just as long as they can appeal to the public's desire for excitement or sensation. But their very craft or calling is significant too—this strange restless activity which repeatedly surges up to a climax of excitement only to descend again. Who are these

> even a little
> more fleeting than we ourselves,—so urgently, ever since
> childhood,
> wrung by an (oh, for the sake of whom?)
> never-contented will? [1-4]

What is it that drives them on? What is the motive force behind the daily routine of training which they have been going through "ever since childhood" and will continue into old age?

The average man's behaviour is motivated by his set purpose in life or the conventions he observes; the actor is guided by the producer; the marionette by the puppet-player; the toy by the fantasy of the child. The child itself, if it is permitted to be really a child, is not directed by anyone, for it simply "is" and "stands" or goes "alone". But what directs these people who are continually in motion? The answer is a "never-contented will". We do not know whose will this is, any more than we know "for the sake of whom" it operates. Again we notice that the human personality has been eliminated and replaced by an impersonal 'it'. Rilke's purpose here is to convey the uncanny and pointless character of the performance.

The lines which follow impress us even more strongly with the restlessness, the futility and the violence of the acrobatics:

> That keeps on wringing them,
> bending them, slinging them, swinging them,
> throwing them and catching them back: [4–6]

This is the pattern formed by the acrobats as they move or, more precisely, as they *are moved*. For these are not people carrying out a movement; they are being pulled and jerked like marionettes, though we must not forget that they are living human beings at the same time. And whereas the human factor detracts from the performance of the actor, it seems to have a different effect with the acrobats. The passage which follows will show clearly that the difference lies in a tragic quality which arouses our sympathy.

So completely have the acrobats surrendered to the power which rules them that we cannot help suspecting that some other factor must contribute to their movement: not just the "will" which brings the movement about, but also the immediate environment in which the movement takes place:

> as though from an oily,
> smoother air, they come down   [6–7]

The air which surrounds them is different from the air around

other people. As we have noticed several times before, Rilke
frequently projects the moods and attributes of inner experience
into external nature. This is why the air around the acrobats
is described as "oily" and "smoother" than elsewhere.

The whole performance—the acrobats, the air and the
driving will—now runs like a machine. The air provides the
well-oiled bearings in which the axle runs. The tumblers are
the twirling components of the machine. The "will" is the
energy which is transmitted along the cable and puts everything
in motion.

After they have completed their turn the acrobats come down
from the air back to the ground,

> on the threadbare
> carpet, thinned by their everlasting
> upspringing, this carpet forlornly
> lost in the cosmos.   [7–10]

The carpet is laid out on the spot where the acrobats display
their talents. It is worn and "thinned" from long use and lies
there "lost in the cosmos". This is a phrase which immediately
touches our feelings and, as was said above, we are moved to
pity by the homelessness and abandonment of the acrobats.
Their carpet lies somewhere in the infinite space of the universe,
without a sheltering roof, for these are poor people who have
to perform their tricks, not in a fine circus, but in the open
square.

And here again there is one of those strange incongruous
images which Rilke introduces into his poetry at quite un-
expected places in order to evoke a striking visual impression.
The carpet is

> Laid on like a plaster, as though the suburban sky
> had injured the earth there.   [11–12]

This acrobatic performance is being presented in the 'suburb'.
It is not the suburb of the prosperous villas, but where the
blocks of tenements stand—the forlorn intermediate territory
between town and country. Here the sky is different from elsewhere—a suburban sky, miserable and unfriendly. There is
certainly "earth" here for the streets come to a stop and lead
into open country. But it is the suburban earth of the building

sites containing rubbish and stunted vegetation—a cross between ploughed field and city street.

This is where the carpet lies and acts like a plaster on the skin—the earth's skin which the heavy sky has injured.

The acrobats descend on to this carpet when they jump:

> And hardly there,
> upright, shown us: the great initial
> letter of Thereness,—than even the strongest
> men are rolled once more, in sport, by the ever-
> returning grasp, as once by Augustus the Strong
> a tin platter at table.   [12–17]

It is the moment just after the completed jump, when the acrobat stands there motionless and invites us with a gesture to look at him and to notice how easy it has all become for him. He summons us to applaud his achievement—"upright, shown us". Again we notice the passive voice: not "he shows himself" but he is "shown".

The meaning of the lines which follow is not immediately evident from the text. Someone who knew Rilke very well for a long time gave me an interpretation which is both simple and profound. This is an example of a form of expression which Rilke is supposed to have been very fond of. If, for example— here I am reproducing exactly what was told to me—Rilke saw a beautiful woman he might have said "she is the initial letter of beauty", meaning that her shape and appearance contained the *first* letter of the word "beauty". Whether or not the other letters would follow, whether the whole word found expression in that particular person, whether she embodied the whole phenomenon 'Beauty'—all this remained in doubt. After the first letter there might be no others, or else something quite different might follow it. This manner of expression is supposed to have sprung from Rilke's sense of the inadequacy of all things. Moreover he was well aware of the outrageous character of the phrase which he called a "metaphysical joke". So the acrobats realize only the "initial letter of Thereness". The word might become complete if they remained in a fixed position of rest. But this they cannot do, for straight away the "ever-returning grasp" forces them, "even the strongest men", into fresh movement.

Finally another, even stranger image is used to convey the whole capriciousness and the senseless violent exertion of the acrobatics. These men are likened to the tin platter which the Elector of Saxony, Augustus the Strong, once bent together with his hands "in sport" for the entertainment of his guests.

III

In the next stanza a new image describes the acrobats as they move or take up their poise:

> Alas, and round this
> centre the rose of onlooking
> blooms and unblossoms.   [18–20]

Now the carpet has become the centre of a rose. We have already encountered this image—the rose with its many petals which lie beside and beneath one another. The epitaph in Raron associates the rose-petals with sleeping eyelids. Here too there are eyes and although they are seeing eyes the implication is the same as before. Just as the epitaph describes a sleep which no one sleeps, so the *Elegy* refers impersonally to the spectators as the "rose of onlooking". There is a clear connection here with the 'pure' spectator of the stage in the *Fourth Elegy*.

The acrobatics in the suburban square are produced then, not by people, but by an abstract "will" which governs the performers like parts of a machine. The "rose of onlooking" which forms around them is equally independent of living people: it is an impersonal activity in space. The image of the rose refers to the people who are constantly coming and going. When they come the circle of spectators becomes complete and the rose "blooms". But when they go away gaps appear in the circle. Indeed, for a time they may all depart in which case the rose "unblossoms".

Now the image is developed further:

> Round this
> pestle, this pistil, caught by its own
> dust-pollen,   [20–22]

This can be understood in two ways. It may mean that the
"pestle" is one of the troupe, perhaps the "man" who is
"clapping his hands" (line 51) and stamping his foot at the
same time so that the rising dust falls back on him. Or it perhaps refers to the whole pattern formed by the group of performers as they confront the spectators. The word "pestle" is
followed immediately by the botanical term "pistil". The root
of the word is the same, though the meaning is different. The
"pistil" is that organ of the flower which receives the pollen,
is fertilized by it and then develops into a fruit. This "pistil",
the centre of the "rose of onlooking", is "caught by its own
dust-pollen". This is intended to express something unnatural
and futile. Since the dust-pollen cannot bloom itself, it fertilizes
its own blossom and produces something negative and worthless:

> and fertilized over again
> to a sham-fruit of boredom, their own
> never-realized, so thin-surfacedly gleaming,
> lightly sham-smiling boredom.   [22–25]

The sentence is not easy to grasp, and this was probably Rilke's
intention. The complicated character of the acrobatic turn,
which produces nothing significant in the end, despite all the
energy expended, is expressed in the very language of the poem.
   The pistil is "fertilized over again to a sham-fruit of boredom". Something new has certainly been created, but it is only
a sham-fruit. It has no stone or pips and cannot therefore
produce life. Nor can it give enjoyment, like that other 'sham-
fruit', the fig-blossom of the *Sixth Elegy*, but only "boredom".
What happens here is a delusion. The word "sensation" would
convey exactly what is meant, for "sensation" does not, like
a marionette performance, arouse pleasure or delight in perfect
movement, but only "boredom", i.e. the protest of our
frustrated desire for 'sense'. This boredom is, however, "never-
realized". The performers of the acrobatic turn do not feel
bored. Deep down within himself, no doubt the artiste is well
aware of his own uselessness and knows that he does not merit
more than the slight esteem which he receives. But this feeling
"never" reaches a conscious level—or as a rule it does not, but
only in certain moments of discouragement. Normally it is

covered up. But even then it is only covered by a "thin surface" which "gleams". This "gleaming" is seen in the artiste's dexterity, the applause which he earns and that smile which he always has on his lips to give the impression that he finds everything easy. But it is not a true smile from the heart, any more than the fruit produced by the whole performance is true. This is a "sham-smile" just as the other is a "sham-fruit". The "truthful" smile which proceeds from truly mastered movement is described in the last lines of the *Elegy*.

In this passage Rilke's intention is conveyed both by the arrangement of the words and clauses in the sentence and by the disappearance of the central idea in abstractions. The very style implies that the acrobatic turn is a complicated procedure resulting from much effort, but created by no one and itself creating nothing.

IV

The "pestle" in the foregoing passage refers to the whole group of acrobats, the central "pistil", as distinct from the 'petals' which are formed around it by the rows of spectators. Now, however, our attention is focussed on one individual:

> There, the withered wrinkled lifter,
> old now and only drumming,
> shrivelled up in his massive hide as though it had once contained
> two men, and one were already
> lying in the churchyard, and this one here had survived him,
> deaf and sometimes a little
> lost in his widowed skin.   [26–32]

This figure is the opposite of the other performers who excel by their self-confidence, their strength and suppleness of movement: this is an artiste who is played out and superannuated, representing the last phase of the acrobats' existence. He is a "lifter", that is one whose speciality is the lifting of heavy weights. Once he himself was "massive", but now the word can only be applied to his skin which is "withered" and "wrinkled" as it hangs around him. He has "shrivelled up" and become thin inside his own skin; it is as if "two men" had formerly occupied this skin, one of whom died together with his vanished strength. The other, however, is still alive and the skin now hangs too loosely around him.

This man is now old and can no longer do anything except "drum", i.e. produce a pathetic sort of musical accompaniment for the other performers. This drumming is particularly wretched because he himself is "deaf" and cannot hear it. The old man is also described as "sometimes a little lost", in fact the very embodiment of human decline and decay.

He stands shrunken up—and here a second image is super-imposed on the first—"in his widowed skin". This second image serves to introduce into the first a faint nuance of meaning—like the spot of colour which the painter adds at a certain point of the canvas to create a particular shade. The spot of colour in this case is certainly a strange one. It links up with the earlier reference to the two men formerly inside the skin, one of whom is now dead and buried. The skin has survived and is here described as a "widow" who must be content with one husband instead of two. Perhaps however this tiny detail does not merit such an exhaustive interpretation as this. Its purpose is simply to heighten our impression of the lifter as someone who is both pathetic and grotesque in his decline.

At the beginning of the *Elegy* the poet dealt with the whole group of performers—the "centre" of the "rose of onlooking", the "pistil" which fertilizes itself in such a meaningless way. The old man is the first of several individual figures who are now picked out from the group. He, as we saw, can no longer do much except beat his drum and he thus indicates the final destination in the lives of the travelling acrobats. Our attention is now directed to his more energetic counterpart:

> And the youngster, the man, like the son of a neck
> and a nun: so tautly and smartly filled
> with muscle and simpleness.   [33–35]

In sharp contrast to the enfeebled old man he is young and strong. He is the member of the troupe who performs the hardest turns. The impression which he makes on us is twofold: He abounds in youthful strength and yet, at the same time, he has about him a certain quiet simplicity and a naive heartfelt quality. These two sides of the young man are, however, fused together perfectly: he is "tautly and smartly filled with muscle and simpleness". The muscles and the simpleness are pressed into him so that his skin is full and tense—in contrast to the old man who is half-empty. The words give the impression of something primitive in which the physical constitution is mingled with undeveloped spiritual qualities. This impression is underlined by the introductory image: it is as if the young man were the "son of a neck and a nun". A "neck" presumably means a man who is only body—perhaps a boxer or a weight-lifter. Again it is characteristic of Rilke to use an attribute instead of saying "a man with a strong neck". But once we have seen the implications of this simile we cannot help regretting it. It was a common practice of *fin de siècle* literature to link together the sacred and the profane in order to achieve certain effects. But Rilke, with his knowledge of the religious life, should have been above this sort of device.[1]

V

In their form the next few lines are related to those which preceded them.

> O you,
> a pain that was still quite small
> received as a plaything once in one of its
> long convalescences. . . .   [36–39]

This sentence, without a main verb, is no more than a form of address: "O you. . . .". In its content it is linked with the *Fourth Elegy* where the "toy" was mentioned and the child which stood between it and the "world". The "world" meant adult life—self-important and dominated by set purposes and conventions. The "toy" is something insignificant in itself but becomes important in the child's imagination. Here the acrobats are called "a plaything"—the same acrobats who were said at the beginning of the *Elegy* to have apparently no initiative of their own, being like a machine directed by an im-

---

[1] This image does not stand alone in Rilke's work. There are one or two other poems which contain a similar distasteful mixture of the religious and the erotic, e.g. "Nun's Complaint" in *Later Poems*, p. 39.

personal will. And now a "pain that was still quite small"—
yet another abstract noun—has replaced both the child and
the will. Thus the process of depersonalization, which we have
seen more and more clearly to be a fundamental feature of the
Elegies, is carried a stage further. Once more there is no person
but an 'It', though since the 'It' is small and, as it were, child-
like, there is a certain warmth in the image.

It is significant that the word in the poem is "a pain",
implying that there are many pains. In the *Tenth Elegy* we shall
meet the "Laments" who act and speak like people. They too
are impersonal and yet vital forces which include both "young"
and "old"; this short stanza perhaps prepares the way for
them. The "pain" in question has been seriously and repeatedly
ill; and during "one of its long convalescences" it received the
acrobats as a plaything so that it could divert itself in the
monotony of the sick-room. Here the "Will" mentioned at the
beginning of the *Elegy* becomes a little easier to recognize.
There is still a certain abstractness about the "pain" but the
abstraction has become half-personified, as if in a myth. It is
a *young* pain, like the "youthful Lament" in the *Tenth Elegy*.
We may recall from our schooldays reading about giants and
other superhuman creatures who treated human beings like
toys. There is, for instance, a poem by Adalbert von Chamisso
in which the daughter of a giant picks up a peasant with his
horse and plough. She puts them into her apron and takes
them home to play with. There follows a moralizing reproof
from her father who tells her that this is not the way to treat
a peasant since it is he who makes the bread we eat. This idea
of mighty creatures who use tiny human beings as playthings
is not unlike the animal monsters in early myths.

The next passage addresses the acrobats at greater length
and develops into a complete sentence:

You, that fall with the thud
only fruits know, unripe,
daily a hundred times from the tree
of mutually built up motion (the tree that, swifter than water,
has spring and summer and autumn in so many minutes),
fall and rebound on the grave: [40–45]

This is directed to one of the performers who is supposed to stand at the very top of certain acrobatic figures and remain there balanced freely. But he cannot do this yet and only falls down "daily a hundred times" in his training.

This image conveys the unity of the acrobatic figure. In the second stanza this figure was likened to the pistil of a rose. Now it has become a tree—a tree consisting of motion: The shape which is visible at any given time has been "mutually built up" in the course of the act from a succession of different movements. The first of the *Sonnets to Orpheus* contains a parallel description:

> A tree ascending there. O pure transcension!
> O Orpheus sings! O tall tree in the ear!

Here again we have motion which is translated from time into space. The time-picture of the song becomes the space-picture of the tree.

Now a second image is superimposed on that of the tree: fast-flowing water. Perhaps it is the same water as that of the fountain in the *Sixth Elegy* which rises up to a high jet and then falls back, forming a visible pattern by its continuous movement. The pattern is fleeting and if the control tap is opened up for a mere instant the water rises swiftly aloft and then sinks to the ground. But the pattern built up by the acrobats, the "tree" of their movement is even more fleeting than the arc made by a jet of water. This tree has "spring and summer and autumn in so many minutes": it grows, bears fruit and then withers.

The boy who is described here performs his part of the movement at the top of the "tree", for he is its "fruit". He ought to release himself at the right moment—the "autumn" of the tree—and jump down so that the fruit of movement may be "ripe" or perfect. But since he cannot maintain his balance he always "falls" prematurely in the "summer" like an "unripe" fruit, making a dull impact or "thud" each time. He is also said to "rebound on the grave". This is a reminder of the dangers inherent in the acrobat's life, for at any time he might suffer a bad fall and get killed. The earth is after all simply a grave.

Now something gentler and less physical tries to find an

outlet amid the relentless violence of this sustained movement:

> sometimes, in half-pauses, a tenderness tries
> to steal out over your face to your seldomly
> tender mother,   [46–48]

These lines refer to a boy who is still closely attached to his mother. When he rests for a moment after falling down—during the "*half*-pauses", because, as we learn later, he is immediately spurred into action again—then he looks across to his mother nearby. He does this from a childish impulse to seek protection: "a tenderness tries to steal out over" his face to the mother. Before this he had no face, properly speaking, but only the rigid mask of exertion or the conventional smile of simulated ease. Now something warm and human, a "tenderness", tries to express itself. In the *Third Elegy* the girl was summoned in similar terms to do an "honest task" for the youth—something springing spontaneously from the heart. Whether the mother responds to the impulse of her son we do not know; all we are told is that she is "seldomly tender". Usually she is hard, worried by the cares of her miserable existence. So we must take it that she dismisses this tentative approach and that the human feelings of the child are not permitted to unfold and express themselves.

The following sentence gives another reason for this:

> but scatters over your body,
> whose surface quickly absorbs the timidly rippling,
> hardly attempted look. . .   [48–50]

Here there is another subtle interplay of ideas. The boy has "timidly attempted a look". The human face is not something ready-made, but expresses a person's changing inner state. The face is the medium through which one person's mind and heart are revealed to another; it is also the place to which the other person directs his attention, perhaps in replying or offering help. The degree of perfection which a face attains depends on the inner depths which it reveals and the purity with which it reveals them. There are faces which express nothing at all, but consist simply of certain proportions between brow, eyes, nose, cheeks, mouth and chin. There are also faces which *seem* to express something, but in which the expression is feigned and does not come from within. The first type is merely an anatomical fact—the structure of the forepart of the head. The second is an artificial shape—the mask. The true face, by contrast, is something which is constantly 'becoming': it is the expression of what is going on inside someone. It acts upon the other person and is affected by him. It is the revelation of the 'I' to the 'Thou'.

Here the boy tries to show a face which is real and true. He does so "timidly", with the timidity of a young person at disclosing part of his inner feeling, in this case a feeling of distress at his own inability. But he could only do this to his mother, and then only if she helped him by showing what she herself feels, namely "tenderness". She, however, does not respond to him and the external force, "the never-contented will", gains the upper hand once more. The boy has hardly tried to give expression to his feeling, the acrobat's mask has barely been dropped to permit the inner person to be revealed, when the "half-pause" is over. The body becomes the most important thing again and the tenderness of the face "scatters over" it. The boy's face which had just begun to express his spirit and mind, becomes simply part of the body's surface once more. The "surface quickly absorbs" it. And whereas a "surface" has only two dimensions, being without depth or height, the true human face has both these qualities as well: it can express heart-felt 'depths' and the 'heights' of enthusiasm or inspiration. But the skin of the body, or at least the acrobat's body which is drilled into precise and elegant performance, is no more than a 'surface' of which the face is merely an extension.[1]

Soon the "half-pause" is past,

> And again
> that man is clapping his hands for the downward spring,
> [50–51]

"That man" is the one who is directing the performance. He is the 'inlet', as it were, for the impersonal energy of the Will. At a sign from his hand the boy must jump up again.

[1] This is the underlying idea of the *Elegy*. It does not mean, of course, that the rest of the human body is incapable of expressing inner 'heights and depths'. See for example, the *Sonnets to Orpheus* on the dancer (*I. xxv, II. xviii* and *xxviii*).

K

and before

a single pain has got within range of your ever-
galloping heart, comes the tingling
in the soles of your feet, ahead of the spring that it springs from,
chasing into your eyes a few physical tears.   [51–55]

These lines drive home to us still more strongly the hardness and cruelty of the life which the boy is fated to lead. For he must not only refrain from showing in his face any love for his mother—he is not even permitted to *have* feelings of his own. Such is the general meaning of these lines. A more detailed interpretation is not easy.

The boy has jumped up and then, losing his balance, he has fallen down again. A note by Rilke on *Les Saltimbanques*[1] suggests that the next few lines have the following meaning. The soles of the boy's feet "tingle" and burn from the downward jump. This is a *particular* pain, different from the *general* pain which comes from the boy's constant training which over-exerts his body and makes his heart "gallop". The latter is the central "spring" or fountain-head of the particular pains which 'spring' from it at different times—in this case the "tingling" of the foot-soles. If the general pain had any seat or location this would be "within range of the heart". However, the particular pain is felt so intensely that it obliterates the more general discomfort and produces "a few physical tears". This is an uncontrollable physical reaction which passes away and is not taken seriously afterwards.

This interpretation may seem somewhat strained and perhaps we are justified in feeling that a little more clarity would not have harmed the *Elegy* itself at this point. However, the passage remains a picture of acute distress and it heightens the impression of urgency and compulsion which the first stanza made—especially since the whole experience is that of someone who is still half a child.

[1] See above, p. 132. "The little son, the grandchild of the old man, . . . is a beginner and his feet hurt from the precipitous jump with which he descends to the ground from his lofty saltos. He has a large face which can contain a lot of tears, but these sometimes well up on the rim of his wide-open eyes. Then he has to carry his head very carefully, like an overfull cup. He is not really sad; not at all. And even if he *were* he would not notice it. It is simply the pain which is weeping and this must be allowed him. In time it becomes easier to bear and finally disappears altogether. The father has not known for a long time what this pain was, whilst the grandfather—no, he forgot it sixty years ago."

> And still, all instinctive,
> that smile. . . .   [56–57]

The pressure and the tension are relentless and the physical
pain is acute, and yet, "still" he smiles. The smile is "all
instinctive". It is a reflex action which springs irrepressibly, in
spite of all, from the heart of the child. The concluding ellipsis
allows the reader to ponder the full meaning of the words.

Finally we may note that there is a theme here which runs
through the whole *Elegy*. The second stanza referred to the
"sham smile" of the acrobats which is only a mask, corresponding to the "sham-fruit" of their futile activity. Here there is a
"tenderness" which "tries to steal out" over the face to the
mother. There is a "look" which takes shape "timidly" and a
"smile" which, though always in vain, is attempted again and
again. At the end of the final stanza a "truthful" smile is
achieved "at last", but only when the land of the dead has
been reached.

The half-smile of the child will not let the poet go. This is
something precious which deserves to be cherished and glorified.
For this reason he now turns again to the final source of
authority in the *Elegies*, the Angel.

In the *Fourth Elegy* the Angel was called upon to direct the
marionette. In the *Seventh Elegy* he is invited to appreciate not
only the pillars, the pylons, the Sphynx, Chartres and everything that "we were capable of", but also, greater than these,
"a girl in love, alone, at her window at night. . .". And here
the Angel is entrusted with the one valuable thing which has
blossomed forth from the futility of these acrobatics:

> Angel! oh, take it, pluck it, that small-flowered herb of healing!
>   [58]

The smile is described here as a "herb"—an image which
suggests something rare and sublime—as in fact it is. The smile
which springs from affliction and disappointment really does
have a healing power. It heals the person who is smiled at and
the person smiling.

The healing herb is "small-flowered". The phrase follows the
style of an apothecary's herb-book, as if this were the small-

flowered variety of such and such a plant, of which there is another variety with larger flowers. This is the herb which the Angel is to "take" and "pluck":

> Get a vase to preserve it.   [59]

The Angel must procure a vase for the smile—one of those beautiful vessels of porcelain or majolica which were once used in apothecaries' shops. The Angel is to take this vase, with the herb inside, and put it in the correct place among all the other herbal remedies. But where does it belong?

> Set it among those joys
> not yet open to us: [59–60]

This is its place: among the joys that are "not yet open to us", which we on earth still cannot understand. Though we cannot appreciate their rareness now, some day we *shall*, as is promised at the end of the *Elegy*, in that "other relation"[1] of the world, the land of the Dead. Even here, however, this smile is "open", in Rilke's sense of the word, so that it has a healing power.

The vessel must also be correctly inscribed:

> in a graceful urn
> praise it, with florally soaring inscription: 'Subrisio Saltat.'.
>   [60–61]

Since the apothecaries' vases date from the Baroque period their inscriptions are "soaring" and "floral" or flowery.

We must also not overlook the fact that in this sentence the "vase" has now become an "urn". It is still "graceful" but none the less a kind of vessel normally associated with burial customs. The inscription which we read on the urn is "Subrisio Saltat.", an abbreviation for "Saltatoris". The general sense is clear from the context of the *Elegy*—"The Smile of the Dancer". One of Rilke's notebooks contains a reference to "Pulv. Saltat.", i.e. "Pulvis Saltatoris". The "Pulv." is crossed out and the word "Subrisio" written above it instead. Rilke particularly liked the Italian word for smile, "sorriso" and this is why he uses the Middle Latin equivalent here.

So among these jars bearing inscriptions like 'Courage', 'Diligence', 'Triumph', 'Calm', and 'Wisdom', there is a special

---

[1] See below, p. 246.

section in the dispensary of life for remedies which cannot yet be used. Here is the urn with the inscription "Smile of the Dancer" or "Dancer's Smile". Here is kept the "small-flowered herb of healing", and, as there is no reference here to 'powder', we may assume that it has not been ground in any mill.

From the boy our attention now turns to a young girl, perhaps his sister:

> Then you, my darling,
> mutely elided
> by all the most exquisite joys.   [62–64]

The boy was prevented by the compelling claims of his artiste's profession from being a child. The girl is likewise deprived of the "exquisite joys" of her age. Her joys never enter her heart and experience, but simply "elide" or pass hastily over her. They are "mute" and neither speak to her nor evoke a response.

We are particularly moved by her joylessness because this child is loveable—a "darling"—as she stands there in all the festive trappings of her performance. She herself gains nothing from all this, but her clothing is sumptuous. Perhaps it can feel some of the "joys" which are denied to the wearer?

> Perhaps
> your frills are happy on your behalf,—
> or over your tight young breasts
> the green metallic silk
> feels itself endlessly spoilt and in need of nothing.   [64–68]

As was clear many times before, there is a peculiar relation in Rilke's poetry between people and things. At first the thing and the person may seem to have separate existences, each in its own right. But both are capable of being absorbed into an inner realm of experience where their attributes become transferable. A thing may be pervaded by a spiritual quality or it may enter the heart. A similar kind of communication between thing and human being underlies the lines quoted above. Perhaps the very "frills" on the little girl's dress are "happy on her behalf" or the "green metallic silk" over her breast has everything which she wants and is "in need of nothing".

Then the simple word of address "You" introduces a sentence which sums up the pathetic fate of the girl-performer:

> You,
> time after time, upon all of the quivering scale-pans of balance
> freshly laid fruit of serenity,
> publicly shown among shoulders.   [69–72]

The mood of the lines is easier to grasp than the structure of ideas. The girl is called the "fruit of serenity", and the word "fruit" here describes her youthful blooming quality. But she does not enjoy that protection which her youth demands, for she is on view in the market where everyone can survey her. She is laid on the "scale-pans" like fruit to be sold. And these scale-pans are in a "quivering" balance, which reminds us again of the acrobats who balance to build up their figures. They too are "scale-pans of a balance" who "quiver" in a more dangerous sense of the word, since they may fall down at any moment. This is the kind of scale on which she, the "fruit", is laid. Indeed, she is laid on *all* such scales: acrobatic figures where the girl occupies a prominent position in order to arouse such feelings as admiration for courage, fear of danger, sympathy for her youthful beauty and every other excitement.

There the girl lies, like the fruit on the scales of the market-woman—the "fruit of serenity". Here the equilibrium of the scales passes over into the equanimity of the mind. The girl can only maintain herself in difficult positions if she has a calm posture which is stabilized from within. It is psychologically a strain to be exposed in this way to the public gaze. She therefore adopts an attitude which is more than mere calm—a cool detached serenity.

The same word "serenity" was used in the *Fourth Elegy* where the spectator in front of the stage said that his father "surrendered realms of that serenity the dead are lords of" in his concern for his son. There the word meant the inner calm of a person who is no longer attached to anything, who desires nothing more and has a "purely proceeding spirit".[1] By comparison with this calm the serenity of the girl is a defensive attitude. But the two are related just as the unsuccessful turn

---

[1] See the *First Elegy*, line 67.

of the acrobats is connected with the "lofty figures" of the spirits at the end of this *Elegy*.

The girl's serenity helps her to bear the ordeal of lying on the scale-pans "publicly shown among shoulders". Perhaps this should be completed to read "publicly shown [held up by the acrobats] among the shoulders". The meaning is clearly that the girl's body should really remain 'un-public', i.e. reserved for herself and her immediate circle, whereas the acrobatic performance brings it into the open market.

VI

The next stanza contains the climax of the whole action. It was anticipated earlier by the reference to the carpet which is "lost in the cosmos". This very phrase evokes a dual sense of location and homelessness, suggesting a specific place situated in a vastly larger expanse. Since the site of the performance which is going on does not fit into any larger whole it too cannot properly *belong* anywhere. This 'space' of external location is now extended in terms of inner experience.

Where, oh, where in the world is that place in my heart   [73]

This is not the same sort of 'place' as that of the carpet. The carpet is something external, whereas the "place" is within, i.e. "in my heart". 'Place' in the ordinary sense can be seen and pointed at—'There!' But this 'place' lies within the movements of the actors, in the symbolical pattern which they create as they perfect their performance. Later it is referred to as the "ineffable spot".

This place never shows itself directly. We cannot seize it immediately, but only by way of the things surrounding it, or, since this is a 'place' within an action, we should say 'by way of what precedes and succeeds it'. It can only be grasped dialectically as something inexpressible between two 'expressibles'. The first of these two 'expressibles' is that phase of the acrobatic performance,

where they still were far from being *able*, still fell away
from each other like mounting animals, not yet
ready for pairing;—   [74-76]

First of all they were not "*able*" and the word is here used emphatically to mean the complete mastering of difficulties. The image itself is quite grotesque. When the acrobats first tried to build up their figure they fell away from each other like animals trying to mate, but without success because they were not correctly matched. And when the weight-lifters and jugglers begin their act they find that the things in their hands are still refractory. This is the stage,

> where weights are still heavy,
> and hoops still stagger
> away from their vainly
> twirling sticks? . . . . .   [77–80]

Weights are, of course, always heavy, but here they are heavy in a particular sense. Their heaviness can be seen in the bodies which are lifting them because they still have not accommodated themselves to the play of the men's muscles. And the twirling movement of the sticks still does not, as it should, make the hoops spin so that they seem to hover in the air. All this is inadequate, or, as it is called later, a "pure too-little": an unequivocal minus. But this is followed by an "empty too-much". First the performers could not achieve enough. Later they do more than is required and an "emptiness" is apparent as the performance turns into routine, the mere mechanical switching-on of a turn. The first phase could be summed up as 'nothing *yet*', the second as 'nothing *left*'. Both phases are essentially empty and insignificant—the equivalent in action of 'Nowhere' in space. But in between them comes the "place" or the moment. The two phases of inadequacy can both be 'told of' and described in logical terms. But this is not true of the moment of perfection which lies in between, for that represents an incomprehensible equilibrium.

> And then, in this wearisome nowhere, all of a sudden,
> the ineffable spot where the pure too-little
> incomprehensibly changes, veering
> into that empty too-much?   [81–84]

First the former, then the latter in quick succession, and somewhere in between there is the sudden "veering". Here is the "ineffable spot" where perfection lies, mysterious and untellable. . . Previously we saw effort and a high degree of energy

expended; and afterwards there is again a high degree—of speed
or record-breaking. In each case there is a "sum" containing
high figures. But in between there is something which cannot
be conveyed quantitatively—something simple which eludes
numerical reckoning:

> Where the many-digited sum
> solves into zero?   [85–86]

But do we not feel a sense of disappointment here? After the
long sentences describing the arduous exercises, after the few
but forceful words about the routine, and after the fervour
with which the poet has spoken of the "ineffable" intervening
moment—ought we not now to feel that the acrobats really *are*
"able"? That something miraculous has come to pass at that
"place" of pure equilibrium which was so difficult to attain—
something which is connected with pure Being? Perhaps a
pervasion of everyday falsity and unreality by something real
and true? But, as is clearly intended by the poet, this does not
happen. The tension is meant to be sustained below the surface
of the next stanza dealing with death, right up to the end of
the *Elegy* where another "place" is mentioned—in the land
of the Dead.

Here then, on a "carpet" in the "suburbs", pure ability
flashes forth for a brief moment in between the long periods
of inadequacy with which life is filled. But the moment of
"veering" is over so quickly that it cannot leave a mark. The
'nowhere' which surrounds the "ineffable spot" is too powerful
for the latter to have any effect. Perhaps we may use Rilke's
terms to say that the "carpet" *remains* "lost in the cosmos".
And there will be no change in this respect until we reach the
land of the Dead.

VII

And now the same theme of abandonment in the cosmos is
taken up again in a passage which is a strange mixture of
grandiosity and tastelessness. But it is characteristic of Rilke's
style in this *Elegy* to say the most serious things in scurrilous
terms.

> Squares, O square in Paris, infinite show-place,   [87]

This sentence mounts quickly to a climax. First "squares" in general—those strange places which people enter and leave in all directions. Each person is led on by a thread of fate, or perhaps trails a thread or "ribbon" behind him. . . Then "O square in Paris", meaning the 'big city' which might equally well be Rome, Berlin or Vienna. And finally "infinite show-place", the word 'infinite' meaning here the same as final, absolute or unqualified. This is the square where everything is finally "shown" as if it were on a stage presided over by the Angel.

Suddenly there is a strange transformation: this square is a workshop,

> where the modiste Madame Lamort
> winds and binds the restless ways of the world,
> those endless ribbons, to ever-new
> creations of bow, frill, flower, cockade and fruit,
> all falsely coloured, to deck
> the cheap winter-hats of Fate.
> . . . .   [88–94]

This is certainly a grotesque picture, but impressive, almost as if it had been painted by Max Beckmann. The great square is the workshop of a modiste whose name is "Madame Lamort" or 'Madame Death'. It is remarkable that in French, as in Italian and Latin, 'death' is feminine, whereas the equivalents in Greek, German and English are masculine. It would be difficult to decide which gender is more appropriate. Where the word is masculine it suggests the lightning from above, the striking of a blow, the plucking away of life and the tragedy of death. Where it is feminine it reminds us of death's sudden-ness, irrationality and perhaps its capriciousness; it may also be associated at a deeper level with the earth which brings forth life and takes it away.

In the *Elegy* Rilke evokes the capricious side of death and her wilfulness bordering on frivolity. Death here is a being who deals with human existence at her own convenience. Death directs the destinies of human beings and weaves them into the most fantastic shapes. Once more we seem to be back in the illusory world of the performing acrobats. Everything is a "show-place" over which people are continually scurrying, each with his own life. But they do not notice that they are

really in the hands of "Madame Lamort", Death. Nor do they
see that she is a dishonest woman who makes something false
and foolish out of humanity's sufferings and cares: "cheap
winter-hats of Fate" with stupid "bow, frill, flower, cockade
and fruit, all falsely coloured".

But Madame Death, who treats human life and destiny in
this way, is surely a grotesque counterpart to the Angel of the
Fourth Elegy who manipulates men like puppets! Perhaps she
is also the scurrilous embodiment of that "Will" which makes
the acrobats jump in the suburban square. For is there much
difference between "winding and binding" human life into
"bows, frills and cockades" and "wringing, bending, slinging,
swinging" human bodies or making living people dance like
marionettes? It cannot be said that each image is a logical
continuation of the other, but certainly all these images spring
from a common ground and contribute to each other's meaning.
The abiding impression which they leave is that men are in the
hands of powerful beings who are playing with them. These
beings may be sublimely indifferent, like the Angel, or capri-
ciously cruel like the phantom milliner. In passing, it may be
pointed out that the "hats of Fate" in the above passage are
winter-hats, intended to be worn in the last of life's seasons, old
age and death. In this context the words "cheap" and "falsely
coloured" take on their full meaning. They describe forms of
death which are radically different from that 'precious' and
genuine death which is referred to in the *Book of Hours*.[1] They
represent an inexpensive conclusion to life's course which has
been improvised in a haphazard way.

In both the *Fourth* and the *Fifth Elegies* we notice that there
is a performance. In the former the heroic but 'selfless' man
sat watching his own life being performed on the stage in front
of him. Here there is an "infinite show-place" and spectacle
and we are not told who is looking on.

There follows a long ellipsis, the purpose of which can be
understood well enough. The whole stanza is like an outburst

[1] O Lord, grant each his own, his death indeed,
   the dying which out of that same life evolves
   in which he once had meaning, love, and need.
              (*Selected Works*, II, p. 90.)

of indignation at death's futility which we do well to ponder.
But it might also be worth considering precisely what part is
played by ellipsis in the *Elegies*, for it occurs frequently, though
this is the only passage where it occupies a whole line. Its
function is clear enough: it is meant to suggest something inexpressible. Yet from the aesthetic point of view it presents a
problem. No doubt it has its proper place in a draft or fragment. But can it be allowed in a literary work written in a lofty
style such as the *Elegies*? It is the same question as whether it
is permissible to use such devices as italics in verse, or to insert
fragments of prose like "Subrisio Saltat.". Here the means
which Rilke employs to express certain inner experiences foreshadows the work of T. S. Eliot, Gottfried Benn, W. H. Auden
and others.

VIII

However complicated and loose in structure this *Elegy* may
seem to be, it still preserves a perfect underlying unity. The
tension which begins in the first line is sustained up to the last.
The whole poem is dominated by one particular situation,
namely the presence in a certain place, either in space or in
life as a whole, of beings who are trying to act or portray something to an audience of spectators. This situation is disclosed
at various levels of attainment and in various realms of existence—until it reaches the point of perfection.

First of all the "place" is the carpet, lying in the suburbs
and "lost in the cosmos", where the acrobats display their art.
Their art, however, proves to be vain and empty, as becomes
apparent from the superficiality of the entertainment which
they provide and in the falseness of their accompanying smile.
The forlornness of the place "in the cosmos" is now transferred
to our inner impression of the performance: it becomes the
"ineffable spot" where the "too-little" of dexterity turns into
a "too-much". Between these two phases there should be a
pure equilibrium and perfect facility, but this 'place' is swallowed up by the inadequacy of what precedes and follows.
Finally the 'place' assumes gigantic dimensions and becomes
the "infinite show-place" of Paris, where the players are simply
humanity in general. Here Death, intangible and yet irresist-

ible like the "Will", but false and capricious as well, weaves
men's fates into follies.

Is this the final word?

Angel: suppose there's a place we know nothing about, [95]

One last reference to a "place" is made here, though now it
is cautious and qualified by the word "suppose". We do not
know whether this place exists. We only know that it might,
indeed *should* exist: "suppose there's a place . . . .". The heart
knows what sort of place this would be, for the heart carries it
within itself.

and there,

on some indescribable carpet,   [95–96]

In this place, too, there would be a carpet—a base on which
someone would display his arts. This carpet is "indescribable",
just as the point of perfect accomplishment which never properly emerges in real life was described as "ineffable". But
whereas the latter was elusive and could not be grasped by the
blunt senses of our earthly life, the "indescribable carpet"
represents an extreme perfection both in the art of life and in
the act of contemplation.

On the carpet there now appear those figures whom Rilke
always introduces when he is trying to define final truths—

> lovers showed all that here
> they're for ever unable to manage—their daring
> lofty figures of heart-flight,
> their towers of pleasure, their ladders,
> long since, where ground never was, just quiveringly
> propped by each other,—were able to manage it there,

[96–101]

The lovers have replaced the artistes and now bring to perfection their inadequate performance. They display "daring
lofty figures of flight", though the flights are of the "heart" not
the body; "towers" or high acrobatic structures, but "towers

of pleasure"; "ladders" which lean against one another and where the performer goes through hazardous movements, "quivering" in the face of dangers which are really unsurmountable but are nevertheless overcome.

These ladders are said to be "just.... propped by each other", for they do not stand on anything, not even on the carpet. They float above it and prop each other up. This is a description of perfect equilibrium which needs no support because there is no weight pulling it down nor anything else to disturb its stability. We must imagine an ascending order of movement. At the very bottom lie the inanimate things which are pushed and driven about passively; a little higher there is the unfolding and development of growing things; higher still there are the spontaneous leaps and jumps on firm ground. At the very top we encounter that hovering flight which has no more need of support. Here the bodies concerned are so light that a mere beat of their wings can keep them aloft. In this stanza of the *Elegy* movement attains a new and, in Rilke's terminology, an *absolute* stage. It becomes the "pure" movement of the spirits which is no longer "hindered".[1] This is the smooth motion of souls in "pure space" where earthly laws no longer hold.

The "carpet" has now taken on a wholly 'inward' character and is identical with the "ineffable spot" of the "solution into zero". It lies within the lovers themselves who, being dead, have become "pure Being". What they achieve in this place is perfect performance, for here they can "manage it" at last. These words contain a sense of triumphant release, as if to say "finally attained!". In death they have become completely adept. Their powers, which were tied and fettered during their earthly lives, are now liberated.[2] Their ability, previously inadequate, is fulfilled. Their movements, which were always disturbed on earth, now have free play. What was sealed up within them is now disclosed. The movement which is completed, the art which is displayed, the unparalleled difficulty which has been overcome—all these are forms of loving. The

---

[1] *First Elegy,* line 66 f.

[2] A kind of indirect commentary is supplied by the *Sonnet,* I. xxi. Rarely has the spirit of Spring—the sense of the liberation of the earth and its vital forces, the feeling of a blessed triumph—been so effectively described as in this poem. A climax is reached in the second stanza: "she knows, she knows", and in the final words, "she sings, she sings".

act of loving has passed from apprenticeship to mastery. Its purpose can now be fulfilled absolutely, leaving a remainder of "zero".

Here we may ask whether it is justifiable to associate the heart and its love in this way with the image of these acrobatics which previously seemed so questionable. The answer probably is that Rilke wished to retain a trace of scurrility to the very end of the *Elegy* as a point of style, until it vanished in a final overriding transcendence. Nevertheless we cannot help feeling a certain surprise that this juxtaposition of the ideas of love and performance was possible at all. For the lovers on the carpet are not playing a part. They are not *performing* the love of *Romeo and Juliet* but their own, their "heart-flight", their "pleasure", their "ladders just propped by each other", that is, the whole mystery of the lovers in their intimacy where the one raises the other to the heights of experience. How can this unique thing, shrouded in all the shame of body and soul, possibly be conveyed by the image of a performance? The answer cannot be in doubt. It is because the poet sees love as something divorced from persons. In Rilke's view love may involve strength, passion or tenderness, but these must not be conceived of as personal qualities. This is the same attitude to values as we have noted several times before and it is both false and disastrous.

To whom do the lovers display their art?

before the ringed onlookers there, countless unmurmuring dead:
[102]

The whole action now takes place in the land of the Dead—in that "other relation" of the *Ninth Elegy*—where the things which were uncompleted on earth finally reach perfection. The spectators are dead people—"countless" in number, for how many people have died in this world! And they are "unmurmuring". The word is very evocative: it suggests both the existence of spirits who are not physically perceptible and a sense of vigilance which cannot be distracted.

The spectators do nothing but observe. Now the "rose of onlooking" is complete, and from all sides this centre is watched with an intense piercing gaze which unmasks everything spurious but also acknowledges everything which is true and

'essential'. This is the tribunal before which the lovers have
to prove themselves.[1]

But perhaps this is a premature simplification, for the whole
stanza is preceded by the qualification *"suppose"*. "Suppose
there's a place" and the "lovers showed" their arts, and "they
were able to manage it there". But is there such a place where
this could happen? And *if* there were, would the dead be able
to provide that confirmation which would be a fitting response
to the lovers' ability?

> would not those then fling their last, their for ever reserved,
> ever-concealed, unknown to us, ever-valid
> coins of happiness down before the at last
> truthfully smiling pair on the quietened
> carpet?   [103–107]

If the incorruptible judges saw the proficiency of the lovers—
would they reward them with the right prize, namely "happiness"? Here again something inexpressible has to be conveyed:
that boundless happiness which follows the perfect expression
of the loving heart. This is done by using the image of the
acrobats again, which inevitably brings back a flavour of
scurrility into the poem. The dead would "fling down their
coins of happiness before the smiling pair" of lovers who have
displayed their art. They would have proved before the keen-
sighted judges that they can love, and for this receive their
reward.

The accumulated adjectives serve to describe the rare value
of these coins and the extent of the happiness they symbolize.
These are the "last, for ever reserved, ever-concealed, unknown
to us, ever-valid coins of happiness". These terms of praise make
clear how considerable this achievement of the lovers is which
wins the complete recognition of the judges and the maximum
return of "happiness". Another possible interpretation of the
passage is that a love which has been perfected is so precious
that it deserves unqualified esteem whenever it appears. This
idea would be in agreement with lines 42–44 of the *First Elegy*.

The pair of lovers is described as "truthfully smiling". This
smile could not find expression earlier because it was covered

---

[1] Here again the traditional idea recurs of the dead as beings who cannot be
deceived; it is linked with the other ancient idea of the dead as passing judgment
on those who have just died.

by a sham-smile, and the slightest trace of it was worthy of being preserved by an Angel in an urn. Now at last it has become "truthful" and entered the clarity of "pure Being". The carpet on which the smiling lovers stand is described as "quietened". At the beginning of the *Elegy* this carpet represented the oppressiveness of earthly things, the forlornness of the suburban skies, isolation in the cosmos, the strain of the performing artiste, the distress of the young lad whose soles were tingling and the frustration of the young girl whose life was sacrificed to the illusory acrobatic display. Thus, as so often happens in the *Elegies*, the inner life of human beings passed into the things around them. Now the 'fufilment' of the lovers has passed into the carpet, which is itself "quietened" and fulfilled, at one with itself and in peace. It is now a true "place", serene and sheltered at the same time. The *Fourth Elegy* referred to the "spot which. . . . had been established for a pure event", i.e. the possibility of a perfect event foreshadowed in life's original plan. The child sees this possibility repeatedly, but it disappears when he grows up into the transient imperfect world of adults. The same vision now re-appears in the "quietened carpet" where it is fulfilled at last.

The foregoing is all addressed to the Angel. He is the responsible authority, the steward of the now inaccessible God. He is at home throughout the universe which extends from Here to Hereafter. The fact that the poet again and again addresses his words directly to the Angel indicates that he must be imagined as omnipresent.

Earlier in the *Elegy* the Angel was called upon to preserve something which could not be perfected in this earthly life. Here he is summoned to witness that it has at last reached fulfilment.

THE SIXTH ELEGY

Begun November–December 1912 in Spain; continued
1914 in Paris; completed February 9th 1922 at Muzot

I

THE central figure of the *Third Elegy* was the youth. The youth
was strangely passive in character, for he was simply a person
upon whom forces acted which had originated outside him or
deep down below the conscious level. He is one variety of that
depersonalized existence which we have had occasion to mention more than once before.

The *Sixth Elegy* is different in this respect. Here too there is no
action, properly speaking. But action, after all, is not the aim
of Rilke's poetry where human characters normally think, con-
template or feel much more than they act. Nevertheless there
is in this *Elegy* a character with an active life, namely the Hero,
and it is interesting to see what happens to him in Rilke's poem.

The *Elegy* begins with a strange image:

> Fig-tree, how long it's been full of meaning for me,
> the way you almost entirely omit to flower
> and into the early-resolute fruit
> uncelebratedly thrust your purest secret.   [1–4]

A botanical explanation is necessary for the full understanding
of this image, although there is no space here for more than the
essential facts. The fruit which we know as the "fig" has two
forms, of which the sweet edible one is not really a fruit at all
but a kind of blossom. Strictly speaking, it is the husk of the
flower, the fleshy container inside which there is a large number
of tiny but authentic flowers. This is why it is called in Italian
fiore di fico. The blossoms are fertilized by a very complicated
process and then the fruit proper takes shape, namely those

granules with a nutty taste which also have a fleshy container, the late fig.

Now the text can be understood. The poet finds something strangely impressive and 'meaningful' about the fact that the fig-tree "almost entirely omits to flower". More precisely it does not produce the kind of flower which we are familiar with on other fruit-trees and which blossoms forth into colour and fragrance. The qualification "almost" is used because in fact the whole of the 'early' fig is a mass of blossom. But it does not seem like blossom and at first sight has the character of fruit.

The interior of the "fruit" is the "purest secret". This we may take to be the urge of the living thing towards fulfilment, that is towards becoming fruit. The parent plant then fulfils its highest function as the new plant-to-be is formed. Corresponding processes take place in animal and human life. But this "secret" of living matter also embraces another form of fulfilment which may be mentioned here since it clarifies what follows. This is the progressive fulfilment of its own *shape* through all the phases of growth and development. This process is completed when the last phase of all is realized, that is, in death.[1]

So the way in which the fig-tree seems to produce its fruit straight away, without passing through a flowering stage, is strange and "full of meaning". The underlying "secret" is also described as "pure". This refers to an ontological, not an ethical purity. It means the original integrated character of something elementary which is striving towards self-expression without wastage or distortion.

There is one other feature which is characteristic of the fig-tree's vital urge to grow and produce fruit. It is "uncelebrated", dispensing with any praise or glory. "Praise" and its synonyms —like "achievement" a little later—are among Rilke's favourite words. They meant for him the beautiful revelation of a thing's essence, or the brilliant throwing into relief of inner significance, or the expression of admiration or joy at the abundance of meaning which a thing contains. In the case of trees their "praise" is to be found in their blossom, for "flowering" is that phase of growth which reveals the mystery of life in joy and

---

[1] The dimension of time here asserts itself in what is primarily a spacial pattern, i.e. the combination of parts and their inter-relationship. The shape of growth becomes apparent in the structural shape.

beauty. But the fig-tree renounces this, and we shall see later how this 'self-praise' in the blossom, or the renunciation of it, has an analogy in human life. The period of human "praise" is normally the time of youth when beauty unfolds itself freely without any heart-searchings about the seriousness of life.

The image of the fig-tree is now developed further:

> Like the tube of a fountain, your bent bough drives the sap
> downwards and up; and it leaps from its sleep, scarce waking,
> into the joy of its sweetest achievement. Look,
> like Jupiter into the swan.   [5–8]

A new simile here serves to describe the driving pressure behind the life-urge. The bough of the fig-tree is compared with the "tube of a fountain" which supplies it with water. The supply-pipe first brings water down from the reservoir and then rises up again, though not so high as before, to the fountain. The difference in level between reservoir and fountain produces the pressure which makes the jet of water rise into the air. There is a real similarity here with the structure of the fig-tree's branches. The branch leaves the trunk, bends down in a curve and then rises up again, though not as high as the point where it left the trunk. So the sap within it passes "downwards and up", and the similar shape of the fountain's tube becomes the image of the plant's vital urge which produces the fruit. In Winter the tree still lies in "sleep". Then it begins to put forth its leaves, and the next stage, that of blooming, would represent an awakening and a joyful emergence into the light. But the fig-tree does not stop there. It now "leaps" straight into the "joy of its sweetest achievement", i.e. into fruit, though "scarce waking", since this 'fruit' is really blossom in disguise.

It has already been suggested that the word "achievement" had a particular meaning in Rilke's mind, for he uses it frequently.[1] It had for him an ethical value, meaning intensity of experience and action or the devotion and thoroughness with which something is brought to fulfilment. Joy is an "achievement" of this kind—the blissful joy of penetrating into perfection. In this sense the fruit is the real "achievement" of the tree.

---

[1] *Translator's note*: In the original *leisten*.

Then, as often happens in Rilke's imagery, another simile is added: the "achievement" of the fruit by the fig-tree is as swift and propitious as that of Jupiter when he approached Leda in the shape of a swan. He first transformed himself into a swan. But even before he had time to rejoice in the beauty of his new shape, or to "glory in flowering" as the *Elegy* puts it a little later, he entered into union with Leda.

II

Thus it is with the fig-tree; but with us things are different:

> . . . . . We, though, we linger,
> alas, we glory in flowering; already revealed
> we reach the retarded core of our ultimate fruit. [8-10]

We "linger" in the purposeless state of youth: in the by-ways or the many blind alleys and wasteful projects of our existence. "We *glory* in flowering". We are proud of our flowering stage, but this is really a diversion from the true course of our lives and in following it we lose something precious. Our final aim or "ultimate fruit"—whether it is a single deed or the fulfilment of a whole life-time—always comes too late. The fruit is "retarded". This echoes again the description of the tree and the streaming of the sap into its fruit. "We reach the retarded core of our ultimate fruit", and in doing so we are "already revealed". This means that we are 'exposed', for we placed our trust in flowering and this diverted us from the richness of fruiting.

Only "few" escape this deception. They are the heroes and those who die young.

> In few the pressure of action rises so strongly
> that already they're stationed and glowing in fullness of heart,
> when, seductive as evening air, the temptation to flower,
> touching the youth of their mouths, touching their eyelids, appears:
> [11-14]

There are not many who feel the impulse towards unqualified "achievement" and resist the enticement when, "seductive as evening air, the temptation to flower, touching the youth of

their mouths, touching their eyelids, appears"—when everything invites them simply to rejoice and squander their ener-
gies in an enjoyment of life's bounty. These few are "stationed
and glowing in fullness of heart". This "glowing" means a
fervent readiness for "achievement". The word "stationed" is
more difficult to interpret. It seems to refer to a man who is
called upon to do something and therefore takes up a position
of readiness. His very 'stance' becomes a preparation for action.

Now the *Elegy* specifies those who are endowed with this
attitude:

> only in heroes, perhaps, and those marked for early removal,
> those in whom gardening Death's differently twisted the veins.
>
> [15–16]

Within the hero a vital uncompromising principle is at work
which does not recognize those factors which determine the
average man's life, e.g. sloth, expediency and fear. The ethos
which fills the hero is exceptional, and because of it he comes
into conflict with those values which predominate in the life
around him. Being orientated towards the great opportunities
of life he has time neither for diversions nor for the beauties of
"flowering" and "lingering". His very task gives him his necessary inner impetus and impels him forwards.

Next to the hero stand those who are "marked for early
removal"—those who will die young. Dying is the last achievement of this life. Death issues forth from the end of life's line and
thereby fulfils life's pattern. There are men who die early, but
in such a way as to fulfil themselves in their early death. They
too, like the hero, have had no time for lingering.

Once more the image of the tree is evoked. There are also
men "in whom gardening Death's differently twisted the veins"
—*differently*, that is, from those who are meant to live long lives.
The veins in which the blood flows here suggest the boughs of
the fig-tree filled with sap. They express the way in which a man
is shaped within; they are the tracks of his life, for his fate is
shaped according to the manner of their "twisting". But what
gives them the decisive twist is Death. Here Death is regarded
as 'completing' life since by its terminal position it determines
the whole course of the life which preceded it. Death fulfils the
same function, though in a different way, as "Madame Lamort"

in the *Fifth Elegy* who "bound" the "ways" of men towards
their "cheap" and "falsely-coloured" final destiny. Thus the
way men live shapes the manner of their dying. Here Death
appears in the likeness of a gardener who bends and ties the
twigs of the young sapling in order to decide the way in which
they are to grow and bear fruit.

> These go plunging ahead: preceding their own
> victorious smile, as the team of horse in the mildly-
> moulded reliefs of Karnak the conquering King.   [17-19]

"These" then, the heroes and those destined to die young,
cannot do what other men do—linger, expend their resources
and savour the glory of existence. They must "go plunging
ahead". Their lives are governed by a force which drives them
on to fulfilment. They "precede their own victorious smile".
The act of smiling is a kind of blooming and unfolding of the
self in radiant beauty. With "them", however, the smile does
not appear, or, if it does, it lacks repose. For no sooner has one
heroic deed, which might call forth a joyous smile, been completed than another deed demands performance and the smile
is 'overrun'. This happens not just once, but again and again.
The fundamental pattern of such men's lives is to be swept
forward ahead of the place where they should have smiled.

Like the acrobats in the *Fifth Elegy*, they cannot make the
smile into a reality. But whereas the acrobats' smile faded amid
the simulation of their performance, here the smile perishes because the task undertaken by the hero is so tremendous. This is
expressed here by a reminiscence of Rilke's journey to Egypt.
There he saw some reliefs in the temple of Karnak which showed
the king driving along in his war-chariot. These were bas-
reliefs, "mildly-moulded" with flat slightly hollowed surfaces.
The steeds in the picture gallop ahead so that they always
"precede" the man in the chariot. He is whisked away all the
time from one spot to the next so that he never has time to
linger in any single place. This image of the war-chariot tearing
along is very different from that of the quietly sprouting fig-
tree. But it expresses the same idea: a way of living which leaves
out everything associated with lingering or blooming and
presses on impetuously towards its crowning fulfilment.

III

Yes, the Hero's strangely akin to the youthfully dead. Duration
doesn't concern him.   [20–21]

Once more the Hero is likened to the "youthfully dead"—those
who have died at an early age and who are, indeed, marked by
the very quality of youth as ready for death. As for them, so for
the hero, there can be no "duration". If "duration" meant the
same as the "everlastingness" which "entertained" the child[1] it
would signify something essential like "pure Being". But in the
mouth of the hero this word would mean something ignomini-
ous, synonymous with the "lingering" referred to in the first
stanza—the tarrying on the way towards action and fulfilment.
For the hero "pure Being" lies in the very opposite of lingering,
namely in an incessant storming ahead.

"Duration" or lingering "doesn't concern" the hero. It does
not even tempt him, so powerful is his forward impetus.

> His rising's existence. Time and again
> he takes himself off and enters the changed constellation
> his changeless peril's assumed.   [22–24]

The hero does not know any Becoming. Filled from the very
beginning with his true essence he simply *is*. For this reason the
hero is associated, not explicitly but at least by the context here,
with the star—the heavenly body which is the most effective
symbol of finality and unconditional completeness.

A deep relationship has always been felt to exist between
human life and the stars. And this relationship seems to be
constant and unchanging in character, orderly and eternal in
duration—in contrast to all the things in the world which are
sudden, tempestuous or vacillating. The stars form the opposite
pole to man's vulnerable existence; but, according to tradition,
they also determine the course of his life and thus appear to be a
manifestation of Fate. Now as frequently happens in humanity's
search for a meaning in life, this relationship also has an opposite counterpart—when man himself is considered to have become a star. The human being, in his bloom and decay, is then

[1] *Fourth Elegy*, line 72.

transformed into one of those lofty constellations which stand high above all earthly change. . . In the *Elegy* the hero appears to be related to a constellation in just this way. His birth is called a "rising": he rises like a star and then, like a star, he is already completely realized—unchanging and irresistible. This image describes the essential quality of the hero, that is, his contact with "pure Being". Yet the character of "pure Being" here—compared for instance to the definition which was given in connection with the child—has now swung round into its opposite: "serenity" and the "everlastingness" have been re-placed by an uncheckable forward thrust into heroic action.

What follows demands some explanation. "He"—this hero, Achilles or Siegfried, Alexander or Napoleon—"time and again takes himself off". This means the same as the sentence in the preceding stanza "These go plunging ahead". The hero does not linger in the situation of the moment, but is constantly swept further on by the tempo of his existence. More precisely, he *sweeps himself* on. He possesses a tremendous fund of initiative which is different from that of the king who is carried forward by his war-chariot. For the hero pushes himself ahead and determines his own destiny. In the same way—and here his initiative reaches its climax—he determined his own birth, his very entry into existence (lines 32 ff.).

Yet this heroic existence entails constant peril. With each of his challenging steps forward the hero "enters the changed constellation his changeless peril's assumed". The hero is like a star entering a "constellation". The word "rising", used above, has clearly not yet exhausted its meaning in the *Elegy*, for the star which can most truly be said to "rise" for us is the sun. And in the work of Rilke, who knew his Bible well, we may be re-minded of the XIXth Psalm in which the sun is likened to the hero leaving his bedroom in order to launch forth on his career of action. This sun is always ready to enter a new sign of the zodiac, according to its position in the sky. And in the *Elegy* we read that the hero repeatedly "enters the changed constella-tion". This could mean that the constellation or star altered within itself. But if we keep in mind the whole context and also the elasticity, not to say capriciousness, of Rilke's grammar, we shall probably be more correct in assuming that it means 'an ever different constellation', i.e. the fresh constellation of any given hour with its summons to perform another new deed. Despite their variety, however, all the constellations which the hero enters involve him in the same "peril", a peril which is "his" and changeless. Such is the abiding character of the heroic life.

But how do we know about the hero?

> There few could find him. But Fate,
> grim concealer of us, enraptured all of a sudden,
> sings him into the storm of his surging world.   [24–26]

By his very nature the hero always stands in a "constellation" or celestial sign. He is not simply *under* a certain sign like everyone else, but *in* it, for he belongs with his whole being to the realm of the stars. Up there in the heavens he might be isolated from us and "few could find him". But the world itself—inasmuch as the world is "Fate", i.e. a specific disposition of events—proclaims the hero's presence. This Fate is not concerned with men of average calibre; it despises and "conceals" us "grimly". "All of a sudden", however, with all the incalculability of inspiration, Fate is "enraptured" and prophetic, and "sings him into the storm of his surging world". The world is not simply shaken by the storm. It *is* the "storm" itself, an incorporation of *dynamis* through and through. It is not an external, physical storm, but one which arises in the spirit of time, a disturbance among the nations of the kind which creates history. This world is "his": it is bound to him, dominated and shaped by him. It "surges" like an ocean and into it Fate proclaims his existence.

Perhaps we may also consider this storm in a less abstract light—not merely as a simile but as a real happening. We may recall here the experience which first gave Rilke the inspiration to write the *Elegies*: how he went down to the sea at Duino and there, on the lower bastions of the castle, heard the opening words of the *First Elegy* amid the raging of the *bora*. The way in which Rilke experienced life was not empirical; but neither was it simply fanciful. Indeed, it contains one dimension which, when fully developed, becomes truly visionary. Perhaps an experience of the kind described above contributed to the writing of these lines.

Suddenly the presence of the hero is felt:

None do I hear like him. There suddenly rushes through me,
borne by the streaming air, his dark-echoing tone.   [27–28]

Rilke was acutely sensitive to all sound, and to music. His world
is "orphic": existence for him is the same as sound and therefore
audible to those who are capable of hearing. But he can hear
no sound which so touches his innermost heart as that of the hero.
"Suddenly", without warning, the poet feels the reverberation
of his "dark-echoing tone".

The world is an infinite symphony, and now, born on the
"streaming air" amidst that storm which is also the "rapture"
of "Fate"—wind, breath and spirit in one—the sound of the
hero makes itself heard. It "echoes darkly" with a tragic note
which announces his impending downfall.

IV

This experience strikes the poet at his most vulnerable point.
Again he feels himself to be a child, a boy; and for Rilke those
critical early years of his life were always a bitter problem. He
was convinced that he had never had a proper childhood. Now
this thought overwhelms him again.

And then how gladly I'd hide from the longing: [29]

He is seized by the desire to be a boy again and to have in front
of him once more the vision of a heroic life—to feel the 'heroic
longing' and, with it, the fear of the longing, knowing that it is,
after all, in vain.

Nevertheless, the feeling cannot be suppressed:

                              Oh would,
would that I were a boy, and might come to it yet, and be sitting,
propped upon arms still to be, and reading of Samson,
how his mother at first bore nothing, and, afterwards, all. [29–32]

The lines are given additional force by the initial repetition:
"Oh would, would that I were a boy". They express the melancholy yearning for something which goes to the very depths and
yet cannot be. And what would happen if he really *could* be a
boy again? Then that 'possible' life would stand open before

him which we call future. This is expressed with particular emphasis: not simply he "could" but he "might", i.e. he would have permission from Fate. But for what? To "come to *it*", the "it" here being the fulfilment of the boy's wishes—to be a complete man, a great man, a hero.

Rilke sees himself seated at the table, "propped upon arms still to be". This is another unusual combination of words— his head "propped upon arms" which are still weak, i.e. not yet proper arms because they are "still to be" in the future. But inspired by a vision of what he would like to become, he already feels these arms to be those of a hero, filled with the tremendous strength which he will then possess.

Then, suddenly, one particular heroic figure emerges from the world of the Bible: this is "Samson", whose name in translation means the "sun man", and whose life took such a spectacular and yet tragic course in his fight against the Philistines. The boy reads in the Book of Judges how "his mother at first bore nothing, and, afterwards, all". First nothing, for Manoah's wife was barren. Then, when her husband had offered up a sacrifice, the angel of the Lord appeared and prophesied that she would be the mother of a powerful son. This was fulfilled, and so she bore "all"—a hero.

V

In line 22 of the Elegy it was said that the heroism of the hero was already manifest in his "rising", that is in his birth. But now the *Elegy* makes still greater claims for him. It affirms that he was a hero even in that first beginning which took place *before* birth. He was a man of action and decision from the very outset, even with respect to his own Being:

> Was he not hero already in you, O mother, and had not
> even in you his lordly choosing begun?
> Thousands were brewing in the womb and trying to be *him*,
> but, look! he seized and discarded, chose and was able to do.
>
> [33–36]

The hero is completely the master of his own decisions. By virtue of his primary power of freedom he is capable of making his own choice. This primary power, however, according to the

Elegy, asserts itself not only in his actions but also in his very Being. We may recall here the question which was posed in the *Third Elegy*—"Did he ever begin himself?"—in which birth was considered as marking the youth's entry into individualized existence.

Rilke here tries to penetrate the origins of individual Being. The secondary form of our Being is evident as soon as individual action commences, i.e. in a freely made decision. For a free decision is essentially an action in which the person acting is the prime mover, the master of the action from the very beginning. But can this same freedom be said to exist with respect to our Being? If I am master of my actions from the beginning, am I in a position to decide my Being from the outset as well? If we take into account human limitations the answer must be that this is not possible. Such absolute power would be the prerogative of God. And even in ascribing this power to God we must be clear what we mean. God is certainly the master of His own Being; but not in the sense that He "began himself", which would be an idealistic paradox of the kind which is asserted in Fichte's philosophy. God determines His own Being in the sense that in Him there is no beginning. He simply "is". To assert anything like this of Man would not only be contradictory but *hubris*, unless the speaker failed to grasp the implications of his statement and was simply carried away by an obsession with supreme "power". The truth is that my Being is something which I can only receive. And in my act of accepting it as something set and fixed my destiny is given its foundation. Until I 'am', and 'am myself', I am unable to act.

Nevertheless, there remains a temptation to regard freedom as something all-embracing which extends all the way back to the origins of Being. Rilke does this by subjecting the Self to a somewhat strange analysis. On the one hand there is the purely formal *ego* without any attributes—the mere fact *that* I am myself. In contradistinction to this there is the *ego* with its content—*what* I am in my essential shape.[1] Clearly, neither *ego* can exist without the other. Now Rilke regards the purely formal *ego* as possessing the power to make a metaphysical choice. This *ego*

[1] Comparable to some extent with the distinction drawn in the Buddhist doctrine of reincarnation between the point of individualization and the form in which it is embodied.

chooses from all the possible selves that self which it wishes to realize in Being. The potential selves are conceived of as kinds of creatures, or shadowy forms which surge up in the *ego* in order to be realized in it. They are countless in number: "thousands were brewing in the womb". The womb of the mother contains all the potential selves which might have developed and is itself associated with the womb of Being—the source of human potentiality. This relationship is not unlike that which, according to the *Third Elegy*, exists between the individual's instinct and that of the species. Here again we note that the integrity of the human personality is called into question.[1] The potential selves were "trying to be *him*", the hero. Normally, in Rilke's view, the ego is overpowered by one of the potential forms during its transition into Being, i.e. it does not choose but is chosen. But the hero—the words "but look!" make us aware of the enormous claim which is being made— was different: he "seized and discarded, chose and was able to do". He was master "already" there. He made an absolute choice even before he received his Being.[2]

This, for Rilke, is the ultimate root of heroism: the "beginning" before the "rising". Significantly, he returns to the figure of Samson:

> And if ever he shattered columns, that was the time, when he burst out of the world of your body into the narrower world,
> where he went on choosing and doing.   [37–39]

The Bible relates how Samson, after he has been blinded, is led into the house where his enemies are feasting and is called to make sport for them.[3] Then he prays that God may restore his former strength to him. He is led towards the two pillars which support the roof and pushes them apart so that he and his enemies are buried. This is what Rilke's lines refer to. The pillars which are pushed apart here are the confining walls of the mother's womb. The hero does what Samson once did: he breaks forth from one form of existence into another. It is true that there is an important difference. Samson was transported

---

[1] The *Third Elegy* also refers to an "innumerable fermentation" which strives out of the depths into light, from insubstantiality into concreteness (line 68 ff.).

[2] The more radical form of existentialism maintains something similar, except that it attributes choice not to the beginning of Being, but to the content of Being.

[3] *Judges*, xvi, 23 ff.

by his death out of the narrowness of this world into the spaciousness of the "other relation". But when the hero was born he was
taken out of an expansive world into a narrow one, for, as the
Third Elegy implied, the world of the womb is larger than that
of the earth. The womb is the realm of the possible, of the
"innumerable fermentation". Birth is a passage into the narrower world of defined form.

Yet in this narrower world the hero continues what was always
his prime concern: "to choose" and "be able". Now, as before,
he masters himself by his decisiveness and dominates his environment through his deeds.

Following the praise which he has accorded to the hero,
Rilke then strikes an elegiac note: a note of praise and lament
at the same time. He does not lament the hero, who stands
beyond all pity, but those who come into the orbit of the hero
where they either suffer or perish.

> O mothers of heroes!
> Sources of ravaging rivers! [39–40]

The mothers are mysterious figures, impressive and yet deserv-
ing pity. After the introductory pathetic "O", the words rise to
a pitch of acclamation. The mother of the hero is the "source of
a ravaging river", unfathomable and powerful. But at the source
of such rivers violence occurs. The interior of the womb is now
transformed into a landscape, reminding us of that other landscape in the depths of the unconscious which is described in the
Third Elegy. This landscape is a gorge, ravaged by the river
which seeks to make a course through it.

The mother is not alone in being caught up by the tragedy
of the hero's existence. There are other figures too—others who
are filled with love as they turn towards him.

> Gorges wherein,
> from high on the heart's edge, weeping,
> maids have already plunged, victims to-be for the son.
> [40–42]

These are the maidens who will later love the hero. Like the "girl" in the *Third Elegy* they are associated with the figure of the mother.

The events of later life are here envisaged as taking place before birth, in a foreshadowing of future existence. Indeed, the hero's whole life is considered metaphysically rather than empirically. The *Third Elegy* portrayed mothers and girls in the radiance of their helping love. Here, however, they have a tragic character. No one can be helpful to the hero, for he is entirely self-dependent, completely alone in his starry orbit where he carries all before him. So mothers and girls inevitably become "victims", unless we are to take these lines as meaning that the mother demands the sacrifice of the girl for the sake of her son. In any case the sensitiveness and humanity of the girl must be overridden by the superhuman hero so that he may flourish. The cruelty of the maids' fate is heightened by the fact that there are several, indeed many, who will have to suffer in this way.

The death of the maids is conveyed in a twofold image. One is that of the gorge over the edge of which the girl plunges to her death. The other is that of the heart which is described as "high", though the word connotes 'depth' of feeling as well. The 'height' of the heart is identified with the edge of the gorge so that the maids are said to fall down "from high on the heart's edge".

> For whenever the Hero stormed through the halts of love,
> each heart beating for him could only lift him beyond it:
> turning away, he'd stand at the end of the smiles, another.
>
> [43–45]

For the Hero all his loves are merely brief delays on his stormy forward path. Indeed their very function is to make his impetus still greater. "Each heart beating for him", every impulse of love which others feel for him, simply heightens the pitch of his life and increases the essentially active quality of his existence. So he is "lifted beyond it"—beyond the passing moment into a fresh onward thrust. He has no sooner recognized the smile which is intended for him than he turns away, becomes "another" and forges ahead.

VI

We cannot help asking here how such a heroic life as this can possibly be treated in an elegy. For an elegy is essentially the expression of grief at the sadness of life—grief, not so much at a particular sad event as at the whole sorrowful nature of existence, above all its transience and the subjection to Fate of all that is noble and beautiful. But the grief is experienced in such a way that it is finally overcome. Rilke's own way of overcoming grief is to accept it, to welcome Death in the hidden recesses of the heart, and to praise the kind of life which becomes one with death and grief. But how can the Hero inspire any experience of this sort? For is he not made up entirely of toughness, bravery and the will to strive and struggle? This is why the epic and the tragedy, the heroic song and the ballad seem the appropriate literary forms for describing his actions. Can the hero be the subject of an elegiac poem?

Part of the explanation is no doubt that the heroic figure fulfils a specific function in the view of life which the *Elegies* present. There is a sonnet on a similar subject which Rilke wrote for Frau Grete Gulbransson and which we may quote here:[1]

> The Hero's one. The Hero's merely power.
> He bows the world: Time rushes to the tryst.
> From some red clay where veins of metal twist
> and drops collected from the thunder-shower
>
> his master's fingers must have clenched his fist.
> He'll stand there, visible from far, and start
> round a new centre every circling fate;
> step, like an umpire, raging without hate,
>
> to fallers-out. And when he loves, what heart
> shall make that primal mover hesitate?
> At last, with nothing further to achieve,
>
> his flight will fling him to the constellations,
> to move within their measures, and receive
> the mildness of their infinite gyrations.

The very first sentence of this poem tells us what Rilke intends in the *Elegies*: "The Hero's one". In a world where everything

[1] *Later Poems*, p. 144.

M

is in conflict with itself, he is unambiguous and self-contained. This is precisely what the *Elegies* say of the puppet, except that the puppet is not alive and can only be given a meaning by man. The same thing is also said of the child, except that the child can be 'shaken' out of its security by the grown-up—quite apart from the fact that he will, in any case, grow up later and lose this security. The lovers too possess an inner 'unity', but it does not last beyond the initial period of their experience. Then a duality intrudes into their lives too. Lastly there is the dying man in the *Eighth Elegy* who is said to stare ahead into openness "with large brute gaze" and who occupies a border-line position in the literal sense of the word.

Fundamentally then, only the Hero stands as a complete figure possessing inner unity. This is how he is presented in the *Sixth Elegy* which brings him into proximity with the stars. Like the Sun-god who appears in so many ancient myths he presses unerringly along on his course; he is unequivocal from the beginning and unbroken to the end. And this 'end' itself is only his "ultimate birth", the revealing of his eternal shape.

Thus the Hero, together with the animal, is the one figure in the *Elegies* who stands out from all others, and against whom all the unreal and provisional features of existence are thrown into relief.

Nevertheless we cannot rest satisfied with this heroic figure. The more often we read the *Elegy* the stronger our objections to him become. The following is an attempt to define them.

In particular, it seems incorrect to say simply that the Hero has nothing to do with "duration". There is ample evidence to the contrary in myths, in legends and in history. Heracles, like Siegfried, conquered the monsters of chaos and made the earth habitable. Achilles—superficially the very embodiment of youthful bravery and desire for glory—was involved in the struggle against Troy, i.e. in the atonement which was demanded for the outrage committed by Paris. At Thermopylae, Leonidas tried to stem the asiatic flood; and Samson, who appears in the *Elegy* as an example of heroism to be praised, secured a period of freedom for his people after long years of oppression. If we had to sum up the essential character of the hero as concisely as possible we might say simply that he extends the bounds of human life against the powers of chaos. It is true that he is not concerned about his own 'duration'. But it is precisely this unconcern which enables him to create something which really endures. This is what distinguishes him from the adventurer who loves danger for its own sake or because it raises his feelings to a pitch of excitement. Like Don Juan in love, the adventurer lacks content. And the true hero differs from the adventurer in the same way as the true lover differs from Don Juan. He serves life at the points where it is most imperilled. For him danger is only the reverse side of his great mission. The Hero of the *Elegy* on the other hand is driven on merely by the dynamic of the deed, not by its content—by the danger itself, not by the life-service in which it is incurred. He is a hero for the sake of heroism. This is an absolute heroism, dissociated from ends and hence strangely devoid of meaning. There is something futile about this Hero of Rilke's. His tragedy, like that of Don Juan, is that of his ultimate hollowness. To this extent he conforms closely with Rilke's doctrine of 'self-less' contemplation and objectless love. Their dialectical counterpart is the absolute unqualified activity of the Hero.

We can express this in a different way. The idea of a Hero, as a meaningful figure in human existence, includes a number of possibilities. He may have a universal significance, in which case he stands for the power of light which gives order to things, shines on them or makes them fruitful; then he is like the sun in its ever-recurrent victory over the chaos of darkness. Or he may have a historical significance, in which case he subdues the chaos of wild lawlessness or inhuman destructiveness; his actions are then of the kind which establish order and lay foundations. In fact he sows the seeds of "duration".

The hero of the *Elegies* is supposed to be seen in a historical perspective. He is meant to have the seriousness and sense of responsibility of a historical figure, as is clear from the second stanza. And yet this heroic figure remains quite unhistorical. It would be truer to say that his character is cosmic and that consequently he tends to be abstract, lacking the quality of real life. He is asserted to be this or that, but his character does not emerge. He is a star, but without any of a star's tranquillity. He is a turbulent constellation.

To put the matter still more plainly: the true hero with a historical significance is nothing like as heroic as the Hero of the *Elegies*. He is a human being, with fine and admirable traits, but with weaknesses as well. And it is these weaknesses which heighten the tragedy of his life. He yearns for the companionship of others and he is capable of love—real love, not merely as a means of kindling the fire of his own Being. Rilke's *Elegy* builds up a tone poem of a Hero around a single note, whereas it should rest on a chord.

One thing finally becomes clear. This heroism is of the kind which might be conjured up by a man who is not himself a hero in the active sense of the word. Rilke's personality was extremely complex, woven through with inhibitions and cleavages. He was sensitive and capable of great suffering. One kind of inner initiative was so alien to him that he could seriously extol the puppet as an ideal in the *Fourth Elegy*. And when he came to describe his Hero he painted a picture in which all those qualities appear which he himself lacked—in rather the same way as Nietzsche drew his portrait of Zarathustra. Lines 29–32 of the *Elegy* are in fact an admission that his picture was born of nostalgia. This is why Rilke omits those very traits which, in a strange way, were undoubtedly heroic in himself: his persistence in living out his chosen values—in life and work —to their final conclusion, even, indeed particularly, when he was helpless and suffering.

The Hero of the *Elegy* arouses a strange feeling within us. We pity him for his violence and his lack of purpose and orientation. He is really like a star which shines as it follows its orbit but cannot feel; which courses through empty space far from the vulnerable, pain-ridden but living atmosphere of the earth. He is a non-human Hero.

This very fact seems indirectly to give the Hero a place in the world of the *Duino Elegies*. For he himself is far less convincing than all the transient and unintegrated figures with whom he is contrasted. He impresses us the less because we are bound to esteem imperfect and suffering creatures which are *alive* more highly than an ideal figure from which life is absent.

THE SEVENTH ELEGY

Composed at Muzot, February 7th 1922

I

THE *Seventh Elegy* takes up two themes which were already touched on in the *First* and recur later in the *Ninth*: one theme is that perfect love has no object; the other is that the real world of truth has to be built up from our inner experience. We shall also encounter here again an idea which is familiar to us from the first two *Elegies*, namely the gulf separating Man from the Angels. The distinctive feature of the *Seventh Elegy* is the contrast which it draws between the abundance of Spring and Summer on the one hand and the sad fate of those who are excluded from life's riches on the other.

> Not wooing, no longer shall wooing, voice that's outgrown it,
> be now the form of your cry;   [1-2]

"Your cry" here means the cry of the poet. This is clear from the beginning of the second stanza which expresses the same idea in the first person. The poet feels impelled to call out, to utter a "cry" of elemental longing. But this "cry" must not be a "wooing" or a solicitation to another human being for he feels that his heartfelt desire may "no longer" seek to be satisfied. His desire must advance from its earlier form of "wooing" to that state of perfection described in the *First Elegy*: it must be directed beyond the other person into "the Open". His voice will then have "outgrown" wooing: it will have developed beyond the immature stage of possessiveness to a state of freedom.

> though you cried as pure as the bird
> when the surging season uplifts him, almost forgetting
> he's merely a fretful creature and not just a single heart
> it's tossing to brightness, to intimate azure.   [2-5]

The poet does not renounce his earlier cry of solicitation because of any discordancy or impurity which it might contain.

181

On the contrary, he feels that he could sing like a "bird" and his "cry" would be the natural and pure expression of an inner need. In the next fifteen lines there follows one of the most beautiful descriptions of bird-song in our literature—more beautiful, or at least richer in imagery than Shelley's famous poem "To a Skylark".

Rilke's "bird" is also a lark—one of the earliest song-birds of the year. The lark sings in flight, while it is ascending, and its song is thus closely associated with the high open skies of Spring which hang so propitiously over the earth. The whole freshness of life is perfectly expressed in the soaring ascent and inexhaustible song of this bird.

The "surging season uplifts" the lark. The impulse to fly aloft does not arise within the little creature itself but is part of the whole surge into life and abundance which we call Spring. This surge is so powerful that it seems "almost to forget" the lark's limitations. From being a tiny "fretful creature" struggling pathetically through life the lark is seemingly transformed into a "single heart"—a being that consists of "heart" and nothing else. Spring releases the bird into life, fills it with joy and longing, and gives it the strength to sing and fly.

The season "tosses" the little bird into the bright expanse which hangs over the still empty earth. The lark enters the "intimate azure" of the sky. The use of the word "intimate" is significant here. Normally when we refer to the sky we mean the lofty distance above us. But sometimes when we gaze calmly up at a very clear sky we may also feel that there is a dimension of depth within that height. The sky still stretches above us but our eyes are drawn inwards as well as upwards. Nietzsche describes a similar impression of 'depth within height' in a passage of *Zarathustra* where he refers to the "midday abyss" of the "sky above us". The ominous threatening quality of Nietzsche's "abyss of light"—varying in colour from blue to dark green or black—is absent from the *Elegy*. Here the sky is a bright and "intimate azure", though we have to remember that in Rilke's usage the words "intimate" or "inward" mean not only familiar and close, but powerful and compelling as well. That dimension which receives *into* itself the quality of Being is called "*in*timate". The "intimate azure" of the *Elegy* means the sky of that 'true' world which should emerge anew and afresh from the encounter between Man and things. Into this heaven the lark ascends.

The rising song of the lark is a "wooing" or mating call—the clear, strong "voice" of Nature. And the voice of the wooing poet would be akin to this, so he believes.

> No less
> than he, you, too, would be wooing some silent companion
> to feel you, as yet unseen, some mate in whom a reply
> was slowly awaking and warming itself as she listened,—
> your own emboldened feeling's glowing fellow-feeling.   [5–9]

At first this wooing is not directed at any specific creature. The "companion" is still "unseen". She is somewhere, but her feelings are still unmoved by the song. At last, however, the song touches her and a "reply slowly awakens". This is the "fellow-feeling" which becomes ever stronger, "warming itself as she listens" until it glows into fire. The bird's call-song evokes the response of his mate; "feeling" has been answered by "fellow-feeling".

The above passage refers to the lark and the poet at the same time. The bird is the subject of the immediately preceding lines, 2–5, and of those which follow line 10. The words "you, too" in line 6 show that the intervening passage refers to the poet. But what is said of the poet is so coloured by the description of the lark that man and bird seem to merge into one another. In the last line both are lost sight of for a moment and we are left with the pure abstractions of a "feeling" without a subject to which a similar "fellow-feeling" responds.

Then, from out of this interplay of call and response the shape of the singing lark emerges again more clearly.

> Oh, and Spring would understand—not a nook would fail
> to re-echo annunciation.   [10–11]

Here "Spring" is not simply a season of the year. Spring

becomes a presiding power as well, the spirit behind certain
processes, a 'Someone'—like the figure of Pan who conjures
up everything that stirs and moves at noon on a Summer's
day.

The Spring would understand the meaning of the lark's
ascent and the "cry" of the poet if he uttered it. Then the bird's
flight and the poet's words would have not only an external
location but also an 'inner' dwelling. They would find harmony
with the spirit of Spring in that realm of "intimacy" or "inwardness" referred to above. "Not a nook" in that bright expanse "would fail to re-echo annunciation". Again we notice
how Rilke's poetry has more than one level of meaning. The
space of the external world is filled with the sweet song of the
lark. But the song has a meaning as well: it is the "annunciation" or message of Spring which fills every "nook".

There is no doubt that the above passage refers to the lark.
But since the whole sentence is in the conditional tense—"Spring
would understand . . . . not a nook *would* fail. . . ."—there is an
implied reference to the poet. Both in these lines and in the
description of the lark's song which follows we must still keep
the poet's wooing in our minds.

> 　　　　　　　　　　　　　Re-echoing first the tiny
> questioning pipe a purely affirmative day
> quietly invests all round with magnifying stillness.　　[11–13]

The poet takes for granted that the reader has already heard
the short spasmodic notes which are the bird's first tentative
utterance, whereas later his song has a unique flowing quality
and coherence. The majority of birds sing in the form of a short
melody which breaks off again and again. But the lark's song
swells forth inexhaustibly. At first there is no sign of this—only
a few notes which seem to pierce the great silence with a question: 'Will it soon be time?' or 'Can I begin now?' This is the
"questioning pipe", a prelude, as it were, to what will follow.

The piping of the bird is surrounded by the silence of "a
purely affirmative day". Here again the world is conceived of
entirely in terms of sound: this is an 'orphic' world which has
to be heard. This "day"—the very word sums up everything
in the countryside around, the air, light, height and breadth,
life and growth—is full of "stillness". The "stillness" which

surrounds the tiny sound is said to "magnify". This word has a twofold meaning. On the one hand the stillness magnifies the sound of the "questioning pipe". On the other hand the still-ness magnifies *itself* as the bird-song breaks through into the silence and makes it seem all the more profound. The second interpretation assumes the omission of a reflexive pronoun which is quite possible in Rilke's use of language. This Spring day, with the "magnifying stillness" which it contains, is "pure" and "affirmative". Everything is in harmony.

The bird now breaks out into its song proper. After a few initial attempts—coinciding with its attempts at flight—the song ascends.

> Then the long flight of steps, the call-steps, up to the dreamt-of
> temple of what's to come;— [14-15]

Anyone who has observed a lark's flight is bound to know this feeling: that the bird will go on rising higher and higher, all the more so since its flight is not a regular ascent but divided into phases of rising and falling. This is true of its song as well as its flight. Our impression of the lark's continual ascent is due not to its upward movement alone, but also to the apparent increase of the bird's inner power as it sings. And since the song is a "wooing" and a "calling", the stages by which the bird ascends are described as "call-steps".

At this point another image makes a fleeting appearance—a high temple up to which these "steps" lead. This is the "temple of what's to come", i.e. the coming fulfilment of life, which is "dreamt of" or yearned for. Again we are aware of how this world which Rilke evokes is dependent on sound, and how the visual image of the ascending bird is merged into the auditory image of the rising melody.[1]

The climax of the bird's movement is now attained:

> then the trill, that fountain
> grasped, as it rises, by Falling, in promiseful play,
> for another thrusting jet. . . [15-17]

[1] Compare the "startled bird" and the "owl" of the *Tenth Elegy* (lines 68 ff. and 82 ff.).

There is in fact a certain point in the song of the lark when the long drawn-out rhythmic phrases cease and are followed by a number of shorter notes in quick succession. This is the "trill" which is here likened to a "fountain". The above passage has several layers of meaning. The image of the temple standing on a mountain sprang from the feeling that the bird-song was moving upwards to a climax. The "trill", a purely musical concept, maintains the level attained. The "fountain" suggests both a soaring sound made up of tiny tonal elements and also something which can be visualized—the rise of the sound to a climax and the descent which follows.

This is a highly subtle description of sound in visual terms. The fountain is "grasped, as it rises, by Falling . . . for another thrusting jet". The "thrusting jet" is the rising arc described by the leaping water. But we can see the curve of the water's descent or "Falling" at the same time. This makes us anticipate the fall of the water even while we gaze at its rising.[1] The whole rise and fall is called a "promiseful play": it is a *play*, because there is no immediate objective in view, and this is an example of pure movement; it is *promiseful* in the sense that the beginning of the movement always contains the promise of its end.[2]

II

Now the prospect opens out into the future—that is, the season which will fulfil Spring's "annunciation"—"Summer". In the following thirteen lines the *Elegy* now rises to a second remarkable climax. The passage is full of rich imagery and feeling.

> And before it, the Summer!
> Not only all those summer dawns, not only
> the way they turn into day and stream with Beginning.
> Not only the days, so gentle round flowers, and, above,
> around the configured trees, so mighty and strong.
> Not only the fervour of these unfolded forces,
> not only the walks, not only the evening meadows,

---

[1] The image reminds us of the "tree of mutually built up motion" in the *Fifth Elegy* where there is also a reference to the speed of water (lines 42 ff.).

[2] Compare the *First Elegy* where the youthful dead do not "interpret roses, and other things that promise so much, in terms of a human future" (lines 70 ff.).

not only, after late thunder, the breathing clearness,
not only, evenings, sleep coming and something surmised. . .

[17–25]

The lark and the wooing poet are each a part of Spring. They
have Summer before them—the season which holds an immeasurable fullness in store. Summer is as immeasurable as any
period of time can be when we look ahead at it: like a day
which we look forward to in the early morning or the life
which lies before youth in all its richness.

The above passage reaches a climax through the repetition
of the same words again and again. The phrase "not only"
occurs eight times and on each occasion it serves to introduce
yet another of Summer's beauties. Each quality of the season
is excelled, or else heightened by the one which follows. Just as
the "intimate azure" of the sky added a new dimension to its
height a few lines previously, so here the evocation of Summer
gains both in intensity and in depth. The climax proper is
indicated by an ellipsis and the main weight of the passage
finally falls on the beauty of the Summer nights and the stars.
At the very end of the stanza there is a suggestive transition into
the "other relation" of Death, which for Rilke means the realization of life.

The first example of Summer's abundance is the "dawns"—
the cool beginning of each day which is all the more precious
in view of the great heat and light to come.

The second example is the transformation of the dawn "into
day". This is the delicate turning-point which still retains some
of the coolness of the night but also anticipates the later warmth.
The dawns are said to "stream with beginning", just as we
might say that a person beams with happiness.

This is the beginning of the day which is "so gentle round
flowers". Such are the days of Summer when the heat of the
atmosphere still has not become close and oppressive. At such
a time as this the contours of things are sharply and delicately
defined. The whole mysterious quality of outlines and contours
is well indicated here. A contour is essentially a line which
marks off the physical limits of one thing from another and also
defines the character of the thing itself. But the contour may
also reveal to us the borders or limits of earthly existence, on
the other side of which lies the Divine. This impression may be

overwhelming when we see a flower in front of us, "gently"
surrounded by light, or a tree with its masses of foliage standing
out against the brightness of the sky "mighty and strong"—
when the light assumes a different quality around each separate
thing and reveals a mystery which is all-pervading and ever
new. The religious aspect of this phenomenon is referred to
specifically in "the fervour of these unfolded forces", for this is
what they really are—"forces" or powers which are fervent.
This may mean either that they inspire man with fervour, or
that the forces themselves are fervent, in the sense that they
celebrate the mystery of existence and thus verge on the realm
of sacred things.

The "walks" and the "evening meadows" are now mentioned briefly, without any attempt at description. Nevertheless, the bare words standing alone are sufficient to conjure up
the picture of a path leading through meadows which are cool
and fragrant with life.

There follows the "breathing clearness" which is apparent
after "late thunder". When everything cried out for the refresh-
ing rain the thunderstorm broke at last—though "late" according to our reckoning. Now that the thunder and the downpours
are past life can breathe again and shine forth.

Finally, after the day has run its course, we feel "sleep
coming and something surmised" in the evening. The close of
day anticipates the release from all tension and the indescribable peace to come.

All these things are part of the abundance of approaching
Summer. Each section of the above passage seems to augment
the richness which fills the day from beginning to end. The
culminating point is reached in the next two lines:

> No, but the nights as well! the lofty, the summer
> nights,—but the stars as well, the stars of the Earth! [26–27]

The most magnificent thing about this season is the "lofty
summer nights".[1] On such nights we can feel the sky's expanse
rising above us; we can see the stars standing out in the clear
air which is cool but still vibrant from the day's warmth. Yet
this is not a simple contrast between the earth at night and the

---

[1] Rilke frequently mentions the "night" in his poetry, either as the "nocturnal
hour" or as the time, space or power of the night.

stars in their heavens. The *Elegy* mentions first the "lofty summer nights" in which space seems to rise *away from* the earth, and then the "stars of the earth" which seem to draw the sky *downwards*. This unity of the upper and lower spheres in the magic of a Summer night is one of the most sublime things imaginable and to experience it fully demands infinite feeling.

Any other poet would probably say at this point, "Oh, to have to die and not to be able to see these things again!". What Rilke says is different:

> Oh, to be dead at last and endlessly know them,
> all the stars! For how, how, how to forget them!   [28–29]

Mortal man is not capable of the degree of feeling which would correspond to the glory of the earth and the stars. First of all he must escape from the limits of earthly existence into the realm of the dead. Only then will he partake of real existence. For after death the "inwardness" or "intimacy"—which enables us to feel things in our hearts and to give them reality and fulfilment—will become an objective condition. After death we shall "know endlessly", that is, infinitely and with an intensity corresponding to the greatness of the universe.

The final words of the stanza are like a sobbing, or the final imploring note in the song of the lark: "for how, how, how to forget them!" The silent stars sparkling in the Summer night have penetrated the poet's heart. He has felt the mystery which surrounds them—the tremendous fact that they are so inaccessible and yet so near to us.[1] This gives the full meaning of the phrase "endlessly know them". The "endlessness" has nothing to do with measurement; it is not an 'infinity' of feeling but rather a quality: the experience of something *numinous*. In the *Ninth Elegy* the word recurs in the sentence: "they .... want us to change them entirely, within our invisible hearts, into— oh, *endlessly*—into ourselves!" The word is intended to convey the mystery of the message which Rilke has to proclaim.

---

[1] Compare a passage from Rilke's correspondence: ". . . the Infinite passed into him from all sides so intimately that he imagined that he felt the gentle presence of the stars which had entered his breast."

III

The early part of this *Elegy* culminates in a mood of radiant serenity which, associated with the image of the lark, cannot fail to impress us. What follows is a rapid descent into the depths of human misery.

At the beginning of the *Elegy* the poet said that he could no longer "woo", but *if* he did, then his "wooing" should be "pure", like that of the lark. But in that case, the poem now tells us, the consequences would be fateful. In order to woo an individual person one would have to presuppose the *presence* of such a person with a self of his own. But from the earlier *Elegies* it is abundantly clear that Rilke does not believe in the existence of such a being. In fact, for him the whole fulfilment of existence lies in renouncing any claim to such a person. The *First Elegy* shows Man as a creature who is capable neither of 'using' nor of '*being used*' by another. The *Second Elegy* deals with the evanescence of our Being. The *Third* attempts to show that it is only possible to exist as a person in the limited world of the conscious. As soon as this conscious existence is relinquished everything else vanishes with it. The *Fourth Elegy* divides Man up into the two aspects of observer and observed. The *Fifth* shows him in the grip of an impersonal force which treats him like part of a machine. The *Sixth* portrays the Hero with whom we can have no contact because he passes through the world like a star in the sky. And the *Seventh Elegy* states that no "wooing", not even the "purest", could possibly call forth a response from another human being.

> Look, I've been calling the lover.   [30]

Here the poet is speaking as if he had made the attempt to woo "the lover". And *if* he had, he says, the outcome might have been very different from what was anticipated. Would the lover have come at all? And if she came—would she come alone?

> But not only she
> would come . . . Out of unwithholding graves
> girls would come and gather. . . For how could I limit
> the call I had called?   [30–33]

"But not only she would come". The human call has not the precision and discrimination which is attributed to it. The *Third Elegy* said much the same thing: when the beloved girl touched the heart of the youth, the dead awakened in the depth of his being and tried to force their way to the surface. Now the position is reversed. If the lover called his "mate", his call would open up the realm of the dead at the same time. "Out of unwithholding graves girls would come and gather . . ." The graves would be too weak to hold back the dead as they break their way out. "Girls" would come and "gather" there, waiting, pleading and insistent.

This would be fearful—but how can the lover's call become "limited" and selective? Twice the word "how" is used—in sharp emotional contrast to its use at the end of the preceding stanza. Previously it expressed a hopeful longing; here it expresses helpless perplexity.

Here again we note that process of depersonalization which Rilke turned into such a fateful virtue. Once more there emerges the same deep-rooted incapacity to realize the "I" by addressing the "Thou" in the other person and maintaining this relationship. It may well be that the person who calls "Thou" inevitably calls to others as well. But we cannot enter here into this problematical aspect of human relations. It may present a problem, a task, or a danger, but it is not the important thing and should not affect our innermost feelings. In so far as I really acknowledge the personality of someone whom I call "Thou", and in so far as I have the courage to orientate my own life towards that person—to this extent I can direct my "call" to him or her. This may be a "limitation" but it springs from a regard for truth and human dignity, *not* from narrow possessiveness.

> The sunken are always seeking
> Earth again.—   [33–34]

Compared to the end of the third stanza or the last stanza of the *Fifth Elegy*, this passage shows a different aspect of the Dead. The Dead are now those who were still unfulfilled when they made their unwilling departure from the earth. Dying was not for them a transition into perfect Being, but something negative —a 'sinking'. They have no peace but are still "seeking Earth";

they wish to return to the realm of the living again so that they
may attain fulfilment.

Now the poet speaks as if the possibility had become a reality.
He has uttered his call and those whom he did *not* summon have
appeared. He is seized by a profound pity for them and
endeavours to console these girls who stand before him with
questing eyes: they are mistaken, he says, if they think that
their lives were unfulfilled. In reality they *have* their fulfilment,
if only they look for it in the right place.

> You children, I'd say, a single
> thing comprehended here's as good as a thousand.   [34–35]

The poet is friendly and kind to them as one might be to young
people who are full of bewilderment and grief. He encourages
them to take heart; they should realize that the *number* of things
which they experienced on earth is less important than the
quality of their experience—even if only "a single thing" were
"comprehended". If this is really accomplished—if we have
"comprehended" or assimilated "a single thing" into our inner
experience here on earth, then this is "as good as a thousand".
Rilke returns to this same train of thought in the *Ninth Elegy*
where we read of certain "things" which "we can live with".[1]

Two "things" of this kind are now specified:

> Don't think Destiny's more than what's packed into childhood.
> How often you'd overtake the beloved, panting,
> panting from blissful pursuit of nothing but distance!   [36–38]

The fulfilment of life is its "Destiny", that is, your experience
of existence. You think that this means unusual or extraordinary
happenings and imagine that these are more important than
"what's packed into childhood", which anyone can experience.
But you are forgetting that the way in which you lived as children—at one with yourselves and "packed" with your personal
experience—was itself a fulfilment.[2]

You also forget that moment when you were walking along
beside your beloved and suddenly felt overwhelmed; and how
you began to run and the movement of your body was matched
by the movement of your heart; how the impetus of your run-

---

[1] *Ninth Elegy*, line 44.
[2] Compare the *Fourth Elegy*, lines 65–85 and *Eighth Elegy*, lines 19–21.

ning—conveyed here in the repetition of the word "panting"—
carried you along beyond your beloved so that you "overtook"
him and blissfully pursued "nothing but distance". Again
Rilke's conception of love is apparent, according to which it
attains perfection when it is directed, no longer towards any
'Thou', but out and beyond any person or thing. You have all
experienced at least one such moment in your lives and that,
he says, is sufficient. Remember that moment and understand
that it contained everything. Then you will be aware of your
fulfilment.

The words which follow sum up one of the fundamental
dicta of the *Elegies* in a sentence:

Being here's glorious!   [39]

Rilke takes up this thought again in the *Ninth Elegy* when he
tries to resolve the question of life's meaning in the sentence
"being here amounts to so much" and in the poetic fugue on
the theme of "once" which follows. It is not necessary to specify
this or that particular action or event in life. The very fact of
existence here on earth, in time and space is sufficient.

Inside ourselves, so Rilke says, we know it well enough. We
are aware of the tremendous fact that we are here. But this
awareness is overlaid by a restlessness, a desire and a yearning
for something more obvious, more tangible—something which
everybody can see and recognize.

> Even you knew it, you girls,
> who went without, as it seemed, sank under,—you, in the vilest
> streets of cities, festering, or open for refuse.
> For to each was granted an hour,—perhaps not quite
> so much as an hour—some span that could scarcely be measured
> by measures of time, in between two whiles, when she really
> possessed an existence. All. Veins full of existence.   [39–45]

This is what the poet says to those who have responded to his
call—those who "went without, as it seemed" and yet were in
fact fulfilled by a moment of genuine experience. But because
they did not "comprehend" their experience inwardly they
"sank under" a sense of life's futility. Rilke claims that this is
true even of those who lived "in the vilest streets of cities", in
dishonour and squalor; those who went to rack and ruin,
N

"festering" with dreadful maladies of the body and soul; and those who were "open for refuse". This phrase is not easily interpreted, but we can sense the association with refuse-bins and rubbish-tips: it clearly means people who seem to be just waiting to be discarded. Each of them, too, had their "hour", or perhaps a little less—"not quite so much as an hour"—or perhaps much less—"some span that could scarcely be measured by measures of time, in between two whiles". This fleeting moment between two short spaces of time is a similar concept to the "ineffable spot" in the *Fifth Elegy* where the 'not yet' jumps over into the 'no more'. Everyone has had such a moment in her life. It was then that she really "possessed an existence. All. Veins full of existence".

In our hearts we know this to be true.

> But we so lightly forget what our laughing neighbour
> neither confirms nor envies.   [46–47]

It is difficult to make this inner knowledge our own and to be satisfied with it alone. We are always in need of the "neighbour" —the other person. For we are only sure of those things which are universally acknowledged, when other people "confirm" our possession of them, or concede them to us, or "envy" us for them.

We want to see our life's joy lying palpably in front of us:

> We want to be visibly
> able to show it; whereas the most visible joy
> can only reveal itself to us when we've transformed it, within.
>   [47–49]

It must be "visible". We want to "show" it like a buried treasure which has been lifted out of the earth. But in reality "joy" is not this sort of thing at all. A joy may stand "visible" and glittering before our eyes and yet the essential quality of the joy may remain hidden. It "can only reveal itself to us" after "we've transformed it within". This means when we have received it, through the purity of our thought and experience, into our innermost hearts. This condition of inner realization is actually referred to later as "invisibility".[1]

This point marks the beginning of Rilke's message which runs

[1] *Ninth Elegy*, lines 65–70, where the word occurs four times.

through the following stanzas and is taken up again and developed more fully in the *Ninth Elegy*.

There remains, however, one final consideration. What Rilke
says contains much truth. Life here is really "glorious". It is
an unimaginable grace to be here on this earth, living in space,
time and form: not to *have to* be here from any empirical or
metaphysical necessity, but to be *permitted* to be here as a privilege—and also as a trust. At the same time we cannot help feeling that Rilke's message, which is meant to console and edify
us, raises one fundamental question. What reply would his
message elicit from someone whose life was actually like that
of the people addressed in the *Elegy*? Can the experience which
Rilke describes in fact outweigh the real terrors of such an
existence? Is this not a variety of aestheticism? Does this message not simply secularize a Christian idea and thus deprive
it of content? It is certain that one single moment of true contact with God can outweigh a life which has been wasted. But
can there be any connection between an experience of "existence" in Rilke's sense, however profound, and such frustrations
of life as this *Elegy* describes? Is "existence" not invested here
with a power of meaning which it can never have, except for
God? Such ideas as these—which recur frequently in the literature of our late modern period—draw sustenance from a
religious faith which has been abandoned and thus they become merely 'literature'.

IV

Let us now resume our interpretation. Unless the form of
address, "beloved", in the following passage is singular, the
poet is presumably still addressing himself to those who stand
before him, yearning for the joy which was denied them in their
earthly life.

> Nowhere, beloved, can world exist but within.
> Life passes in transformation. [50-51]

The "world", in the proper sense of the word, is something
which only comes into being through man. He receives some-

thing which has Being into his contemplative spirit, his sensitive heart and his formative hands. He then produces his 'works' —tools, adornments, buildings, music and everything else he creates. This is the process of "transformation". Man absorbs into himself the things from the outside world, gets to know them thoroughly, feels his way into them and then endows them with form. Thus it was from the very beginning.

But then all was changed. Things no longer entered his creative centre from outside to emerge again as finished works. A new process began which the *Ninth Elegy* calls the "imageless act". Things lost their inner significance and were only esteemed for their utility. The resultant product was what Rilke calls here an "invented structure". Houses, tools and gadgets were now fabricated by a process which led directly from the raw material via the machine to the finished product. This process by-passes the "transformation" into "invisibility" by the heart within. On the contrary everything now remains without. The calculating reason and the purely utilitarian way of thinking has no 'inwardness'. This 'inward' or 'intimate' quality is only found in the mind which contemplates and grasps inner truth, in the heart with a feeling for values, and in the soul which is open and receptive to its very depths.

Man's works have now taken on a different character:

> And, ever diminishing,
> outwardness dwindles. Where once was a permanent house,
> up starts some invented structure across our vision, as fully
> at home among concepts as though it still stood in a brain.
>
> [51–54]

However great the mass of material which has been disciplined into shape, however powerful the energy which has been applied, however enormous the achievements realized—everything continues to lose more and more of its real greatness and significance: "ever diminishing, outwardness dwindles". The real merit of a work does not depend on quantities which are measurable but on its quality and on the 'inwardness' which has gone to its making.

When a man used to build a house, it was something "permanent". This does not mean simply that it stood for a long time, for a modern ferro-concrete structure can be permanent in this sense. It means that the house embodied the *quality* of something valid and firmly established, rather like a family which is firmly rooted in marriage. In the older sort of house life developed on a firm and orderly basis. New generations grew up and were sheltered in its walls. It gave dignity to the present by continuing the past and preparing for the future.[1] What makes an old house so valuable is the fact that it is *more* than merely a place which satisfies practical needs.[2] Now, in its stead, "up starts some invented structure"—a forceful but vivid description. Instead of a real house something else sprawls across our vision—something high, broad and straight which obscures the higher things of life. It is simply "invented" because it comes straight out of someone's head. It is thus "at home among concepts"—i.e. those things which anyone who has a methodical turn of mind can create for himself. The "structure" stands out there before us just "as though it still stood in a brain". It was not produced from the inner creative centre and therefore lacks the dimension of true inner life. It is —to use a word which expresses exactly what Rilke means— completely 'cerebral'. This is a problem of technical civilisation with which Rilke, despite all his efforts, never came to satisfactory terms.

In this *Elegy* he admits that our age has gigantic achievements to its credit and that it has discovered and mastered tremendous new forces:

> Spacious garners of power are formed by the Time Spirit, formless as that tense urge he's extracting from everything else.   [55–56]

The "Time Spirit"—the spirit of the present age—forms "spacious garners of power", huge reservoirs of energy, by exploiting the resources which lie inside water or oil or, more recently, the atom. But these works are "formless"; they have

---

[1] The same values which Adalbert Stifter defended.

[2] The letters in which Rilke described his arrival at Muzot show how important this little castle was for his life and his work. In a letter to Lou Andreas-Salomé of February 11th 1922 he wrote: "I went out, and this little Muzot which has safeguarded it (i.e. the completion of the *Elegies*), indeed *granted* it to me, seemed like some huge old animal which I had to stroke." It is significant that Rilke never had a "permanent house" in his own sense of the words. At Muzot too he was only a guest.

no living form, any more than that "tense urge"—electricity—
which is their final product.

The man who has become inwardly acclimatized to the
modern age will no doubt object. He will say that the new structures are not formless at all and that we simply have to open
our eyes to the particular character of their construction. He
will say that the ultimate aim of technology is not merely
utilitarian, and that technical progress will shape the world
anew in such a way as to express the values of a new historical
situation. As the next stanza makes clear, there is a gulf here
which divides the views of two separate generations on this
question. A new world is certainly in the making. But this does
not alter the fact that there are many things in it which are
soulless and ugly; that some exquisitely beautiful things of the
old world are falling into decay and that much which could
once be created by man will never take shape again, because
the necessary pre-conditions no longer exist.

Rilke puts all this into one sentence:

> Temples he knows no longer.   [57]

Here again 'modern' man may well object that "temples" have
been built and are being built today—at least the first experiments in such temples. Buildings have taken shape which express both grandeur and reverence. There may not be many,
but there *are* some, and these give us a glimpse of what *can* take
shape if the right will is there. But for Rilke such buildings did
not count—assuming that he saw them at all. For him the
structures of the technical age were purely external: they were
produced, not by way of "transformation" but through calculation; not through the contemplation of form by the spirit or
the inward perception of the heart, but from a mere functional
need. Hence, in his view, the "world"—in the true sense of the
word—must no longer be sought outside; it must be created
within.

> We're now more secretly saving
> such lavish expenses of heart.   [57–58]

The "expenses of heart", here referred to, are those things which
are not created for utility but for revelation—things which are
alive, sublime and holy—in this case the "temples". By econo-

mic standards these are purposeless. The "*saving*" of the expenses
does not refer to the object of expenditure or to the money
saved but to man's characteristic 'lavishness' as such. Now the
"lavish expenses of heart" can no longer be made openly amid
the prevailing utilitarian spirit of the age. They must be "more
secretly saved" or replaced by private hidden actions. We must
achieve within our hearts that transformation which is no
longer possible outside.

Nowadays, when we *do* encounter a work which has been
produced by the older process of "transformation" it seems as
if it were out of its element and ready to depart into another
realm.

> Nay, even where one survives,
> one single thing once prayed or tended or knelt to,
> it's reaching, just as it is, into the unseen world.   [58-60]

When such a work survives, having withstood the onslaught of
technology, it produces a strange feeling in us. The words
which follow are tortuous but strangely impressive. They describe something which was once "prayed . . . to", which grew
out of prayer and subsisted in the continuance of prayer. The
old churches first sprang out of the contemplative life and were
real as long as this life went on. They were "tended"—protected and sustained in piety. These buildings were "knelt to":
the kneeling builder erected the buildings which then kept their
reality in the kneeling of those who prayed there. All this is
perfectly true. And in spite of all his disavowals Rilke's sentiments here are those of a Christian and a Catholic. Old churches
are just like this, the only trouble being that modern man cannot see them in this light. He thinks that the old buildings are
not light enough, not hygienic enough and dismisses them just
because they are "old". So something new must be erected
which will be more practical and more convenient and 'modern'.
An old work of art can no longer claim a place of its own in the
modern world. It passes away, and is indeed already "reaching
into the unseen world"—into that inward sphere which springs
from "transformation".

There is a profound sadness in these words. This is an elegiac
experience—grief at the passing away of beautiful things, and
also a desire to salvage them and give them their proper place.

Modern man has become quite incapable of looking at old things which, in his view, can only content out of date romantics and idealists:

> Many perceive it no more, but neglect the advantage
> of building it grandlier now, with pillars and statues, *within*!
>
> [61–62]

There might well be a legitimate way of "perceiving it no more", in the case of someone who knows that the real work of art does not stand outside but within, and who realizes that the physical structure which can be touched and measured is only a medium for conveying a fundamental experience from the artist or designer to the beholder. Anyone who possessed this understanding would be reading the signs correctly and would be justified in recreating the essential work of art or architecture within himself. This might also enable him to bear more easily the loss of the external world.

That would be satisfactory enough. But this is not the case with most people. The majority no longer look at the exterior of an ancient building or work of art, simply because for them it is old lumber. And even when they look at it their first reaction is to anticipate its inevitable destruction by technology, new communications or by war. So the majority do not share that "advantage" which anyone capable of contemplation can derive from the urgency of the situation—the "advantage", that is, of concentrating all the more intensely on the inner shape of things.

V

> Each torpid turn of the world has such disinherited children,
> those to whom former has ceased, next not yet come, to belong.
> For even the next is far for mankind.   [63–65]

Today we stand in the middle of such a "torpid turn of the world". This phrase implies a change of direction. The idea which underlies it is not that of progress—pointing onwards and upwards in a straight line. Here the direction in which the world moves is seen to have changed, and it is open to question whether the new course is a good one. The old course produced the works of art of a culture which, in Europe, lasted up to about the middle of the last century. But the direction of the new course which replaced it has been determined more and more by the natural sciences and technology. This "turning" is still "torpid". It is fermenting below the surface of events and no one knows whither it will lead.

At such a time as this there are always "disinherited children" who can no longer appreciate the works of the past, but who are not in a position to create anything genuinely new either. They thus no longer possess the "former" nor what is "not yet come". They lack a cultural home and heritage. They might have such a heritage if they could cling to the past, or if they could take a step forwards and anticipate a stage in the course of history. But this step is not easy, for even "the next is far for mankind". The dividing factor is not simply an interval in time or space. It is qualitative—a difference which affects our whole way of living and feeling, the patterns of our behaviour, the shape of our houses and tools, and the arts and crafts we practise.

Rilke himself tried to take this forward step. This is evident from some of the *Sonnets to Orpheus*[1] and the *Elegies* show traces of the same endeavour. But he did not succeed. Indeed, at bottom he never wanted to. He clung hard to the past and was thus not one of the "disinherited children".

> Though this
> shall not confuse us, shall rather confirm us in keeping
> still recognizable form.   [65–67]

Rilke here states his allegiance to "what has been". Characteristically he advocates the "keeping", or preservation, of "still recognizable form", thus inviting anyone who shares his feelings to maintain a 'conservative' attitude. Of course this attitude has no political significance. This consummate individualist was never concerned with political activity. What he meant by "keeping" and conserving was the retention of the older meaningful patterns of work and behaviour—an attempt to assimilate the "form" of the past age and thus to preserve its "Being".

This "form", according to Rilke, deserves to be saved:

[1] *Sonnets, I, xviii* and *xxii; II, x.*

> This *stood* once among mankind,
> stood in the midst of Fate, the extinguisher, stood
> in the midst of not-knowing-whither, as though it existed, and
>   bowed
> stars from established heavens towards it.   [67–70]

The old works "*stood*"—the italics are Rilke's own—"among mankind", in the flux of life. They had that staying power which derives, not from durable material or massive bulk, but from the intrinsic truth of spirit and form.

The same point is emphasized again: "This . . . stood in the midst of Fate, the extinguisher"—amidst the destruction of old things which goes on continually to make room for the new; amidst the "not-knowing-whither"—the human perplexity and bewilderment about the future. The great works which were fashioned by Man *stood* in their allotted places and remained there. This "standing" quality, reiterated three times, conveys a sense of that power which springs from something which has reached complete fulfilment. And when Rilke says that a thing stood "as though it existed", he means that it was justified in its existence by its own right and might—that the inner nature of the universe was made manifest through it.

This power and meaningful quality of the older works of man is also expressed when Rilke says that "this . . . bowed stars from established heavens towards it". This reference to the "established heavens" contains an echo of the ancient concept of the "firmament" or "fastness" of Heaven. For no earthly power can influence them. Their majesty is expressed in the stars, and here both stars and heavens are conceived of, not just astronomically, as spaces or groups of stars observed from the perspective of the earth, but mythically—as images or dwellings of numinous reality. The older works of Man are so powerful that they "bow" or attract the stars out of their orbits. They compel the recognition of the very stars and, indeed, may be considered as belonging to the stellar universe themselves. Perhaps there is an underlying idea here that they share in the magical influence of the stars on human Fate—the power to conjure up and to ward off destiny.

Finally the Angel is addressed once more as the representative of ultimate reality in the *Elegies*:

Angel,
I'll show it to you as well—there! In your gaze
it shall stand redeemed at last, in a final uprightness.
Pillars, pylons, the Sphinx, all the striving thrust,
greyly from fading or foreign town, of the spire!   [70–74]

This "Angel" is not a particular one among many but stands for
the whole angelic order—unless there is a reminiscence here of
that significant Old Testament figure, the "Angel of the Lord"
who is the messenger of God and God himself at the same time.[1]
At all events he can distinguish between genuine and false,
worthy and unworthy, Being and non-Being. It is to him that
the poet calls "I'll show it to you as well—there!"

Man's works are thus submitted to the supreme test. For if
the Angel says "it is worthless" then the work is rejected. But
the poet knows that the Angel will acknowledge its value and
take it up into his "gaze". In this angelic "gaze", which is
focused on the world, the whole value of things is revealed and
whatever has proved its worth is preserved. The same thing
happens in the *Fifth Elegy* (lines 57–61), where the Angel is
called upon to preserve the smile of the acrobat child in a
"graceful urn". Here too there is a trace of Biblical thought,
namely the idea that all earthly events take place "in the face
of God" or "in God's sight" where their value is assessed once
and for all. A thing only has Being in so far as God knows it and
affirms it. The Angel here takes the place of God.

Even if a thing is doomed to perish on earth it may be
"redeemed at last, in a final uprightness" when it is seen by the
Angel. So the final act of the 'inward' process is performed,
now not simply by Man in his heart, but by this perfect being,
the Angel, in his "gaze". Here the work reaches fulfilment and
takes on that quality of Being which is described in Rilke's letter
to Witold von Huléwicz.[2]

It must be pointed out for the sake of truth and consistency
that the "Angel" could never really give a human work that

---

[1] E.g. see *Exodus*, xxiii, 20–22 and *Genesis*, xvi, 13, where Hagar says of the angel
of the Lord: "I have looked after him that seeth me" and even calls him "the
God that sees".

[2] See below, p. 211 f.

final "redemption" which Rilke expects from him. This could only be granted by one who is in the position of judge and lawgiver. Despite all the *Elegy*'s fervour there is a fundamental lack of seriousness underlying what is claimed and asserted here.

The author of this interpretation does not find it hard to imagine how those readers who respect Rilke as a religious visionary must feel about this way of treating the poet's ideas. Or how those readers will feel who hold that a poem must be considered *either* simply as a poem *or* in its historical context— but *not* according to the truth it contains. But today even those critics who should be concerned with the latter question seem to lack discrimination and judgment. Someone therefore has to accept the thankless task, even at the risk of being condemned by some as unscientific, by others as aesthetically blind, and probably by all as narrowly 'dogmatic'.

The *Elegy* proceeds to specify some of the greatest human achievements which are doomed by the "turn of the world" to perish—either by being physically destroyed or by losing their inner meaning. This is a continuation on a grander scale of the list which commences with more homely things in the *Ninth Elegy* (lines 31–33) and concludes with the "pillar" and the "tower". The list in the *Seventh Elegy* begins with "pillars" and "pylons" and is continued later (lines 81–85).

First of all the "pillar". There is the powerful Doric column, filled with primitive strength and designed to support weight; or the slender rising Ionic column which blossoms out at the top into such wonderful freedom. How beautiful they are, these components of old architecture—relics of bygone life! Perhaps it is worth pondering—and lamenting—the fact that in modern structures, with their girders, struts and ferro-concrete which can be adapted to any desired purpose, there is no longer any place for a pillar. Then there is the "pylon", the fortress-like offshoot of the temple-gate which does not serve any purpose but simply stands upright, looming up as a warning symbol. And there is the "Sphinx", that enigmatic being with the lion's body and the human head—a gigantic shape crouching in the desert, big enough to hold a temple between its paws. The

Sphinx is an image of eternity still cast in the form of riddle and myth.[1] Finally there is the "striving thrust of the spire". Perhaps we shall only realize fully what a spire means when the evil destructive tendency of the age—either in the shape of creeping urbanization, or in the catastrophic shape of war—has obliterated all these symbols of man's striving towards God, these embodiments of man's impulse to pray. Many still stand, "grey"—and here we may already think of Chartres which is mentioned a little later: the cathedral whose wonderful grey stone assumes ever-changing colours as the sun moves round and which stands there like a symbol of coming transfiguration.[2] They tower up now, either from "fading town"—one which still has old buildings but is losing them one after another—or from "foreign town", i.e. one which has already become quite modern in plan and only retains the spire superficially as something alien for which there is no real place.

These are the things which the Angel must take into his gaze:

> Was it not miracle? Angel, gaze, for it's *we*—
> O mightiness, tell them that *we* were capable of it—my breath's
> too short for this celebration.   [75-77]

There is something very moving in this appeal to the Angel to endorse the poet's belief in the grandeur of human achievements, however transient they may be. For Rilke feels that it *can* be endorsed. It is because he is so aware of the shortcomings of all finite things by absolute standards that he expresses himself in a rhetorical questioning which demands confirmation.

Man was "capable" of these mighty things—"*we*" men in all our fragility. The same note is struck again in the *Ninth Elegy* where we read that transient earthly things need *us*—"us, the most fleeting of all".[3] The Angel is asked to acknowledge these works, to "tell" of them, or, as the next line implies, to "cele-

---

[1] Compare Rilke's treatment of the Sphinx in the *Tenth Elegy* (lines 73-79).

[2] It may be noted in passing that the word "grey" has quite different associations here from the "grey bread" and the "greyish draught" of the *Fourth Elegy* (lines 78-79 and 31).

[3] *Ninth Elegy*, line 12.

brate" them. These human works are so great that they transcend mere human limits. They were perfected within the confines of space, the transience of time and the limitations of
human energy and yet they tower above Man himself with a
validity of their own. So there is, after all, some justification for
Man's urge towards self-transcendence despite the commenda-
tion in the *Second Elegy* of the virtue of *sophrosyne*.

> So, after all, we have *not*
> failed to make use of the spaces, these generous spaces, these
> *our* spaces. (How terribly big they must be,
> when, with thousands of years of our feeling, they're not over-
> crowded.)   (77–80]

This earthly existence has not then been in vain. Here again
Rilke's style is strange and provocative. He does not say that
'we have not wasted our *time*', but our "spaces". By this he
means the realm of earthly life which, in the *Ninth Elegy*, is also
described in spacial terms—"being *here* amounts to so much".
These spaces are "generous" for they give the pre-conditions of
earthly life, providing opportunities for creative activity among
people and things. We have not had these opportunities in vain,
so runs the poet's plea for Man. On the contrary, we have used
them to create something valid and lasting.

The sentence in brackets is enough to counter any possible
charge of *hubris* here—and indeed if we take this word in its
fundamental meaning it is quite irrelevant to Rilke's message.
How "big", indeed how "terribly big", these spaces must be if
they can contain thousands of years of human feeling—the same
feeling which produced those works. By any realistic standards
this is, of course, nonsense, for feeling cannot be contained in
space. But Rilke is clearly referring here not to outer but to
'inner' space. To be precise, he is referring to that *cosmic* space
which embraces both the outer and the inner realm, as described in the *First Elegy*. This space is "terribly big"—two words
which express religious fear and awe in the face of the *tremendum*
and are sufficient to correct any impression of hubris.

Once more the *Elegy* gives expression to a sense of mankind's
greatness:

But a tower was great, was it not? Oh, Angel, it was, though,—
even compared with you? Chartres was great—and music
towered still higher and passed beyond us. Why, even
a girl in love, alone, at her window, at night. . .
did she not reach to your knee?— [81–85]

A tower is great. We may think here of those belfry towers of
romanesque churches in Italy which stand apart from the main
structure—perhaps that of the *Pomposa* which is so beautiful in
its simplicity and detachment—or perhaps of Gothic spires
soaring up into the infinite—like arrows, or *flèches* as they are in
fact called in French. A tower includes many things. It may be
a fortified defensive tower built for warfare; it may be a symbol
of duration and power; a look-out, or a place from which the
bells ring out. Nor can we forget the titanic associations of the
tower as a symbol of revolt against the authority of Heaven. It
was not by chance that the rebellion against God took the shape
of the Tower of Babel. The "tower" is thus a real manifestation
of grandeur, "even compared with" the Angel.

Then the *Elegy* mentions a particular human achievement—
the cathedral of Chartres which is really one of the most beautiful things on earth. Rilke knew Chartres well, living as he did
for such a long time in Paris. He left a fine poem as a memorial
of the impression which Chartres made on him: it describes the
angel with the sundial which stands on the right-hand corner of
the cathedral front.[1]

Next, Rilke turns to that realm of creation which, for him,
stood even above architecture: "Music towered still higher and
passed beyond us."

Finally he leaves the great achievements of Man and returns
to the ordinary human life mentioned in the earlier stanzas of
the *Elegy*. "A girl in love", filled with feelings of love, as she sits
"alone, at her window", is greater still. She is so great that she
"reaches the knee" of the Angel.

VI

As the poet addresses the Angel in tones of urgency and fervour it is as though a question suddenly arises in his mind,
interrupting his appeal: 'But what am I doing now?'

[1] *L'ange du méridien* in *Selected Works*, II, p. 159 f.

> Don't think that I'm wooing!   [86]

With this line the *Elegy* returns to its opening theme. The "outgrown voice" of the poet should not "woo", but should simply
go out into the 'Open' without any object or purpose. But what
was the poet doing just now if not wooing? Did he not intend
that the Angel should join him in admiring the grandeur of
human achievements?

This he denies. But even if something of the kind had been
partly intended—after all, the whole of the first stanza deals
hypothetically with such a "wooing"!—he solemnly renounces
it now. Even if he had made the attempt it would have failed.

> Angel, even if I were, you'd never come!   [87]

This is similar to the opening lines of the *First Elegy*—"Who, if
I cried, would hear me among the angelic orders?" It does not
mean that any shortcoming on the part of the Angels would
prevent them from hearing, but simply that they are too great
to do so: their very order of Being has no relation with individual man and his desires.

> For my call
> is always full of outgoing; against such a powerful
> current you cannot advance. Like an outstretched
> arm is my call. And its hand, for some grasping,
> skywardly opened, remains before you
> as opened so wide but for warding
> and warning, Inapprehensible.   [87–93]

The Angel has a relation to the universe as a whole, for this is
his sphere of existence. But he is incapable of entering into any
relation with an individual creature, or of communing with
something that is *in* the world. The Angel's deafness to Man in
the *First Elegy* is simply another aspect of this same incapacity.
Indeed, it would be a calamity if the Angel attempted to hear,
for Man would then "fade in the strength of his stronger
existence".

Yet Man himself is incapable in just the same way, of this
the poet feels sure. Let us imagine, he says, that someone called
and wooed the Angel—what would happen then? His call
would inevitably be "full of outgoing". Instead of summoning
the Angels nearer, this call could only take the shape of a

"powerful current" driving him away, for there could be no reciprocal countermovement hitherward.

This is again the familiar problem of the relationship between one person and another. Another person can only be my 'Thou' if I am prepared to be his. The 'I-Thou' relationship is dialectical. But here there is something unique and frightening which makes the communion between 'I' and 'Thou' impossible. The impulse of the human 'I' to make the Angel into his 'Thou' would really exclude the possibility of a response on the part of the Angel. And why? Because the earthly creature recoils in fear from a being who can only have relations with the infinite and the universal. This is the fear of being destroyed mentioned in the *First Elegy*. Fundamentally it is probably the same fear which Malte speaks of in the *Notebook*— the "fear of being loved", and especially by such a being as this! So the wooing call becomes an attitude of defence, if not of rejection—"against it you cannot advance". Rilke here projects his incapacity for personal relationships into the realm of metaphysics.

"Like an outstretched arm is my call". This too is ambiguous, for an outstretched arm may mean either "come here!" or the opposite, "keep away!" And Rilke deliberately plays on this ambiguity and exaggerates it. "And its hand, for some grasping, skywardly opened"—the hand which is open and could decide to grasp and draw someone near—"remains before you as opened so wide but for warding and warning, Inapprehensible". The gesture which was potentially a "grasping" and pulling closer now turns into the exact opposite—an *avoidance* of grasping and a warding off. And now the Angel, to whom the inspired poet was about to submit the glory of human achievements, inviting him fervently to accept them, becomes once and for all the "Inapprehensible" one—a being who stands beyond any possibility of recognition or love.

The two words "warding and warning" are coupled together in a peculiar way. The meaning of the former is clear: he who is threatened *wards* off the "terrible" Angel.[1] At the same time, however, he warns the Angel against doing something which might be dangerous to himself. Perhaps the reason is that a boundary for Man is also one for the Angel. It defines

[1] Cf. *First Elegy*, line 7.

o

allotted territory which neither may leave. For the man such a move would involve destruction; for the Angel perhaps a sacrilege against that law which was given by the impersonal supreme power who is unnamed in the *Elegies*.

This sets the final seal on Man's loneliness. And just as he has to make a virtue out of his inability to "use" people or things, so it now becomes his task to make a virtue of this final renunciation.

THE EIGHTH ELEGY

Written on February 7th and 8th 1922 at Muzot

I

With all its eyes the creature-world beholds
the open.   [1–2]

THE "creature-world" of the first line is creation. And, as the next few lines show, this means primarily the world of animals —animals with "eyes". The eyes as bodily organs fulfil their immediate function when they see the things and events around them. In addition, however, the "creature" does something else with its eyes: it looks out into the "open". And it is a cardinal point in Rilke's definition of human existence that, in his view, Man lacks this power which the animals possess.

What is meant by this concept of the "Open"?[1]

In the letter to Witold von Huléwicz of November 13th 1925, already quoted, Rilke says: "*Affirmation of life and of death prove to be* one *in the Elegies*. They proclaim that the admission of the one without the other would be a limitation excluding everything infinite once and for all. Death is the *side of life* which is turned away from us and which we cannot illumine: we must seek to achieve the maximum possible consciousness of our being which is at home in *both these unlimited spheres* and is inexhaustibly nourished from both. . . . The true pattern of life stretches through *both* territories. The blood with the greatest circulation surges through *both: there is neither a Here nor a Beyond, only that great unity* in which those beings who surpass us, the 'Angels', are at home. . . . We of the Here and Now are not for one moment satisfied in this world of time, nor are we confined within it. Continually we overflow towards those who came

before us, to our origins, and to those who will apparently come
after us. In that mighty *open* realm all people simply *are*—one
cannot say 'simultaneously', for it is precisely the disappearance
of time which determines that they *are*. Transience plunges
everywhere into a deep Being . . . Not into a Hereafter, the
shadows of which darken the earth, but into a Whole, into *the
Whole*."

Here 'openness' is the quality of that 'realm' which, as the
Elegies proclaim, results when Man adopts the existential attitude which is demanded of him.[1]

So far the idea seems to be a theoretical one. Fresh light is
cast on it, however, by a strange experience which is recounted
in an extract from Rilke's notebook which he sent to Lou
Andreas-Salomé: "Later he thought he could remember certain moments in which the power of this one[2] was already contained, as if in a seed. He recalled the hour spent in that other
garden of the South (Capri) when a bird-call sounded simultaneously outside and within himself. The bird-call seemed not
to be refracted on the barrier of his body, but to collect both
spheres together into one continuous space, where there remained, mysteriously protected, only one single spot of purest
and most profound consciousness. On this occasion he closed
his eyes, so as not to be distracted amid such a magnificent
experience by the contour of his own body; the Infinite passed
into him from all sides so intimately that he imagined that he
felt the gentle presence of the stars which had settled in his
breast. . . . He still did not know how apparent his far away
state was to the others. As for himself, it was only with this
experience that he gained a certain degree of freedom towards
other people; for the small beginning of poverty by which he
was lighter gave him a peculiar mobility among these people
who were full of cares and hopes for one another and tied together in life and death. He still felt a temptation to weigh his own
light unburdened state against their encumberment, although
he soon saw how he would deceive them in this. They could
not, after all, know that he had attained a kind of triumph—
not (like the Hero) in the things which bound them or in the
heavy air of their hearts—but outside, in a rare space so lacking

---

[1] See especially the *Ninth Elegy*.
[2] i.e. 'this moment'.

in human qualities that they would simply have dismissed it as
a 'void'."

Finally a third passage, taken from one of the prose fragments
called *An Experience*.[1] This contains an account of a man who
was leaning against a tree "in a castle garden which sloped
down fairly steeply to the sea" and there "experienced something marvellous". It seemed as though "almost imperceptible
vibrations were passing from inside the tree into him". The
passage continues: "He felt that he had never been filled with
more gentle motions; his body was, as it were, being treated
like a soul and enabled to receive a degree of influence which
would not have been perceptible to it in its normal clear-cut
physical condition. . . In his constant endeavour to account for
even his slightest experiences, he asked himself urgently what
was happening to him; and almost immediately he found an
expression which satisfied him, saying to himself that he had
'reached the other side of Nature'. . . Filled as he was, everywhere more and more uniformly, with this impulse, which
recurred at strangely deep-felt intervals, his body now became
indescribably moving to him, and useful only to stand inside,
purely and cautiously, like a ghost—a ghost which, belonging
to some other place, had entered sadly into this gently discarded
body only in order to belong again, though distractedly, to this
once indispensable world. Looking around slowly, without
otherwise altering his position, he recognized everything again,
smiled at it with a kind of distant fondness, and then let it go on
its way like something obsolete which had once had some share
in him under different circumstances. He followed a flying bird
with his eyes; he considered a shadow; the very path which led
away and lost itself in the distance, filled him with a thoughtful
insight which seemed to him all the purer since he knew that
he was independent of it. Apart from this he would not have
been able to think of where he actually was. But that he was
only *returning* to all this here and was standing in this body as if
he were looking out from behind a deserted window—of *this* he
was so convinced for a few seconds that the sudden appearance
of someone from the house would have disturbed him in a very
painful fashion, whereas he was inwardly quite prepared to see

[1] For a complete translation of *An Experience* see R. M. Rilke, *Selected Works, I*,
Hogarth Press, 1954, pp. 34–38.

Polyxène or Raimondine, or any other deceased member of the house, emerge round the turn of the path. He understood the silent supernumerous nature of their appearance; he was familiar with this fleeting unconditional use of earthly shapes. The pattern of their habits dispelled from within him all else that he had learnt. He was sure that, if he moved in their midst, they would not find him conspicuous. A periwinkle which stood near him, and whose blue glance he must have encountered more than once before, now touched him from a more spiritual distance, but with inexhaustible significance, as if there were nothing more to be concealed. He noticed in general how all objects now seemed more remote and yet somehow more true, though this was perhaps due to his gaze which was no longer directed straight ahead and diluted there in the open; he now looked back at things, as if over his shoulder. Their existence, which for him was finished, now gained a sharp sweet flavour, as if everything had been lightly spiced with the blossom of departure."

The man of whom this is recounted is Rilke himself, as is clear from the *Memoirs* of Princess Marie of Thurn and Taxis. The castle is Duino, and the "experience" took place at the time when the early *Elegies* were being written. We are therefore probably justified in assuming that it left some mark on his poetry. The following is the account given in the *Memoirs*: "Rilke was strolling one day, dreamy and without any set purpose, through briar and thickets, when suddenly he found himself in front of a huge, very old olive tree which he had not seen before. How it happened, I do not know, but suddenly he was leaning with his back against the tree, standing on its gnarled roots, and resting his head against the branches, and,—I can only say what he repeated to me more than once—immediately he was overcome by a very strange feeling which made him stand silent and with beating heart. He felt as though he had entered into another life, into a period of time long past—everything that he had lived, loved and suffered here now came back to him, surrounded and engulfed him, as if it sought to live, love and suffer in him again. 'Time' did not exist: there was no difference between the Once which had returned and the dark formless Now. The whole air seemed animated, seemed to oppress him strangely and ceaselessly. And yet this unfamiliar life seemed somehow near to him; he had to partake of it. Teresina, Raymondine, Polyxène—did they surround the poet, did he feel their presence and perhaps also the proximity of other restless vanished forms which had once been happy and loved? I do not know. When Rilke spoke of this phenomenon, which had appeared and vanished with such suddenness, he was extremely excited. 'Strange', he repeated, 'strange'. He never trusted himself to return to this secluded spot and even touch the tree. 'I did not know whether I should come back then' he said softly."

The last two passages describe inner experiences which, though not entirely similar, are obviously closely related and seem to elucidate the letter to von Huléwicz.

In the extract from the notebook Rilke refers to a sense of unity, in which the distances of space seem to be abolished in such a way that "the stars had settled in his breast". In the *Experience* he describes a similar feeling of all-embracing unity, but with the addition of certain new details. There is, for instance, the awareness of not being at home in his body like a living person, but of occupying it temporarily "like a ghost" and observing all things with "distant inclination", that is with the detachment of someone who no longer has any relation to them. He would therefore have been "disturbed" to see "someone from the house" approaching, whereas he was "inwardly quite prepared" to see people coming along who had once belonged to the house but were now dead![1] This means that the Here and the Hereafter have been merged in a single unifying experience. They are not mixed, but fused together in such a way that a "more spiritual distance" determines our inward

[1] It was already stated above that Rilke did in fact have para-psychical experiences of this kind. The *Memoirs* give some account of them: "And really it seems to me that Rilke lived at Duino among the shades. He not only felt the presence of Teresina. There were two other figures—sisters of my mother—who were as really present to him as if time had stood still: Raymondine, who had died at the age of twenty shortly after her marriage, and Polyxène, who had been only fifteen years old. We possessed pictures of both girls. Of Raymondine we had a very beautiful bust and charming miniatures, and Serafico (i.e. Rilke) gave the best one of these a place of honour in his glass-case. The poet was particularly pleased by the pale face with the finely inclined nose, the large blue eyes and the magnificent black plaits. My brother once told me that he had asked Rilke whether he would like to spend another winter at Duino. After thinking for a long time Rilke hesitantly answered yes; he would like to, but it was so unsettling. One must take into account so many things, particularly on account of Raymondine and Polyxène, whom one always had to be concerned about."

relations to earthly things, and "with inexhaustible significance". How this takes place is then described in greater detail and, it must be admitted, in a way which is confusing at first. The gaze is no longer "directed straight ahead in the open" where it would be "diluted". It has not the form of a beam going out into the infinite, and it is directed at specific things. But this happens in such a way as to release the vision from the action of focusing directly. It now perceives things "as if over his shoulder", backwards and indirectly in space. The things themselves are no longer constrained by the gaze in search of its object but now become free and "somehow more true", i.e. more intense and meaningful. They have a "silent supernumerous" quality: their shapes have a transcending value and an "inexhaustible significance".

The concept of "openness" apparently means a transcendence of the barriers between the Here and the Beyond, between Life and Death—and, at the same time, a breaking-down of the spacial, temporal and qualitative differences of our normal world. This is not a blurring of the differences, such as might be produced by a magical or fantastic delusion.[1] The differences are still present, absorbed as it were in the Whole, but they now operate as vital tensions rather than as divisions. "Openness" would thus be a state of existence synonymous with "completeness or wholeness of Being"—the "deep Being" which absorbs all transience.[2]

The *Sonnets* create the appropriate *numen* of this condition in the figure of Orpheus. He is responsible for, indeed he *is* the constant "metamorphosis" within our world (I.v.), that larger metamorphosis between Here and Beyond (I.vii;ix), and finally, running through both of these, the metamorphosis between the multitude of *beings* and the single *Being*. Music—"Once and for all, it's Orpheus, when there's song" (I.v)—expresses this "intimate lasting transformation" which takes place constantly in the fervent heart of the man of pure feeling.[3]

The experience described in the above passages lies outside the bounds of the normal. It presupposes a condition of complete release and detachment. All mental reflections have

[1] See *Sonnets*, I. vi.   [2] See above, p. 212.   [3] See below, p. 261.

ceased and given place to a simple receptivity which is "only
one single spot of pure and profound consciousness".¹ This
consciousness is, as it were, 'at the disposal' of the cosmic influences from which it attains self-knowledge without hindrance.
All desire and all purposeful willing disappear, being replaced
by a selfless benevolence towards everything that exists. There
is in addition something which seems to have its origin in the
cosmos, namely a sense of the oneness of the universe which
would be unattainable in normal life, amid the obtrusiveness of
things and events. This is an awareness of something which lies
below or behind or above the divisions of space, time and form.²
Under certain conditions even the average man is filled with
something of this experience, though he does not value it and
it only lasts a short time. But the *Elegy* gives three examples of
this experience in the child, the dying man and the lover.³

II

We will now return to the opening of the *Elegy*:

> With all its eyes the creature-world beholds
> the open.   [1–2]

Only in Man has this relationship with the 'open' realm the
character of something unusual or temporary. With the
"creature-world"—that is, with animals, though later the same
is asserted of flowers and fountains—this relationship is the rule.

> But our eyes, as though reversed,
> encircle it on every side, like traps
> set round its unobstructed path to freedom.
> What *is* outside, we know from the brute's face
> alone; for while a child's quite small we take it
> and turn it round and force it to look backwards
> at conformation, not that openness
> so deep within the brute's face.   [2–9]

¹ See above, p. 212.
² There is a very revealing parallel to this experience in the work of the Danish
poet Anker Larsen, *With the Door Open—My Experience*. The pattern of his 'experience' is the same as that of Rilke, often down to the very details and the turns of
phrase in which it is described. In particular the idea of the 'open' seems to have
the same meaning as for Rilke. The same value is attributed to the transcendence
of Space and Time, the idea of Being, oneness, etc. One could almost call this
work a religio-psychological commentary on this aspect of the *Elegies*.
³ The correspondence with Princess Marie shows that Rilke was impressed by
the thought of Alfred Schuler, though Schuler's conception of the 'open' had a
different meaning from Rilke's.

The "eyes" of all living beings are directed into this "openness" —only Man's are not!

The final stanzas of the *Elegy* say that something evil has befallen Man—a calamity through which he was "turned round" inside. The direction of a creature's life should be an unimpeded departure from out of its own centre: not towards some objective, but—and here the connection with the idea of 'objectless love' is apparent—beyond everything confronting it into the 'open'. In this place it would find the things, but they would not be *objects*, since here "Everything" and "itself in Everything" is "for ever healed". Man does not behave like this, for his essential life is egotistical and worldly. His attention is fixed on himself and therefore on his neighbours or things as objects. The movement of his life is not into the realm of simple Being, but either into the object or back into himself. His eyes which should properly be doors leading into the "freedom" of "openness" become "traps" which hem him in and "encircle it on every side". The pronoun "it" means the "creature-world", but whereas this previously meant only the non-human creature, now it includes the 'creature' in Man. Man's spontaneous movement *should* lead through his eyes into the 'open'. But instead, these same eyes serve to hamper his motion.

We can only obtain a reliable picture of the 'open' realm, and of the 'non-object' towards which Man should be orientated, from the attitude of animals. The word "*is*", italicized in line 5, means the underlying reality of "deep Being" where all things become One.[1] The word "outside" which follows does not mean the outer physical world as opposed to the inner world of the mind, but rather 'freedom of Being' compared to what is tied or attached to the Here and Now. There is a tentative approach to this state in the life of the child as well as in the

---

[1] "Those factors in our *worldly* being. . . . which are independent of space and time". Rilke claims in a letter to Nora Purtscher-Wydenbruck (August 11th 1924) that this reality should also be accessible to Man. The letter continues: "Since my early youth I have had an intuition (and as far as I was able have lived in accordance with it) that, at a deeper segment of this pyramid of consciousness, unadulterated Being could become a real event in our lives. By this I mean that inviolable presence and concurrence of everything which, at the 'normal' summit of consciousness, we are only permitted to experience as a 'trickle'. In *Malte* I felt the need to suggest a figure who was capable of grasping things past and things to come simply as present actuality in the highest degree. And I am convinced that this view corresponds to a real condition, however much it may be repudiated by all the agreements we make in our day-to-day lives."

animal. But only in the child who is "quite small", before it comes under the influence of grown-ups who "turn it round and force it to look backwards at conformation". The child would like to complete the simple action of existing, but they make him reflect, confronting him with individual things and his own self, so that he soon falls a victim to their perversion. As we are told later, the same attitude is encountered in someone who is dying; but here it forms the conclusion. And it is also found in the lovers, but merely as an unrealized potentiality. Only the animal has it in a pure form. This assertion clearly derives from a particular impression which the animal makes on Man. The animal's attention is certainly focused on things outside itself—its prey, its enemy or its nest—but in a way which differs altogether from that of Man. It has no awareness of an object as something 'like this or like that'; nor of purpose—'I need this for that'; nor of its own self—'I stand here, opposite him; I am he or she, as opposed to the other'. So there is something un-circumscribed in the animal's attitude. It knows neither subject nor object. This is yet another variant of 'I-lessness' and 'Thou-lessness'. In the last event an animal does not *do* something, but something is *done* in it; its life is not directed towards a certain object but simply "outwards". It is not a 'someone' but a point at which existence breaks through.[1] This impression of the animal's nature becomes particularly clear at the conclusion of the stanza: "a dumb brute's calmly raising its head to look us through and through". Here the animal's relationship to "openness" is most apparent.

Moreover, only the animal is

> Free from death.
> We alone see *that*; the free animal
> has its decease perpetually behind it
> and God in front, and when it moves, it moves
> within eternity, like running springs.   [9–13]

[1] In Rilke's letter to Nora Purtscher-Wydenbruck, quoted above, which deals with her experiments as a medium and with his own attitude to occult phenomena, he recommends "counterweights" to these experiences in such normal activities as "artistic work, house, family, nature—and, not least, in the fact that animals urgently engage your heart and sympathy. Certainly the animals, who share in knowledge of the Whole . . . are most likely to lead us across again and are them-selves close to the mediumistic state". In Rilke's view there is a clear connection between 'subjectless' and 'objectless' attitudes, the form of a child's or an animal's life, the existence of the dead, the mediumistic experience and the concept of "deep Being" in the realm of "openness".

The shape of death, which rounds off the temporal shape of life, is not hidden from Man. He can look at his own life, see it running away and, anticipating the end which will come, he feels fear. The animal, on the other hand, apparently stares away from all patterns and shapes, and away from itself, into the 'open'. It lacks all awareness of its life's passage and of its end in death. For the animal death only exists as an intrinsic feature of life's completion. Its "decease" exists, not as an object to be watched "in front", but as something "behind it" in the unseen. Not fearing death, the animal is said to be "free from" it. Of course the fear of its enemy—and that means really a fear of death—is a continuously active factor in the animal's inner life. But Rilke means that the animal is free of the fear which springs from reflective knowledge of the inevitability of our end.

Thus the direction of the animal's life is outwards into the 'open'. This same concept is now given a number of different names. First Rilke says that the animal has "God in front". What bearing this has on his definition of God will be examined at the end of our interpretation. He then says that the animal "moves within eternity": it "moves"—and here the temporal event is transposed into a non-temporal form—"like running springs". The spring is here an image of the true movement of existence: its water rises out of the inner depths, not towards a specific goal, but simply outwards. "Eternity" and the "Open" are thus synonymous. The passage, already quoted, from Rilke's letter to von Huléwicz seems particularly relevant here.[1]

> We've never, no, not for a single day,
> pure space before us, such as that which flowers
> endlessly open into: always world,
> and never nowhere without no: that pure,
> unsuperintended element one breathes,
> endlessly knows, and never craves.   [14–19]

With Man this is never the case. We never have—and here yet another term is applied to the "open"—"*pure space* before us". This does not mean the physical space of things, nor the realm of the *psyche* occupied by feelings and actions, nor the spiritual realm where the significance of things is revealed. It means that

[1] See above, p. 211 f.

space of Being where everything becomes One, and at the same time the *state* attained by things here as soon as they have made the necessary transition. It implies freedom from Here or There. It is the same space which contained the "place" and the "spot" of the acrobats in the *Fifth Elegy*.

All creatures are orientated towards this "pure space"—even the flowers. By the movement of their life and growth they "endlessly open into pure space". "Endlessly" here does not refer to spacial extension, but to something qualitative—the absolute and final fulfilment of the flowers. The shape of the unfolding flower owes its whole freedom and value precisely to the fact that it is not orientated towards objects. The flower passes mysteriously beyond the limits of space and time and simply is.[1] But we are so fettered that we do not usually notice this "endless" quality. It is only during certain fleeting experiences that we recognize the true nature of life, for *our* "world" is made up of what we see and do and are. Our existence is a closed one of objects, but *not* a "nowhere without no". This too is a definition of 'openness': in contrast to a "here" or "there" 'openness' is a "*no*where". But this "nowhere" is not produced by the sort of negatory "no" or "not" which gives us the phrase "not here but there". On the contrary the "nowhere without no" expresses pure abundance and simple Being which transcend any 'Here' at all.

This abundance is now brought home to us more clearly still as the concept 'Open' is defined in other terms. It is called "pure", that is, uncontaminated by being desired or used functionally. It is the "unsuperintended element one breathes, endlessly knows". There is on the one hand the knowledge of 'confrontation' which observes, judges and 'deals with' an object. But there is also that other knowledge, that vital inner awareness which consummates and fulfils the thing to be known. It is

---

[1] See *Sonnets to Orpheus*, II. xiv:

Flowers. . . . .

To all that would soar our selves are the grand aggravation,
we lay them on all we encounter, proud of their weight;
what terrifying teachers we are for that part of creation
which loves its eternally childish state.

Could someone but take them right into his slumber and sleep
deeply with things, how differently, lightly he'd wander
back to a different day out of that communal deep.

this second knowledge which is referred to here and compared
with the act of breathing.[1] When we give reality to the movement of existence in our very act of breathing we partake of
inward knowledge. This way of knowing, like the unfolding of
the flower, is called "endless". It takes place in a state of perfect clarity by an act of penetration, and it is only possible when
we do not "crave", when we have no objective and "are in
pursuit of nothing".

> A child
> sometimes gets quietly lost there, to be always
> jogged back again. Or someone dies and *is* it.
> For, nearing death, one perceives death no longer,
> and stares ahead—perhaps with large brute gaze.
> Lovers—were not the other present, always
> blocking the view!—draw near to it and wonder. . .
> Behind the other, as though through oversight,
> the thing's revealed. . . But no one gets beyond
> the other and so world returns once more.   [19–28]

The child originally has its own relationship to the 'Open'. In
its earliest years it lives entirely in this 'creaturely' approach.
At the sight of a child's face a grown-up may often wonder what
the child is looking at when it gazes away into the distance. In
fact the child is not looking at anything but just looking forth;
it lives its life looking into openness—breathing and being in all
things with true inwardness. But gradually normal life takes
hold of him and directs his attention to people, actions and
things. Nevertheless it sometimes happens that the child is
suddenly transported away from the presence of grown-ups
and sits motionless. It has "got quietly lost there" and, having
entered the 'open' realm, simply stays there—"there" and yet
'away' simultaneously. But then the child's guardian comes and
shakes it, saying 'What are you thinking about? Don't dream!
Do your work! Pay attention to the game!' The rapture is
interrupted and the child again becomes a little grown-up.

The same tendency is present in the experience of the dying
man for whom 'openness' is not merely an action but a state of
being: he "*is* it". Dying means a departure from this "earthly
relation". As long as we have it ahead of us and know that it

---

[1] See the text of *An Experience* and *Sonnets to Orpheus*, II. i and II. xiv; also the
Seventh Elegy, line 38.

will happen in the future—in years or months, or perhaps, when an illness has taken a turn for the worse, in days—death stands before us on the edge of life, inspiring fear and sealing off the realm of pure space. But as soon as one is "nearing death", or when death has already begun, one no longer sees it. One "stares ahead" into the 'Open'. Then there is nothing more to be observed or planned. Only the 'creature' is left in Man and his gaze is like that of an animal.

The same feeling is shared by lovers. A person in love is capable of insights which would normally be impossible to him. "Behind the other . . . the thing's revealed". But this brief grace, granted "as though through oversight", quickly passes. And the possibilities which it opened up are not realized. The beloved—who opened the lover's eyes to the vastness lying behind space and time, so that his heart felt near to reality and was filled with wonder—now draws his attention back again "and so world returns once more". The "world" here stands for the essence of everything that is 'closed' and compels our gaze towards itself.

> Always facing Creation, we perceive there
> only a mirroring of the free and open,
> dimmed by our breath. Or that a dumb brute's calmly
> raising its head to look us through and through.
> For this is Destiny: being opposite,
> and nothing else, and always opposite. [29–34]

So the possibility is never realized. We never perceive the "open" and "free"—yet another description of reality—for we turn our backs on it and face "Creation", i.e. the concrete world of time and space. We see only the "mirroring" of its light—its mysterious reflection on things; but we never see it itself, for our vision is barred, not by any thing, but by ourselves. Man only perceives the "mirroring" of the "free and open" and imagines that there is nothing else.[1] Now and again, however, he sees a "dumb brute calmly raising its head" and apparently looking

---

[1] A kind of Platonism reminding us of the simile according to which Man is turned away from reality, i.e. the Ideas, and shut up in a cave, so that he can only see its rear wall. Outside, however, behind his back, the forms of existence pass by in front of the cave, refracting the light of the Ideas and projecting their shadows on the wall. Man sees these shadows and calls this sham vision 'knowledge' (*Politeia*, beginning of the Seventh Book).

at him, but really "looking us through and through". Then he
'takes in' the creature's movement and is disturbed by his own
perverseness.

To be turned round the wrong way against the general
direction of existence. To be an observer standing in front of
shapes and scrutinizing them. To be always filled with desire,
wanting things and grasping them. Always being "opposite,
and nothing else"—that is the imprisonment of our existence.
That is our "Destiny".

III

The second stanza is a eulogy of the "animal", but in terms
which are far from 'naturalistic'. Rilke's "Nature" includes a
great deal more than the normal use of the word implies. His
"Nature" is the "creature-world" of "Creation", and these
words—though Rilke would not have agreed—re-echo the
time-hallowed Biblical description of Paradise and the sanctity
of created things. Nature has two sides—one side which is open
to our direct experience and another which is turned away from
us. Compare the passage in *An Experience* which tells of the man
who "reached the other side of Nature". Something of this
other side also plays a part in Rilke's praise of the animal, like
a reminder that it too was once in Paradise.

Perhaps the whole condition which the creature enters into
when it "endlessly opens into pure space" is connected with
Paradise and it may therefore be appropriate to say a word on
this subject here. In modern times 'Paradise' and the primeval
state of 'Nature' are usually identified. In the life of the individual this signifies the period of childhood or, still further
back, the time spent in the mother's womb; in the life of a nation
or of humanity as a whole it is often considered to be the period
preceding rational culture. In each case Paradise is taken to
mean the initial condition when rational order and irrational
instinct were in harmony and humble life was 'innocent'. This
condition ceased as soon as man began to think for himself and
to have a will of his own, thus incurring guilt.

Yet this picture, outlined above, does not correspond to
revealed truth. Revelation tells us that Paradise is the fruit of
direct communion with God—not with the universal spirit of

pantheism but the free Lord and Creator. Paradise certainly does mean a beginning, but it is the beginning of union with the will of God through Grace—life in association with Him. In this condition Man is pure and whole and, through him, things also become pure and whole. Man has mastery over things because he is obedient to the Lord of the Creation. His dominion is thus one of peace in which all things are free and have open access to God.

This happy condition is, however, subject to a trial or test. The test does not consist of a choice between a romantic state of happy innocent tutelage and a mature state of knowledge which has to be paid for through suffering and guilt. That we are intended to attain all stages of maturity and perception is not in doubt. The question is whether this takes place in submission and acknowledgement by Man of his creaturely state *or* in rebellion which seeks to make Man the equal of God. Knowledge itself is not a sin, any more than the union of the sexes— but the fact that these things are desired in revolt against God.[1]

This ultimate truth which is manifest in divine revelation has been obscured by the modern interpretation of Paradise. Now Rilke's view is a long way from that of the Bible. On the other hand his is not the modern 'naturalistic' view either. He stands between the two. He is critical of revealed truth but appropriates its secularized content. From this standpoint he interprets the animal as having pure existence while still partaking of the freedom of Paradise.[2]

> Did consciousness such as we have exist
> in the sure animal that moves towards us
> upon a different course, the brute would drag us
> round in its wake. But its own being for it
> is infinite, inapprehensible,
> unintrospective, pure, like its outgazing.
> Where we see Future, it sees Everything,
> itself in Everything, for ever healed. [35–42]

In the first stanza, which mentioned the flowers, the 'Open' was

---

[1] There seems to be a widespread ignorance of the early chapters of *Genesis* today, otherwise the distorted accounts of Paradise and the Fall which are current would be impossible.

[2] It is significant that the theme of Paradise also occurs in Larsen's *Experience*, where it receives great emphasis.

P

presented as a blossoming richness of meaning. Here it becomes
a force or power. The image is a striking one, although I am
not sure whether the following interpretation is correct. Suppose
someone were walking along in a dark wood when an animal
approached him—perhaps a stag or an elk which had never
seen a man before and had therefore not learnt to fear him.
The animal would then "move" towards him "upon a different
course"—calmly and with a sense of power. If, in addition to
this power, another were added, namely the "consciousness
such as we have", then what would happen? If the silent creature were capable of judgment, choice and volition, then it
would "drag us round in its wake". It would tear Man out of
the wrong direction of his life so that he would cease to be
"turned round" (line 70) and would be forced to follow the
animal's movement towards the 'Open'. This too would be the
effect of a "stronger existence", like that of the Angel in the
First Elegy, only in this case it would be beneficent—a kind of
liberation brought about by the pure "creature".[1] In fact,
however, the animal's existence is incommensurable to Man. It
skirts the fringe of his life, "looking us through and through"
because "its own being for it is infinite". This word, like "endlessly", has nothing to do with physical extension but means
simply the way in which the animal exists, completely justified
in its own right, developing from within itself and radiating
forth its life. The animal is also "inapprehensible, unintro-
spective"—i.e. without reflective power and oblivious of its self
—"pure, like its outgazing". Its whole existence is no more than
a simple movement out of its self into "openness".

Consequently the animal has no "Future" before it. What

[1] Compare Rilke's experience in Spain of which he gave an odd account with
a certain touch of blasphemy: "Oh, I have not got quite beyond expecting the
nouvelle opération from human intervention. And yet to what purpose? Since it is
my lot to pass humanity by and to reach the extremity, the edge of the world as
I recently did in Cordoba. There a small ugly bitch in the last stages of pregnancy
came up to me. It was not a very attractive animal, and certainly it was full of
chance puppies which will not have caused great concern to anyone. But as we
were quite alone she came across to me and, although it was not easy for her,
raising her eyes which were large with apprehension and 'inwardness', she begged
me to look at her. And her gaze really contained everything that passes beyond
the individual and goes out—I know not where—into the future and the incomprehensible. The upshot was that she got a lump of sugar from my coffee, but
incidentally—oh, so incidentally!—we read the Mass together as it were. In itself
the action was nothing but giving and taking, but the solemn meaning it contained
and our whole understanding were boundless." (Letter to Princess Marie of
December 17th 1912.)

will become of it later is never the subject of reflection, hope or fear. The continuance of its life is not something which it 'looks forward' to but something 'behind' it, in the sense that its "decease" is "perpetually behind it". The Past and Future together constitute the unified existence of the creature. This is not unlike the child's relation to death at the conclusion of the *Fourth Elegy*.

The 'Open', towards which the creature is orientated, is now given yet another name. Already, as we saw, it has been called variously "outside", "God", "Eternity", "pure space", "nowhere without no", "that pure, unsuperintended element". Now it is called "Everything", i.e. the place to which *every thing* moves and where it becomes *Everything* and "infinite". This is the "space" where the eyes which have abandoned objects partake inwardly of everything that has being. In this "communal deep"[1] the seeing creature becomes aware of all other creatures—and also aware of itself, in so far as it is within the "Everything". See the passage from *An Experience* quoted above.

In this unifying sphere everything is "healed": healed *of* the compulsion to observe objects, the convulsion of exerting the will and the pain of desiring things. The healing is, however, also a positive process. It leads everything *towards* 'wholeness' and the abundance of "deep Being".

Such is the numinous state described by the word "infinite". This is given a more specifically temporal reference in the last line of the stanza which describes the animal as "for ever healed". But "infinite" and "for ever" mean basically the same thing from different points of view, namely that state of existence which has become abundant, whole and free.

IV

The above lines which praise the animal are followed by a change of tone. Compared to Man, the animal seems to be perfect since it is free in its creaturely 'forward' movement. In one respect, however, it is severely handicapped, and here the eulogy turns into a lament.

[1] *Sonnets to Orpheus*, II. xiv.

> And yet, within the wakefully-warm beast
> there lies the weight and care of a great sadness.
> For that which often overwhelms us clings
> to him as well,—a kind of memory
> that what one's pressing after now was once
> nearer and truer and attached to us
> with infinite tenderness.   [43-49]

The *Elegy* has already said a variety of things about the animal. Its face is "deep"; it is "free"; it has a "large gaze"; it "looks us through and through"; it is sure; it "moves into Eternity".[1] And now it is "wakefully-warm"—words which put us in mind of a living thing with warm blood and its own moods. This prepares us for the "weight and care of a great sadness" which follows. Here the picture of the animal becomes something of a paradox, for this "sadness" shows that the individual creature is still burdened by something from its past origin which holds it back from freedom. So when Rilke says that the beast is "sad" he contradicts what he previously affirmed about its "unobstructed path to freedom". If the beast really could continue along this path it would become free from the bonds tying it to its origin and immune to sadness.

This sadness is a retarding force. Rilke expresses this by calling it a "kind of memory" which painfully fetters the animal. The poet's own unhappiness is betrayed in his lament that it "often overwhelms *us*". He means a memory of some incomplete experience from the past which binds us still—parts of childhood which were not fully realized,[2] or perhaps events still further back in the period before birth. For life inside the womb is a real phase of existence when something important, spiritually as well as physically, takes place. The feeling of sadness seems to be evidence that the release of birth was not complete and final and that life longs to return to the womb. This is clearly the meaning of the statement that "what one's pressing after now" in life was once "nearer to us".

There are two different paths which give access to the transcendental or 'open' realm. One leads upwards into the heights

---

[1] Compare the state of the child in the *Fourth Elegy*, line 71.

[2] Compare Rilke's interpretation of the Parable of the Prodigal at the end of *The Notebook of Malte Laurids Brigge* where the young man returns home thinking of "his childhood which . . . . seemed to him more and more to have been unfulfilled; . . . to take all this once more, and this time in reality, upon himself—this was the reason he, estranged, turned home." (p. 242.)

and the spaces, the other into the depths of inwardness. The 'Open' should therefore itself be manifest in two "places"— above and within. The inner 'openness' is clearly revealed in that section of the *Ninth Elegy* which deals with inwardness, the realm of the heart. It appears there as that dimension where the earth strives to "arise invisibly" within us[1]—where all differentiated things become a simple unity, where "childhood" and the "future" turn into the present and existence is "super-numerous". But inner 'openness' is also revealed in the *Eighth Elegy*, in the realm of physical organic life where the unborn creature is dependent on the life of the mother. Here too there is no separation or division, only inner creaturely movement. Something which man later has to seek far away outside himself is present here in the mother—"nearer and truer and attached to us with infinite tenderness". 'Openness' is now bound up with the proximity of the maternal blood and vital warmth. Once more the key-word "infinite" occurs, again describing not a quantity but a quality.

> Here all is distance,
> there it was breath. Compared with that first home
> the second seems ambiguous and fickle.   [49–51]

This passage characterizes the peculiar position of the animal in life. In front of it lies one realm of 'openness'—that of spacious freedom. Behind it lies the other 'open' realm of the womb which had inner warmth and vitality. Between these two 'opennesses', and unlike either, stands the sphere of actual existence in the world. This is narrow compared to the "free and open" realm ahead, but vulnerable and exposed compared to the "first home". The direction of life is forwards but there is also a yearning *back* to the original state of shelter and protection. Rilke here projects the deep human feeling of sadness into the world of living things and displays its character in the attitudes and movements of animals.

The intermediary realm consists of things which are circumscribed, each of which stands alone and at a distance from its neighbour. Hence all our actions are required to bridge differences and to bring them into relation with one another. In the womb, by contrast, everything was in a state of vital unity which was experienced from within—like "breath". This was a true

[1] See *Ninth Elegy*, lines 67–69.

"home". But what is called by this name in the intermediary realm is something "ambiguous" and undefined, neither a real protection nor a real expanse. Everything here is in a paradoxical state of collision and contradiction, putting life at odds with itself. There depth, calm and silence prevailed. Here everything is vulnerable and "fickle".

The remaining lines of the stanza seem at first somewhat curious. But their purpose is to reproduce the impression which certain animals make as they move, and to interpret this impression in the light of what was said previously:

> Oh, bliss of *tiny* creatures that *remain*
> for ever in the womb that brought them forth!
> Joy of the gnat, that can still leap *within*,
> even on its wedding-day: for womb is all!   [52–55]

In the fragment of a letter to Lou Andreas-Salomé dated February 20th 1918, but never despatched, Rilke wrote: ". . . the fact that a whole host of creatures, produced from seed which has been planted outside, have *this* as their womb—this expansive, excitable open space—how they must feel at home in it all their lives; for they do nothing but leap for joy, like little John the Baptist, inside their mother's womb; this same space conceived them and brought them forth; they never emerge from its security at all. Only with the birds do things become a little more timid and prudent. The bird's nest is like a little womb, borrowed from nature, which it covers instead of enclosing. And suddenly, as if it were no longer safe enough outside, the wonderful maturing process takes refuge within the darkness of the creature and only emerges at a later stage into the world; this it takes to be the second world but never wholly disaccustoms itself from the more inward conditions of the first."

These ideas are expounded at greater length in an earlier letter to the same correspondent dated February 20th 1914: "I have had a marvellous picture of it such as never came to me before: this transposition of the growing creature ever further from the outer into the inner world. This explains the fascinating position of the bird in the middle of this progression inwards. The bird's nest is, after all, almost an external womb granted to it by nature which it simply fits out and covers instead of enclosing it entirely within. So the bird is the creature which has a unique familiarity with the external world, as if it had a secret understanding with it. This is why it sings in the world as if it were singing inside; this is why we can 'take in' the bird's song so easily, as if we were translating it completely into our own feelings. The song may transform the whole world for a moment into inner space because we feel that the bird does not distinguish between its heart and that of the world. On the one hand animal and human life gains greatly by the transposition of the maturing organism inside the mother's womb. For the womb becomes 'world' to the extent that the world ceases to participate in these events (as if it had become less assured the world is deprived of them); on the other hand (taken from an entry made in my notebook last year in Spain—you will remember the question): Where does the inwardness of the creature . . . come from? From the fact that it did not reach maturity within the body, which means that it never really left the body at all. (Has a relation to the womb all its life.)"

These two passages show how much Rilke was concerned with this question, and if we read carefully between the lines we shall understand more clearly his feelings about life as a whole.

The *Elegy* expresses the same idea. The tiny creatures—here the gnats—seem to us to be "brought forth" at maturity, but not born. The space surrounding them and the air which carries them are so powerful by comparison with these little creatures that they seem not to have entered into an existence of their own, but simply to be swept along by the current or wafted on the breeze. The "open space", as the letter says, is their "womb". The next line—"Joy of the gnat, that can still leap *within*"—blends together the picture of a swarm of dancing gnats and the stirring of the unborn creature in the mother's womb. The "tiny creature" is always in the womb, even at its wedding, that is, when it procreates. So for the gnat the intermediary realm simply does not exist.[1]

> Look at the half-assurance of the bird,
> through origin almost aware of both,
> like one of those Etruscan souls, escaped
> from a dead man enclosed within a space
> on which his resting figure forms a lid.   [56–60]

[1] Compare the poem quoted above on p. 85.

In the bird the "ambiguous" and "fickle" character of the world becomes clearly apparent. For the bird only has a "half-assurance". Its flight makes an impression of light dexterity, but also of vulnerability. The explanation of the bird's contradictory nature lies in its "origin". At birth it is both protected and exposed at the same time, for it has come out of an egg. This egg was certainly formed inside the mother's body and then, as Rilke says in his letter, enjoys some protection in the "borrowed womb" of the nest; but here, in the 'nest-womb', the egg is only "covered" by the brooding hen-bird instead of being "enclosed" in it.

As if this image were not complicated enough already, it is followed immediately by another which is taken from ancient burial customs. The Etruscans used to lay the body or ashes of a dead person in a sarcophagus and also portrayed him on the lid outside, so that he was, in a sense, both on the "lid" and "within a space" at the same time. So the liberated soul must have felt that it was leaving behind both the protection of the closed coffin *and* the exposed figure lying on top. The bird's experience is similar. It feels itself joined to the inside of the brooding mother-bird and also to the egg lying in the open. It is thus conscious of peril and protection simultaneously and this twofold awareness passes into its innermost feelings.

> And how dismayed is any womb-born thing
> that has to fly! As though it were afraid
> of its own self, it zigzags through the air
> like crack through cup. The way a bat's track runs
> rendingly through the evening's porcelain.   [61–65]

The paradox is most evident in those creatures which have emerged from a real womb and are then forced to adjust themselves to the outside world. The extreme example given here of a "womb-born thing that has to fly" is the bat. The external "intermediary realm" does not, for the bat, mean the security of the ground, but the unreliable element of the air. So the bat is not merely unsure of itself, but "dismayed . . . as though it were *afraid* of its own self". In fact the flight of a bat does express something like the terror of a creature that cannot adapt itself properly. It "zigzags through the air", twirling and darting rapidly to and fro. Again one image is fused with another, for the

bat's track is "like crack through cup". The "cup" is the evening at the moment when everything seems to become trans-
parent. Through its delicate porcelain the track of the bat "runs
rendingly" in a jagged line.

V

From praising the beasts the *Elegy* has passed to the opposite
extreme. The animal's sadness is now clear enough. There is no
trace left of its earlier calm movements. The beast's fears, its
homelessness and its harassed circling round now come to the
fore. But this does not cancel out the eulogy of the animal which
was originally intended, and between the third and fourth
stanzas we have to insert some such sentence as "All this is true,
but . . .". The memory of its origin *does* bind the animal and
prevent it from completing its movement into the "Open". Yet
the animal still remains superior to human beings.

> And we, spectators always, everywhere,
> looking at, never out of, everything!
> It fills us. We arrange it. It collapses.
> We re-arrange it, and collapse ourselves.   [66–69]

We are much worse off than the animals—and by our very
nature. Even the flight of the bat, despite all its uncertainty,
was directed 'outwards' inasmuch as there was nothing to confront it as an object. But we are conscious of objects confronting
us the whole time. Our constant attitude is that of "spectators":
"always" and "everywhere" we are "looking at" things. We
never complete the *out*ward movement.

The "spectators" mentioned here are different from the
"watching" spectator of the *Fourth Elegy*. His "watching" was
a purely contemplative attitude, so far removed from action
that both subject and object became insubstantial. They were
dissolved into one single relationship by the co-ordinating
guidance of the Angel. But here the "spectators" stand for our
worthless and perverse condition—our "Destiny" of "being
opposite, and nothing else, and always opposite". "Here all is
distance" and we shut ourselves off from the unity of openness.[1]

[1] See lines 33 ff.

We not only stand "opposite" the objects as spectators, but we are confused and overwhelmed by their very number. We lack the inner assurance which can allot a place to every phenomenon.[1] So we have to use concepts and makeshift devices to impose an artificial order on the chaos around us. This seems to be successful. But because this order is purely external it collapses straight away. We "arrange it" a second time, a tenth or a thousandth time, in every re-adjustment of our daily lives. But then we "collapse ourselves"—repeatedly and, in the end, finally.

VI

A bitter mystery. How can this be? Everything after all is part of Nature, or the Earth or the World. How can there be such a contradiction here?

In Rilke's mind the idea of Nature no longer had any of that enchanting power which it commonly has for other poets. Goethe said that if a paradox in Nature seemed insoluble this was always due to our failure to consider the phenomenon in a broad enough context and from a high enough vantage point. If we did this, Goethe maintained, everything would be merged in harmony. There may be tensions in such a view of Nature as this but there can be no real contradictions, least of all such a contradiction as Rilke describes here. And Rilke's problem must be attributed, not to an inadequate synthesis, but to something much more radical—something disruptive which is suggested in the very first line of the final stanza:

> Who's turned us round like this, so that we always,
> do what we may, retain the attitude
> of someone who's departing? Just as he,
> on the last hill, that shows him all his valley
> for the last time, will turn and stop and linger,
> we live our lives, for ever taking leave.   [70–75]

This state of being "turned round" or inverted is not 'natural', nor can it be explained by any dialectic. For the question "Who's turned us round like this?" touches on another sphere altogether which lies beyond our day to day experience. Here

---

[1] Compare the first and last stanzas of the *Fourth Elegy*.

not only Nature is at work, but also a power, a Someone, for the question is not merely "What?" but "Who?" We are inevitably reminded of the doctrine of original sin and that first action of man which separated him from God, brought him into discord with himself and others, and also destroyed Paradise. The same doctrine of which Pascal said that man would be incomprehensible without it.[1] But here the doctrine has become so diffuse that it seems more like the faint echo of a myth. We should perhaps have in mind here Rilke's accusation against Christianity—that the Church "has sold out into the Hereafter . . . . everything which is deeply and fervently Here" and has thus made it impossible to have within oneself the "pure nature of the Earth" as "essential consciousness".[2]

Such is the disaster which accounts for our position in the world. The beast still has its home here, in so far as it is not confused by a memory of its own origin. But Man is without a home, for his relationship to things is a constant "leave-taking". The animal is at home in Being, and this means that it always "moves towards us upon a different course" as it goes out into "openness". We cannot share this assurance. Whereas memory only "clings" to the animal, it "often overwhelms" us and prevents us from moving into the "open and free". We are always orientated towards things, "always opposite" and hence subject to "Destiny". We observe things, judge them, demand them, grasp them and arrange or adopt them, but we still cannot hold them. For real possession of things is only possible through a selflessness which is free from desire and hankering after possession. Hence all our holding and clinging to things is in vain. Again and again we become detached from things, but not in the sense that we are free from them, but in the sense that we have to relinquish them and "take leave" of them. So convinced is Rilke of the truth of this that in the *Fourth Elegy* he makes "Parting"—not from a particular person or place but 'parting' in the widest sense of the word—into the "scenery" against which our whole existence is played. He even claims

[1] Pascal, *Pensées*, ed. Brunschwicg, No. 434: "Chose étonnante, cependant, que le mystère le plus éloigné de notre connaissance, qui est celui de la transmission du péché, soit une chose sans laquelle nous ne pouvons avoir aucune connaissance de nous-mêmes! . . . Le noeud de notre condition prend ses replis et ses tours dans cet abîme, de sorte que l'homme est plus inconcevable sans ce mystère que ce mystère n'est inconcevable à l'homme."
[2] Letter to Ilse Jahr of February 22nd 1923.

that this scenery does not require any special explanation since
it is "easy to understand" for anyone—an assumption which is
a very significant comment on the pattern of Rilke's own life.[1]

The final stanza of the *Elegy* returns to the elegiac mood
proper. Everything passes away, everything must be left behind
or renounced—and yet at the same time there is a final touch
of reconciliation. The bitter sense of futility which filled the
previous stanza now gives way to the sad but homely image of
the traveller taking leave of his valley. As he departs he stops
on the last hill and turns round for a moment to take in the
sight of home with his eyes and with his heart.

VII

In our interpretation of the first stanza of this *Elegy* we said
that the meaning which Rilke gives to the word "God" would
require more detailed discussion. This will be attempted in what
follows.

The key to Rilke's conception of God lies in his doctrine of
love which has already been dealt with above. Rilke's view of
the human "Thou" and human love is intimately bound up with
his idea of God and divine love. In the first stanza of the *Elegy*
Rilke says that, like children and dying people, lovers too have
an inkling of "Openness"—"Behind the other, as though through
oversight, the thing's revealed . . .". The condition of their
hearts raises the lovers above the limitations which beset everyone else. But it is not sufficient to liberate them completely, for
"no one gets beyond the other, and so world returns once more".
The "other", the beloved who has opened the eyes and heart of
the lover, also blocks his way. How could this obstacle be overcome?

The *First Elegy* said that the "forsaken" were "so far beyond
the requited in loving". This means primarily those on whom
Fate imposes renunciation and who rise to greatness by accepting their lot. But it also contains an allusion to the nature of
perfect love. We are confirmed in this view by the conclusion
of the *Notebook of Malte Laurids Brigge*, already referred to in

---

[1] An itinerary of all Rilke's travels would be most revealing; where he lived,
when he arrived, why he did not stay and where he went to afterwards. It would
be an affecting account, as would also a chronicle of his relationships with people.

connection with the *First Elegy*. The reader is therefore asked to
keep in mind what was said there.

According to Malte, perfect love is one in which the lover is
not attached to the other person. His act of love is no longer
confronted by any thing or any person—no 'Thou' at all—but
simply passes into "openness" or, as the *Seventh Elegy* puts it, into
"pursuit of nothing". The same thing should hold good for love
and the response to love. Perfect love becomes 'selfless' with
respect to the 'I' and the 'Thou'. Each should be the means to
the liberation of the other's love. The person has no validity as
such, but becomes simply a channel or opening for the rays
which pass from the heart into 'Openness'. This is why the
Notebook refers to the "transparency" of the beloved.

It might be objected that this is an oversimplification of
Rilke's meaning and that the eye which leaves the "object" in
favour of the "Open" would find its object again precisely there.
For the "Open" is the same realm of "Being" where the animal
"sees Everything, itself in Everything, for ever healed";[1] and
what is true of the animal should surely be true of Man as well.
If he could attain this realm he would certainly rediscover the
"other"—the beloved. Yet, as far as I can see, this is nowhere
explicitly stated. It is certainly claimed that he will find *things*
again, but not the other *person* with his or her individual personality. It appears to be such a relief to Rilke to be no longer
confronted by the person, that he looks forward to rediscovering
"flowers endlessly opening into pure space", but not another
human being.

What the poet says about human love is like a prelude to his
account of divine love.

In the *Notebook of Malte Laurids Brigge*, just before the interpretation of the Parable of the Prodigal Son and just *after* a
description of young Abelone's song, the following passage
occurs: "I had sometimes wondered before that why Abelone
did not direct the fervour of her magnificent passion towards
God. I know that she longed to remove from her love all that
was transitive; but could her sincere heart be deceived on that
score? Did she not know that God is only a direction given to

[1] See line 41 f.

love, not its object? Did she not know she need fear no return from Him?"

God, then, is not someone whom we could confront or recognize or love "transitively", and there is no need to "fear" a return of love from Him. He is in no sense a goal, but only "the endless road"; love of God springs from the "inner indifference of the spirit"—when the "heart-rays" have become "parallel". As soon as the eyes are focused on a specific object the rays of vision intersect; but they become "parallel" when the eyes pass through the object into the infinite. Something similar is true of the heart and its "rays". These meet when they find their objective in the person who is loved. But they become "parallel" when love no longer has an object but passes into infinity.[1] Perfect love is not directed towards a person, but simply passes through him into the "Open". And when love seeks God it tries again at first to confront Him as an object. But when love has been instructed by the "sincere heart" it becomes clear that this relationship is a false one. As is stated in both *Malte* and in the letter to Ilse Jahr, love learns in time to pass beyond God as a confronting object and into the "Open". And when this is achieved the real God is present, for the "Open" *is* God.

Rilke's various statements can now be merged together. The *Elegy* says that the creature which has freed itself from the earthly object proceeds towards the "Open"—it has "God in front". *Malte* says that God is not an "*object* of love" but something which stands beyond everything that can be approached directly: God is only "given" to the extent that the will to confront Him has been overcome. According to the first statement God is that Being towards which all creatures move and in whom everything becomes wholly free and wholly itself. According to the second, God is what becomes manifest when Man renounces all claim on Him as the object of his sublimest passion, love— *and* also the claim to *be loved* by Him in return: when, in other words, he is quite "poor" and "unsatisfied" as far as God is concerned. God is not directly approachable but represents the "Being" which gives everything its fulfilment. The logical consequence of this is that the personal aspect of God disappears —just as the human personality disappears; for the existence of

[1] See *Notebook of Malte Laurids Brigge*, p. 233 ff.

the latter depends on the fact that the Creator calls to his creature. Man is an 'I' because God makes him into His 'Thou'.

There is a short definition of God in *Malte* which places Him still more definitely outside the bounds of accessibility. It says that He is "only a direction given to love, not its object".[1] Here God has no identity at all, but is simply a quality which emerges when love ceases to be "transitive" in order to become "radiant".

Nietzsche says in his *Zarathustra* that the soul is "a something in the body", that is, an ultimate harmony and vitality in it. We could alter this definition and say that, according to the *Elegy*, God is "a something in the world"—a quality of freedom and meaningfulness which breaks forth in the world when the latter has reached final perfection. This is not the traditional pantheistic view which makes the world absolute and infinite. According to Rilke it is precisely the world in its finiteness which should acquire the maximum degree of significance and beauty. As he states in his letter to Ilse Jahr, "the attributes are taken away from God, who is now ineffable, and are given back to the Creation, to Love and Death".[2] The final definition of God would thus be a statement about the world, and in particular about Man and his loving and dying, whenever these actions are unblemished by any 'transitive' aim. The "direction" of this loving and dying—*this* would be God, springing from the (rightly) "breathing heart". What God *might* be apart from this, per se, would remain inexpressible.[3]

[1] *Notebook of Malte Laurids Brigge*, p. 234.
[2] See above, p. 18.
[3] How little Rilke understood of the personal aspect of God and of man's existence as a person—how little he knew, despite his preoccupation with such Christian mystics as Angela da Foligno, Mechthild von Magdeburg, Saint Theresa and others, of what love of God really means, is clear from the extent to which he identifies sacred love and the human *eros*. One passage from *Malte* may be sufficient to illustrate this point: "Did she not recognize the restraint of this deliberate lover, who quietly defers desire so that we, slow as we are, may bring our whole heart into play? Or did she seek to avoid Christ? Did she fear to be held by Him half-way, to become his beloved? . . . . I almost believe so, when I recall how lovers so simple as Mechthild, so passionate as Theresa of Avilla, so wounded as blessed Rose of Lima, could sink back on this alleviation of God, compliant, yet beloved. Ah! He who was a succour for the weak does these strong souls a wrong; when they awaited nothing more but the endless road, once again, expectant at the gate of heaven, they meet a palpable form that spoils them with His welcome and troubles them with His virility. His heart's powerful lens assembles once again the already parallel rays of their hearts, and they whom the angels hoped to keep intact for God flame up and are consumed in the drought of their desire." Anyone who has real knowledge of these matters—based on written texts and on true

It might be objected, especially after the quotation from Rilke's letter to Ilse Jahr, that I have exaggerated or distorted his ideas. However, I do not think that this is true. The poet gives us in this document a kind of report on the development of his conception of God. At first there was a period of youthful confusion which was followed by endeavours to approach nearer to things and animals, in the hope of drawing closer to human beings later. Thus he would be "granted admission into the whole glory of life without any false gaps... But then Russia revealed herself and bestowed on me the brotherliness and darkness of God in whom alone there is real communion. And this was how I *named* him then—the God who had broken in upon me—and I lived for a long time in the antechamber of his name, on my knees". These are the religious sentiments of the *Book of Hours*, according to which God is the mystery in all things, the One who is both given and relinquished, who manifests himself everywhere and yet veils himself behind all things. This period in Rilke's life also came to an end and was followed by that of the *Elegies* and the *Sonnets*... "Now you would hardly ever hear me mention his name, there is such an indescribable discretion between us... What was comprehensible now escapes us and is transformed. Instead of possession we learn the relationship; and so a namelessness comes into being which has to begin with God again if it is to be perfect and free from pretence. The experience of the sensibility [directed towards God] is eclipsed by an infinite joy in everything 'sensible'." The sentence quoted previously now joins on here: "The attributes are taken away from God, who is now ineffable, and are given back to the Creation, to Love and Death."

At first this passage seems to mean that the God who was filled with "darkness" has now become completely "nameless" and "ineffable". This would imply that the new picture of God was the same as the old, but in a heightened form. Such an interpretation would, however, not be in keeping with the

religious experience—cannot help finding such views as are expressed above offensive. If we also take into account the way in which Rilke associates this love of God with the human love of Gaspara Stampa, Louisa Labé or Marianne Alcoforado, our distaste is only increased. We are forced to assume that Rilke did not really know the meaning of love for a person. His view of love leads quite naturally to the conclusion that anyone who is concerned with the reality of existence must decide "never to love, in order not to put anyone in the terrible position of being loved".

profound sense of something new and decisive which runs
through these lines and indeed the whole period of the *Elegies*
and the *Sonnets*. There is more to it than this. There seems to be
a new conviction behind the words "Instead of possession
we learn the relationship", especially if we take into account
the two statements which follow: that "the experience of the
sensibility is eclipsed by a joy in everything 'sensible' "; and
that the "attributes" of divinity are "given back to Creation",
in particular the ontologically significant events of "Love and
Death". The "relationship" in this context is not the relationship between the 'self' and the confronting object or between
the 'I' and 'Thou'. It means the relevance of something which
is not directly given to us, or, in the terms of *An Experience*, a
connection which has been established "as if over one's shoulder".

What has been said above does not claim to reproduce
Rilke's whole conception of ultimate religious truth—or, let us
say, the whole 'relation' which he felt to be there. In any case
his later view of this relation was influenced by his earlier ideas
of it. Moreover, we must not forget that Rilke was not a philosopher but a poet whose thoughts are 'polyphonic' in character,
containing many overtones and undertones. Here we have been
simply concerned with that one tone which seems to be dominant in the *Eighth Elegy*.

THE NINTH ELEGY

Completed on February 9th 1922 at Muzot, including
two fragments from the years 1912–1913

I

IF we look at the *Elegies* as a whole the *Ninth* will probably impress us as having the most satisfactory inner balance since its mood of confidence is matched by the beauty of its lines. This view may, of course, be merely subjective. But it has been confirmed again and again over a period of years, as I have learnt to appreciate the *Elegies* more deeply. The following interpretation may show the reason why.

> Why, when this span of life might be fleeted away
> as laurel, a little darker than all
> the surrounding green, with tiny waves on the border
> of every leaf (like the smile of a wind):—oh, why
> *have* to be human, and, shunning Destiny,
> long for Destiny? . . .   [1–6]

This is the great question: Why does Man exist? What justifies his strange existence? If the word "life" sums up the content and meaning of existence in this world—why should humanity exist as something apart? Since there are already so many forms of the 'non-human'—animals and plants—are they not sufficient? The laurel, for instance, the sight of which greatly impressed the poet as he was once strolling through the bushes of a southern hillside. This noble tree, with its firm, clearly defined branches, the precisely set berries and the beautifully shaped leaves with wavy edges suggested to him the subtle simile— "like the smile of the wind". For the whole form of this leaf, between whose two edges runs the straight line of the principal vein, is similar to that of two lips lying close together. So each fragrant leaf seems like the mouth of the wind as it blows through the laurel bush and curls its 'lips' into a "smile". Rilke saw this in the glow of the sun and understood then why

Daphne was transformed into a laurel and why a laurel-wreath was a symbol of high honour.

If there has to be life—why is it not sufficient that the laurel lives in all its purity and nobility? Why should there be this strange thing called *human* life? Why should a creature exist who "*has* to be human" and who has a "destiny", indeed who creates a destiny, which we shun because it is painful and yet yearn for because it is human?

> Not because happiness really
> exists, that precipitate profit of imminent loss.
> Not out of curiosity, not just to practise the heart,
> that could still be there in laurel. . . . .   [6–9]

"Happiness" does not provide the justification, if only because it does not "really exist". Happiness subsists merely as the fleeting prelude to something real, in the form of something "precipitate" or premature. This word must be read together with what follows—the "precipitate profit of imminent loss"—meaning that happiness is like a sample fragment which anticipates a later 'whole' or the glittering vanguard of a drab army which is to follow it. This is reminiscent of the description of "Beauty" in the *First Elegy* as the "beginning of Terror we're still just able to bear".

"Happiness" does not justify human existence, any more than "curiosity" or expectations about the future, or the "practice of the heart" in joy, grief, loneliness and longing. "That could still be there", Rilke says, "in the laurel." Let us leave aside the question of whether or not he is here attributing human emotions to plants. What he does claim is that even without Man there would still be some happiness, curiosity or other feeling which would justify existence. So the reasons for Man's particular sort of life must be sought elsewhere.

> But because being here is much, and because all this
> that's here, so fleeting, seems to require us and strangely
> concerns us. Us the most fleeting of all.   [10–12]

The fleeting aspect of life is now contrasted with something else—"being here". This means not the mere fact that we belong to the realm of the earth, as opposed to that of Death, for this would also apply to the laurel. It means *having a place* on this

earth—our whole trust or mission in being here and the "Destiny" which this implies. The plant has none of this. It is reserved for Man.

Man, however, is not "here" for himself alone, but also for "all this that's here"—all the things which he encounters as immediate 'reality' in the world. The whole point of Man's "being here" lies in his importance for this 'reality'. It "requires" him.

But it is strange that the weakest and most vulnerable creature on earth should be "required" in this way. His mission has to do with the "fleeting" character, the transience of all things. Instead of being imposed on the creature most capable of resisting this transience the mission is given precisely to the one who feels it most keenly—"Us, the most fleeting of all". The *Elegy* states later that "these things . . . . fleeting, they look for rescue through something in us, the most fleeting of all". This is like an echo of the sombre note of the *Second Elegy* but now followed by a modulation. The more intense a creature's life is, the more fleeting its existence. Man not only passes away more quickly than other living things, but in a different and tragic way, because he knows his own fate. But it is precisely this which equips him to rescue "all this that's here".

The lines which follow are a kind of poetic fugue on the theme of irrevocability:

> Just *once*,
> everything, only for *once*. *Once* and no more. And we, too,
> *once*. And never again. But this
> having been *once*, though only *once*,
> having been *once* on earth—can it ever be cancelled? [12–16]

As we read these lines it is as though we hear the same cry sounding forth from all existence—"*Once* and no more". And we cannot help repeating "We too, only *once*". Grief at life's transience seems to submerge everything else until it is relieved by the final challenging question: "But this . . . having been *once* on earth—can it ever be cancelled?"

Here Rilke takes the opposite to the dionysian point of view according to which everything was revocable. For Dionysus the supreme force was "Life" from which everything sprang and into which everything passed. Whatever is born must pass away, but before passing away it brings forth more life. According to this view the individual does not matter, but only the main current which goes on its way. Indeed the individual fulfils himself precisely by being merged in the whole. Nothing finally has a special validity of its own and there is no place for memory. Against this Rilke puts the consciousness of life's irrevocable character—the fact that we recognize the significance of our "only once". The finite nature of our lives can *never* be "cancelled". The "only once" of life is merely a contingent truth—a 'fact' of existence—but as such cannot be altered or revoked.

We might continue by saying that this is 'history'. But here a qualification is necessary. The pattern of events we call history depends ultimately on the human person acting in freedom and with a sense of responsibility. But as we have noted again and again, the human person, in this sense, is far from conspicuous in the *Elegies*. So we are left with something which is 'historical' in character but depersonalized. There remains, to use the language of *Malte*, only the single "place" or "spot" where existence attains consciousness and things are realized within.

In the last sentence of the stanza a word occurs which sums up the whole pathos of Rilke's message. Our existence takes place "on *earth*". This foreshadows the great invocation to the "Earth" at the end of the *Elegy*. What is 'earthly' is the same as "all this that's here". And for Man, who dwells in the 'here and now' this constitutes his mission and justifies his "being here".

II

And so we keep pressing on and trying to perform it,
trying to contain it within our simple hands,
in the more and more crowded gaze, in the speechless heart.
Trying to become it. To give it to whom? We'd rather
hold on to it all for ever. . .   [17–21]

We cannot help feeling that we have a task to perform. We want to do justice to it and to fulfil this infinitely important thing which depends on us. But how can we set about it? By

striving to 'excel'—the word runs implicitly through the whole
stanza—even if this means no more than excelling in ordinary
everyday actions and feelings.

The way in which we "press on" in our attempts to "perform"
our earthly task is suggested three times. We try to "contain"
it, i.e. make it our own, first "within our simple hands", then
"in the more and more crowded gaze" and finally "in the speechless heart". We are most dexterous with our hands, for they can
grasp the tangible form and cling to it. Our "gaze" has a larger
scope: a profusion of shapes rushes into it and "crowds" it more
and more. The "heart", finally, is overwhelmed by infinity and
falls silent.

But even this is not enough, for we even try to "become it".
There is a continual progression here between the ideas of
'containing', 'gazing', 'feeling' and 'becoming'—a movement
towards union through appropriation. And when the 'here and
now' has finally become ours, to whom shall we give it? The
answer is that we would rather have it and 'be' it so completely
that we can "hold on to it all for ever".

The ellipsis following the last word expresses the painful
realization that this is impossible if not foolish. Yet the question
recurs again:

> But into the other relation,—
> what, alas! do we carry across? Not the beholding we've here
> slowly acquired, and no here occurrence. Not one.
> Sufferings, then. Above all, the hardness of life,
> the long experience of love; in fact,
> purely untellable things. [21–26]

The sense of these lines is not immediately apparent. They might
be taken to mean that we can only answer the question of what
is really important in life by making it refer to the final experience of death. What can we take over into that "other
relation"? The "other relation" means the realm of the ultimate and the essential. What can still retain a meaning over
there? The answer would be: "Not the beholding we've here
slowly acquired",—i.e. the correct way of seeing things—because the things themselves disappear in death. Nor can we
take across any "occurrence" from here either, for that belongs
to the past. Nor "sufferings", nor "the hardness of life", nor the

"long experience of love", for these things are all "untellable" and cannot be expressed. In other words, we can take nothing at all with us.

But, if we take the above passage together with the one that follows, it seems more correct to interpret the lines differently. If we ask someone what he would like to take with him after death he does not think of "the beholding" or seeing, that faculty by which man discriminates among the shapes which surround him. Nor does he think of the "occurrence" here, i.e. the events of life, the day to day encounters, actions, tasks, etc., although all these form the real substance of his existence. He would not consider any of them important enough to be taken across. The only important thing is something which stands out in life and makes an impact on it—the "sufferings", the "hard-ness", the "long experience of love", in short, the "purely un-tellable things". "Untellable" here means much the same as 'unusual' or 'extraordinary'.

Such is our opinion. But it is an error. It is not the 'extra-ordinary' which is important, but something else.

> But later,
> under the stars, what use? the more deeply untellable stars?
> [26–27]

"Later", with an absolute lateness beyond that decisive final point against which everything that is *relatively* 'earlier' or 'later' must be measured, after death, in fact—and "under the stars", when we have quitted our earthly sphere,—the things we now hold to be important will prove to be quite trivial. "Under the stars" does not mean 'beneath' them on earth, but *amidst* them in the cosmos. This is the spacial form of the "other relation", just as the "later" is its temporal form. Here again the stellar space referred to should not be confused with the sky which we see at night. The latter is astronomical space, whereas the former is the "other" space of the constellations. The stars in it are those of mythical tales, like that of Andromeda trans-figured.

In this realm the "more deeply untellable things" are in their proper element. They have a quality which would really make us rapt and speechless. Hence it would be foolish to try to take *our* 'untellable' things there.

Now there follows an image which is every bit as strange and vivid as the "smile of a wind" with which the laurel was compared. This image also stirs the imagination and touches our feelings:

Yet the wanderer too doesn't bring from mountain to valley
a handful of earth, of for all untellable earth, but only
a word he has won, pure, the yellow and blue
gentian.   [28–31]

"The wanderer" who returns from the mountains and wants to carry back some precious rarity to his friends in the valley does not usually take a mere "handful of earth". He might discover a delicate plant sprouting from soil in the fissure of a rock and this soil would seem very precious at the time. But if he took it home to his friends they would not regard it as any rarer than the earth in their fields. Admittedly the earth is "for all un-tellable"—a mysterious and vital source of life—but we only appreciate its value when it is scarce. So the wanderer is expected to bring back something which is unknown in the valley —in fact a "word he has won". This means something that has impressed his mind, filled his heart and has been finally expressed in language. The "word" constitutes the most elementary human 'achievement' in Rilke's sense and is the opposite of what was previously called the "speechless heart", for the word is spoken precisely by the voice of the heart. But it can only express what is "tellable"—the simple thing or event. And the word must be "pure", that is, clear and free from dross or adulteration.

The content of such a word may perhaps be a "gentian" which the wanderer has found. But this does not mean that he should *describe* the "yellow and blue gentian" to people. He must *bring* it. The word which is "pure" and has been really "won" does not merely refer to the thing. It *is* the thing itself. If the wanderer says "Look, I have found some gentian" and shows the blue and yellow flower in his hand at the same time, then the words in his mouth and the gentian in his hand are one and the same thing. But this is only if he has really *seen* the flower and if it has really stirred his heart and soul. Then the word is no longer a mere name. Rilke here revives the old magical unity between word and thing.

Are we, perhaps, *here* just for saying: House,
Bridge, Fountain, Gate, Jug, Fruit tree, Window,—
possibly: Pillar, Tower? . . . but for *saying*, remember,
oh, for such saying as never the things themselves
hoped so intensely to be.   [31–35]

We are not here to experience anything extraordinary or
unusual. If we did it would simply run through our "simple
hands" or "crowd our gaze" and make the heart "speechless".
On the contrary we are here to experience the things that can
be really "contained", seen and therefore "said" or told about.

There follows now a remarkable list of such "tellable" things
which we can "say". First of all those things which can be taken
for granted from "House" to "Window". Next those of larger
dimensions like "Pillar" and "Tower". In each case the bare
word stands alone without an article giving a maximum intensity of meaning. The list does not continue any further and it
seems that we are intended to be satisfied with it as it stands.
Apparently only the day to day things are accorded to us for
the "saying". But these things, which are finite and earthly and
have clear-cut relations with one another, must be "said" or
"told" with such *in*tensity as to give them parity with the *ex*-
tensive grandeur of the rare phenomena of life. In this way a
thing may assume an intensity of meaning which it could never
have attained alone. As soon as the "pure" word is spoken the
things imagine that they now 'are' for the first time. This does
not mean merely a natural external existence, but existence in
the sense of being "inward" or "intimate". From Rilke's point
of view the question of whether the laurel has feelings and
consciousness which was posed above must be answered in the
affirmative. For him all things are alive and capable of knowing
and feeling. More than that—they can communicate with
Man's heart and in the process of being made 'inward' they
attain the fullness of conscious Being. This idea is complementary to what was said in the *First* and *Second Elegies* about the
dimension of depth which man's soul can give to things. This
is possible because there is, beneath the superficial divisions of
our world, an inner realm of "deep Being" where all things are
united.

Here at last an idea is developed which we have often encountered before, namely the 'Becoming' of the real world

within the human heart. In his letter to Ilse Jahr, already quoted,[1] Rilke describes how, in order to reach the right relationship with God, he tried first to make contact with people, but above all "*things* which were the real confidants of my early childhood". He wrote in a similar strain "To a Young Girl" with reference to *Malte*: "For these things (as he often said in our few intimate conversations), whose essential life you wish to reproduce, first of all ask *you*: 'Are you free? Are you ready to devote all your love to me? To share a bed with me as *Saint Julien l'hospitalier* shared a bed with the leper, in that ultimate embrace which can never be fulfilled in the ordinary fleeting love of one's neighbours, but which is motivated by *Love*, the whole of *Love*, all the *Love* which exists on earth?' And if such a thing (so Malte told me) sees you occupied, even with a fraction of your interest, then it will close itself up to you. It may bestow on you a word of precept, or make you a slight sign of friendship, but it will refuse to give you its heart, to entrust itself to you with patience and that starlike constancy which brings it so close to the constellations of the heavens. If a thing is to speak to you, you must accept it for a time as the *only* thing which exists, as the one and only phenomenon which, thanks to your diligent and exclusive love, finds itself in the centre of the universe, where the angels serve it every day in that incomparable place. What you read here, my young friend, is a chapter from those lessons which I received from Malte, my only friend in the course of so many years full of suffering and temptations." If what Rilke demands actually takes place man will receive the "thing" into his innermost being and, so he claims, bring about that transformation which is discussed a little later— the transition into "invisibility". At the same time, as is proclaimed in one of the *Sonnets*,[2] the thing on which he has bestowed his interest will also lead man into a deeper fruitful realm.

It is this 'inward' transforming process which decides what we can "take across" into the "other relation". Here once more a fragment of Christian belief seems to have been translated into secular terms: the creation of a new world by the spirit of God which created the first, the birth of a new man, a new Heaven and a new Earth through the fervent heart of the

[1] See above, p. 240.   [2] *Sonnets to Orpheus*, II. xiv.

believing Christian.[1] This idea—consciously or unconsciously, directly or indirectly—seems to lie at the bottom of Rilke's view of things. Since he was born a Catholic it is not surprising that Biblical concepts should have gone on influencing his work, even after he had, as he emphasized so strongly," withdrawn more and more passionately from Christianity". But as he "withdrew" he incorporated the Christian concepts into myth —a process which is continually going on in the development of Western thought. He took away their real meaning and secularized them, giving everything, which he accused the Church of having "sold out into the Hereafter", back to the Earth.

At first sight this might seem to be a gain. The Christian revelation is done away with and the world seems to have acquired a new dimension which it did not possess in ancient times, namely that of 'inwardness'. But in the long run we cannot retain the ray of light and do away with the star which sends it forth. We cannot preserve the goodness of the heart without the heart itself. For a time the light will go on shining and the rays of warmth will still radiate; but as soon as our link with the source is finally severed the power which issues from the source disappears as well.

The foregoing remarks will probably not meet with general agreement. They may be misinterpreted as an attempt to demonstrate the Christian foundation of Rilke's work and thus to belittle the originality of his message. But what is claimed here is that there is still no such thing as a completely independent non-Christian man in the West. For even the most radical anti-Christian—and Rilke described himself as such in the letter to the Princess of Thurn and Taxis already quoted—still stands in some sort of relationship, even if it is an antithetical one, to Christianity. We have not made any attempt at all to claim Rilke as a Christian poet or thinker. He belongs to the line of writers who proclaim a message of finite and autonomous reality, and we have already suggested the sort of problems which faced him when he came to clarify his views on God. We have also referred to the dissatisfaction which any clear thinking reader must feel at the repeated appearance of Biblical figures and even of Christ in Rilke's poetry. But the capacity of

[1] *Gen.* i, 2; *Rom.* viii, 16–26 and *Rev.* xxi and xxii.

man's mind is very large and one of the most important devices which help him to go on living seems to be that of inconsistency.

> Is not the secret purpose
> of this sly Earth, in urging a pair of lovers,
> just to make everything leap with ecstasy in them?
> Threshold: what does it mean
> to a pair of lovers, that they should be wearing their own
> worn threshold a little, they too, after the many before,
> before the many to come, . . . as a matter of course!   [35–41]

The feeling which prompted the "wanderer" to bring back the gentian, the feeling which moves anyone who really sees a thing and tries to seize its inner essence, is also shared by the lovers. The significance of this feeling for the earth is that everything "leaps with ecstasy in them". Love is an experience which makes even the most uncreative person creative, because all things are transformed in the lover's mind. He finds everything anew in the beloved partner and she seems to be looking at him from every thing. In addition the "sly earth" teaches men to love so that the world may attain consciousness of itself through their feelings, and pass from a provisional unreal state into final reality. A new word is used to describe this transition—"ecstasy". The lovers feel "ecstasy" and this quality is transmitted to all the things which cross their path.

The general truth is now followed by a particular example. In the doorway lies the threshold which the lovers cross when they enter their house. How naturally—"as a matter of course" —they seem to "wear" this threshold with their feet, after so many have done the same before them, and with so many others to come after them. This is something of little importance, a minor detail in the insignificant pattern of daily life. And yet it is also something unique which will never happen again. It will never be "cancelled". And since it is across this threshold that the lovers enter into their life-partnership, the threshold itself becomes "inward" and thus qualified to be taken across into the "other relation".

Here the earlier pessimistic picture of Man has given way to a brighter vision. The *Eighth Elegy* stated that the realm of inwardness was a form of that "openness" from which Man was cut off. But the mood of the *Ninth Elegy* is happier: "inwardness" is now granted to Man and hope becomes possible. The very act of experiencing things deeply and expressing them in the "pure" word permits us to find freedom. The urge of this "sly earth" brings about precisely that "movement" into Being which was referred to in the *Eighth Elegy*. But whereas there the movement was common to all creatures *except* Man, here it is precisely man who is entrusted with the "rescue of things".[1] And this is all the more necessary because, as the *Seventh Elegy* laments, everything is becoming deprived of its proper place and content by technical progress. Therefore an appeal has to be made to the heart of man, not his scheming will or reason, to salvage what would be lost without him.

III

This is the beginning of Rilke's answer to the question of "Why?" which was raised at the beginning of the *Elegy*:

> *Here* is the time for the Tellable, *here* is its home.
> Speak and proclaim. [42–43]

Rilke's earth is not like the dionysian universe which streams with an infinite abundance of "life". The "earth" means "Here", this sphere where we accept our trust and fulfil it, where we experience our destiny and endure it, where something finite but unique and irrevocable takes place which decides what can be taken across into the "other relation". The trust which is imposed on Man is to "speak and proclaim". But he can only do so after he has learnt the right way of holding, seeing and feeling the things around him. Then he is qualified to "speak" and "tell" of them.

The words "speak, proclaim" mark the beginning of a short climax, the next stage of which is represented by "praise"[2]— another word which recurs in the *Sonnets to Orpheus*. Speaking, proclaiming and praising are all rising gradations of the "pure" word. Speech is the concern of everyone who has something to say. Proclamation is necessary in critical moments of decision. But "praise" is the task of the poet.

---

[1] See line 64.   [2] See line 52.

                                                   More than ever
things we can live with are falling away, for that
which is oustingly taking their place is an imageless act.
Act under crusts, that will readily split as soon
as the doing within outgrows them and takes a new outline.

                                                          [43-47]

Speech and proclamation are always necessary because they
give a meaning to our "being here". But in our own time they
are particularly necessary, for this is a period of emergency when
things—and here we may anticipate a line which comes later—
"look for rescue through something in us, the most fleeting of
all". The "things" are in danger, for due to technical advances
their *true* shapes have been replaced by others which are arbi-
trary. House, Bridge, Fountain, Gate, Jug, Window, Pillar and
Tower are all things which we can "live", taking them into our
inner heart and hearing the depths of meaning in the words.
But with a machine, so says the *Elegy*, this is not possible. One
may admire its efficiency or be impressed by its power or precision, but this is not the same as the impression we receive of
the "things" listed above. They are fundamental elements of
existence and hence always new and inexhaustible. A machine,
on the other hand, and whatever is made by the machine, is
something artificial. The machine makes us aware of the problem of construction, and once we have understood this problem
it is settled. The older works of man had an inherent importance
and value which they retained under all circumstances. But the
machine is designed and planned for a specific purpose. It
satisfies our sense of function and utility, but when this has been
satisfied it is of no further importance.[1] Why is this so? Because
life in this technological age is an "imageless act".

---

[1] In his letter to von Huléwicz of November 13th 1925 Rilke wrote: "Even
for our grandparents a 'House', a 'Fountain' or a familiar tower, even their very
clothes, their cloaks, meant infinitely more to them and were infinitely more
intimate. Almost everything was a vessel in which they found humanity and to
which they added some of their own. Now there come pouring across from America
empty indifferent things, spurious things, mere *counterfeits* of life. . . . A house in
the American sense, an American apple or vine have *nothing* in common with the
house, the fruit or the vine on which the hopes and meditations of our forefathers
were fixed. . . The things which are animated and experienced by us and which
share our thoughts are entering a decline and can no longer be replaced. *We are
perhaps the last to have known such things.* We bear the responsibility of preserving
not merely their memory (which would be a small and unreliable thing) but also
their human and 'laral' value (laral in the sense of household gods)."

The word "image" can mean much the same as 'picture', 'representation' etc. But the problems of our time suggest another shade of meaning which is more appropriate here. The difference between human culture *before* the incursion of technology and human culture *since* that process began is that in the earlier period "images" still had power. And this power seems to be all the greater the further back we go in time—greater and more mysterious until we reach the period of magic and myth. Those who love and cherish the older culture may often say things which are only of aesthetic or antiquarian interest. But fundamentally they have grasped the essential thing—they feel that formerly there was a power at work which is necessary to life and which has since fallen into decay. This was something 'canonical', not just for taste or thought, but for life itself, the spirit and inner order of things. That is why it is so tragic when an ancient town decays or an old traditional custom is forgotten. For together with these things something else disappears which is hardly to be found at all—or perhaps has not been found *yet*— in the new order of things, namely the "images".

A great deal has been said about this in recent times by psychiatrists and psycho-analysts. The study of dreams has led to the discovery of the part played by images in the unconscious. In myths the psychologists and historians discover those same images which, they maintain, once used to govern men's lives more openly, whereas today they have been obscured or suppressed by our rational consciousness. But what the rationalism of the past regarded as progress is now proving to be a dangerous deviation from the vital conditions of life.

What, then, are the "images"? They are the archetypes of our perception which enable us to introduce order into the manifold universe around us. They are not intended to lead to theoretical knowledge; they simply give us a chance to take our bearings in practice as we live and act. Examples of such images are the Higher and Lower realms (or Heaven and Earth), the Path, the Line, the Spring or Source, etc. These images are man's natural heritage—not as ready-made concepts with fixed meanings—but potentially there and ready to be used as soon as we make our first encounters in the world. The above are the elementary images. But they are the foundations of others which are more complicated and specialized—the fundamental forms of our world, our culture and existence such as occur in the *Elegy*: Fountain, Gate, Window, Pillar, Tower.

These "images" seem to be connected with what Plato called 'ideas'. The latter are the prerequisites of all possible knowledge; the former are the prerequisites of life's fulfilment; they provide the conditions of a rightly ordered life and also give this life its meaning. They provide the means whereby the arch-enemies of life—Chaos, Error and Desolation—are conquered and they also bring the reward of this conquest, namely wisdom. 'Ideas' and 'images' seem in fact to be different aspects of the same thing. Both are emanations of the logos by which God establishes and governs the finite order—through the clarity of consciousness above and from the depth of life within. The ideas enable human thought to perceive truth; without them it would go astray and be deceived. The images are what give life its form, shaping its course through a multitude of events; without the images life would lack content and direction. This explains the peculiar impression of chaos which modern life presents, despite the increasing amount of thought and planning which go into its making. Why is it that an old town, or for that matter a reasonably preserved village, makes such an impression of orderliness, whilst a modern city, with its huge technical and organizational apparatus, still suggests a chaotic disorder which is being contained with great difficulty? The difference does not lie in any temporary inadequacy in the city, such as a still unsolved traffic problem. It lies in the fact that buildings, implements, customs and festivals, patterns of behaviour and religious life have all been deprived of their images which are now lost in the unconscious.

Something of this sort seems to be meant by the reference to the "imageless act" which replaces "things". Previously there was an act *with* images—images which directed and expressed human action. The image united the thing and the word. It held sway deep down in man's soul and in his works outside, so that his heart could be equally at home in the external and the inner world. But now man's industry can only produce "crusts" or veneers—i.e. superficial organizations or structures. These have no original form of their own and as soon as they cease to be held together by the function for which they were designed they "split". This they do "readily", almost 'willingly', as if they did not care. In the old days, when a work created by man fell into disuse, an image of it still survived; it became a ruin, full of history—a form which, for those with eyes to see, still retained its significance even in decay. But when a modern 'technical' structure is discarded what remains is only fit for the scrap-heap, for it was merely a functional "outline"—not an organic expression of life.

The lines which follow provide a counterweight to this threat:

> Between the hammers lives on
> our heart, as between the teeth
> the tongue, which, in spite of all,
> still continues to praise.   [48–51]

Even from the point of view of metre this passage stands out from the rest of the *Elegy*—four short lines in solemn measure, like an inscription on the wall of the poem. They contain two similes which at first seem strange, but these become readily understandable as soon as they are recognized as an antithesis to the menace referred to above. Inside the mouth are the teeth which are hard and capable of crunching and wounding in their bite. Enclosed within is the tongue and one might imagine that this defenceless organ would be destroyed by the teeth. But the tongue survives and is able to utter speech and "praise". Similarly "between the hammers", the hard structures of technical civilization—in the factories and among the machines —our heart continues to beat, unharmed. It is not by chance that the image of the tongue occurs here, for it is the tongue which, in Rilke's terms, shapes the "pure" word of "praise" which springs from the "heart".

Just as the tongue continues to "praise"—"still" and "in spite of all"—so the heart continues to feel, despite the hammers. The heart retains its "inward" or "intimate" quality and still cherishes those things which have survived. The *Elegy* does not say what will happen when the "hammers" have triumphed all over the world—whether a dire fate can be warded off by the discovery of fresh "images". This prospect seems to be at least anticipated in the *Sonnets to Orpheus*.[1]

Sonnets, I. xviii and xxiii; II. x.

IV

Praise this world to the Angel, not the untellable: you
can't impress him with the splendour you've felt; in the cosmos
where he more feelingly feels you're only a novice. So show him
some simple thing, refashioned by age after age,
till it lives in our hands and eyes as a part of ourselves.
Tell him *things*. He'll stand more astonished: as you did
beside the roper in Rome or the potter in Egypt.   [52–58]

The earlier challenge was to "speak and proclaim". Now the
call, for those who hear it, is to "praise this world to the Angel".
Previously the poet was concerned with what would happen
"*under* the stars". Here the Angel who dwells *among* the stars
is invoked.

Men are only concerned with "all this that's here" during
their lifetime; the dead only with the "other relation". At the
point where these two realms intersect stands Orpheus, the seer
and singer who binds both together. But the Angel embraces
the whole universe in his existence; according to the *First Elegy*
Angels are "often unable to tell whether they moved among
living or dead". The Angel is the 'cosmic partner' who is
capable of "feeling" and "achieving" on a universal scale.
Hence the "untellable" things which pass beyond our grasp are
for him the very substance of life. If Man is to praise the world
to the Angel there is no point in his mentioning those things
which are marvellous by human standards. In the 'angelic'
universe all human experience fades away into insignificance.
So he must praise that which is peculiar to the earth—the simple
thing which is passed on through the eyes and the hands from
one generation to the next.

"Tell him *things*". At this point we may recall some late nine-
teenth century painting which shows nothing more than a chair,
a bowl of apples or a flower blooming at a window. This is
different from the traditional 'still life'. Not an 'interior' but
simply a table or a jug; no overflowing abundance of fruit or
flowers but merely a few twigs or a single plant. Here we
experience the "thing" itself and all its mysterious power. The
thing emerges in its individuality and isolation—sometimes to
such an extent that it may appear to be a symbol of poverty.

And it is when he is faced with poverty and loneliness of this sort that man discovers his ultimate resources of strength. It is no coincidence that Rilke should have been an admirer of the poet Francis Jammes who wrote so feelingly about the 'things' of poverty. Man is entitled to speak of these things to the Angel because they belong to his own sphere of responsibility. Indeed Rilke prophesies that the impact of these simple things on him will be so great as to "astonish" the Angel.

Two examples are now given of "things" which struck Rilke himself very forcibly: the "roper" of Rome and the "potter" of Egypt.[1] One has good reason to feel impressed when one first sees a ropemaker at work, knowing that he is practising a craft that will soon die out altogether. As his hands twist together the strands which come off the wheel, we may be reminded of Oknos twisting the rope of life. He is like an "image" which is rooted in history and the depths of the human soul. But how different everything is where the craftsman has been replaced by the factory and the only consideration is output per day. And the potter is no less significant as he shapes the vase or bowl on his twirling wheel: he is like an archetype of human creativeness, reminding us that God once fashioned the human body from the dust of the earth.

It is things of this kind which contain "images" that Man should show to the Angels.

> Show him how happy a thing can be, how guileless and ours;
> how even the moaning of grief purely determines on form,
> serves as a thing, or dies into a thing,—to escape
> to a bliss beyond the fiddle. These things that live on departure
> understand when you praise them: fleeting, they look for
> rescue through something in us, the most fleeting of all.
> Want us to change them entirely, within our invisible hearts,
> into—oh, endlessly—into ourselves! Whosoever we are.   [59–66]

The Angel must be shown the mystery of the thing—the fact that it can be "happy", "guileless and ours". This does not

[1] Compare the letter to Alfred Schaer of February 26th 1924: "But I often ask myself whether the most important influence on my development and creative work was not exerted by something which, in itself, was not outstanding, namely my meeting with a dog; or the hours I spent in Rome looking at a ropemaker as he went through some of the oldest movements the world has known in the practice of his craft. . . . just like that potter in a little Nile village; to stand beside his wheel as he worked was indescribable and in a most mysterious way fruitful for me."

mean an untouched 'thing' in its natural surroundings, for precisely that is *not* ours but, to quote Hölderlin, "wild" or alien to Man. Rilke means rather a thing which has entered into a close relationship with Man: the thing as it is when it has been rightly seen and cherished and has thus become "inward". Not when it is irreverently pressed into service, but when it has been approached with love and respect so that it gains a new freedom. It is then that it finds access to the human heart and becomes properly itself for the first time.

A thing may possess such power in all its simplicity that it can help human "grief" to take on "form" and thus to transcend itself. For the worst aspect of grief is that it has no precise dwelling in a place or a shape. But grief may, if we wish, be changed into a "thing" which "serves". It may be the dish of food given to a poor man or the implement which helps to keep a house in repair. Or grief may "die into a thing" and rise again from it in a new shape—perhaps when a man projects his sadness into his violin and it emerges "beyond" the instrument, i.e. after it has been transformed by it, as music. Then the "grief" is said to be blessed or "blissful" at its liberation through the thing.

Things "live on departure", that is, they live on the very stuff of transience and for this reason they turn to Man. And we are even more "fleeting" than things because we are aware of our transient state. Despite this, or perhaps because of it, they hope for "rescue" through us.

This "rescue" takes place when we understand things, loving and "praising" them. The *Elegy*'s clearest description of this process is that we "change them entirely, within our invisible hearts".

External things are visible and present in a solid shape. Each is separated from the other according to its position in time and space, and one shape excludes the other. "Invisibility" on the other hand is the dimension of the heart, the realm of feeling, though this 'feeling' is spiritual rather than sentimental.[1] The "heart" is that part of the spirit which is near to the blood. It is the "inward" realm of the spirit whereas the reason and the understanding are its heights and breadths. In this inward

[1] Rilke thus belongs to the same tradition of the "philosophy of the heart" as St. Augustine, St. Francis, Dante, Pascal and, later, J. Joubert and Max Scheler.

realm there is no longer any division of things. Although the
things retain their shape and order, their manifold diversity is
"changed" or transformed into a simple unity.

Rilke regards this "change" or transformation not merely as
something in the mind but as having objective reality. As soon
as we receive a thing into our hearts with love and understanding he asserts that it is really transposed into another form
of being. A new form then takes shape in the world which is
nor merely thought or felt but real. The following passage from
Rilke's letter to von Huléwicz makes this clear: "So we must
not only refrain from debasing and depreciating everything
here, but, precisely because of the provisional character which
they share with us, we must grasp these phenomena and things
with our innermost understanding and transform them. Transform? Yes, for it is our task to imprint the mark of this provisional perishable earth so deeply, so painfully and passionately
on ourselves that its essence may rise up again in us 'invisibly'.
. . . The 'Elegies' show us at this work, the work of constantly
transforming the beloved visible and tangible things into the
invisible vibration and excitement of our nature, which will
introduce new frequencies into the vibrations of the universe.
. . . The earth has no other refuge except by becoming invisible:
in us, who partake of the invisible with a portion of our being,
or at least have share certificates in it and can increase our
holding of invisibility during our stay here—*in* us alone can
this intimate and lasting transformation of the visible into the
invisible take place—into a state which no longer depends on
being seen and touched, just as our own destiny is constantly
becoming *both more actual and invisible* within us. The *Elegies* set
up this norm of existence. They are an assurance, indeed a
celebration of this awareness. . . . All the worlds of the universe
plunge into the invisible realm as this is the next depth of reality.
*There are some stars which increase immediately and then fade away in
the infinite consciousness of the Angels—, others are dependent on creatures
which transform them slowly and laboriously, and in whose fears and
delights they attain their nearest invisible realization. We are,* let it be
emphasized once more, *in the sense of the Elegies, we are these trans-
formers of the Earth; our whole existence, the flights and falls of our love
—everything qualifies us for this task* (beside which no other is
worthy of the name)."

The emphasis with which Rilke expresses himself here shows beyond all doubt that he is not concerned with mere feelings but with serious affirmations of truth. He refers to a first "provisional" world—that of "visible" reality or a reality which can be grasped by the senses. This reality has to be taken up into the "invisible", i.e. the spiritual sphere of the heart, through our right perception and attentive love. This produces not merely conceptual ideas or a sense of values but something that is "more actual"—more real and at the same time "invisible" or 'inward' and spiritual. It is only then that the 'real' world—in the true sense of the word—takes shape. According to the purity of its inner state and the degree of strength it possesses, every living being participates in the evolution of this world. Indeed, this process of 'Becoming' is the true content of human existence, in the life of the individual as in history; this is our "task, beside which no other is worthy of the name".

So the world is constantly passing out of its provisional visible state into final and *in*visible Being—a view which seems to be a strange compound of the Pauline and Johannine message of a new Creation, the pantheistic and idealistic concept of a third phase in the universal process, and magical ideas about the spirit's transforming power. The latter throw new light on the figure of the Angel. The section from the letter quoted above shows him to be still active in the work of transformation; the sentences which preceded this passage define his nature in the following terms: "The Angel of the *Elegies* is that being in which the transformation of the visible into the invisible, which we carry out, already seems to be completed. To the Angel of the *Elegies* all the towers and palaces of the past are existent *because* they have long been invisible; whereas the towers and bridges of our world are *already* invisible although they are still solid and lasting in our eyes. The Angel of the *Elegies* is that being who guarantees the recognition of a higher degree of reality in the invisible world."

The last line of the stanza contains a cry of joy—"oh, endlessly—into ourselves!" The meaning is similar to that of line 16 in the *Eighth Elegy* where flowers "endlessly open into" pure space. What mysterious creatures we men are, in whom this is to take place—all of us, "whosoever we are".

V

Earth, is it not just this that you want: to arise
invisibly in us? Is not your dream
to be one day invisible? Earth! invisible!
What is your urgent command, if not transformation?

[67–70]

The final stanza is the culmination of all those that precede
it. The Earth wants "to arise invisibly in us": this is her will, her
"dream" and her "urgent command". Three times the word
"invisible" occurs—interrupted by tremulous questions and
exclamations but linked together by the words "want", "dream"
and "command".

At last the question which was raised at the beginning of the
Elegy is answered. The short "span of life", filled with a yearning for, and a fear *of* destiny, offers us an opportunity to fulfil
the command of the Earth. We can receive the Earth into our
hearts so that she may "arise invisibly" within us.

Earth, you darling, I will! Oh, believe me, you need
no more of your spring-times to win me over: a single one,
ah, one, is already more than my blood can endure.
Beyond all names I am yours, and have been for ages.
You were always right, and your holiest inspiration
is Death, that friendly Death.

[71–76]

These words are the deepest expression of Rilke's piety, his faith
and his ready acceptance of the "command". There is a significant heartfelt note running through the lines. They are like an
intimate dialogue, coloured with tenderness in the words
"Earth, you darling, I will". This mood becomes a shade more
intense in Rilke's *Sonnet* on Spring[1], and it is significant that
Spring is also mentioned here in his tribute to the Earth. But
here the "spring-time" is incidental to the inward acceptance
of the finite world which follows. The final decision to accept
the Earth is "beyond all names"—that is, so serious that no
words would be adequate to describe it. This 'namelessness'
suggests a religious solemnity of purpose just as the declaration

---

[1] *Sonnets to Orpheus*, I. xxi.

"have been for ages" suggests a hard-won religious conviction. It is as if all the earlier insecurity and distress had now been left behind. The sense of homelessness has given place to a feeling of protection. All is now well: "You were always right."

In his acceptance of the Earth and everything in it as "right" Rilke also tries to accommodate the most formidable thing of all—Death. "Friendly Death" is granted a place in the 'inward' realm as the Earth's "holiest inspiration". Here Rilke tries to deal with the same problem as Nietzsche in his doctrine of the 'eternal return'. He does it by turning his most vulnerable spot into a strong point from which further conquest becomes possible. It may be left to the reader to decide whether Death can be overcome by adopting the attitude described here, and whether the words of the *Elegy* correspond to the true reality of Death in human existence.

> Look, I am living. On what? Neither childhood nor future
> are growing less. . . . . Supernumerous existence
> wells up in my heart.   [77–79]

The last lines express a serene acceptance of the present. "Look, I am living". It is as simple as that. Life remains transient as before. Childhood is past. The future is still to come. We glide imperceptibly through the present. But everything has been transformed from temporality into "deep Being". Neither past nor present is "growing less".

The sort of existence described here which "wells up in the heart" is called "supernumerous".[1] It is finite by nature, as before and yet it transcends the normal measure of human life. The infinite, the eternal and the absolute, which were renounced for the sake of the Earth, return again as the inner qualities of this new transformed existence. But this transformation is only possible through an acceptance of the Earth which has existed "for ages" and is "beyond all names". The *acceptance* is, as it were, the 'mystery' in Rilke's religion. According to his message, Man's new vision can only emerge when he has renounced any personal relationship to God the Almighty and any hope of eternal life rooted in His love. Yet we cannot help asking ourselves the same question as we do when faced with Nietzsche's

---

[1] Compare the reference to the "silent supernumerous nature of their appearance" in *An Experience* (quoted above, p. 214).

proclamation of the Superman. Supposing that we omit from Rilke's vision everything which derives from the Christian message of the New Man, the New Heaven and the New Earth which will come through the power of the Holy Spirit—in that case what is left?

THE TENTH ELEGY

Composed on February 11th 1922 at Muzot; the first
twelve lines written at Duino in 1912

I

THE reader may approach the last *Duino Elegy* in the anticipation that it will finally knit together the various themes which
have emerged in the nine *Elegies* which precede it; one might
now expect the tensions which have arisen between heart and
mind to be resolved and all discords to be merged in a single
tremendous harmony.

These hopes are justified by the poet himself who held the
Tenth Elegy in particularly high esteem. In one of the letters
which he sent in Spring 1922 to announce the successful completion of his work Rilke wrote to Lou Andreas-Salomé: "Lou,
dear Lou, at this moment of Saturday, February 11th, at six
o'clock, I lay down my pen after writing the last completed
Elegy, the *Tenth*: the one (even then it was destined to be the
last) with the opening which I wrote at Duino—'Some day,
emerging at last out of this fell insight, may I lift up jubilant
praise to assenting Angels! . . .' I read what there was of it to
you then, but in fact only the first twelve lines have remained;
the rest is all new and, yes, very very very beautiful!"

This is no small praise. And yet we cannot help being a little
surprised when we come to read the *Tenth Elegy*. Not at the
ideas which it contains, which are significant enough. Nor at
the use of strange and even scurrilous images, for this feature
of Rilke's style is already familiar to us from other *Elegies*,
especially the *Fifth*.[1] Nor do we find anything strange in the
sombre tones of the poem. For here, at the conclusion, it is
from the realm of Death that the colours and sounds must
emerge in full strength. The elegiac form proclaims the passing

---

[1] The strange affinity between the *Fifth* and the *Tenth Elegies* is a structural
feature of the whole work. Both *Elegies* convey the tragic nature of life by means
of strangely artificial but very effective images.

away of all things and it moves us all the more deeply when we
are aware of the abundance and beauty of life. An elegy is a
song about life's transience, but of a kind which helps us to
pass beyond mere grief to an affirmation of life. Here in the
Tenth Elegy the note of lament at life's transience is very
audible although it is finally absorbed by a chord of affirmation
which seems to swell up from great depths.

In my view what really disturbs the reader is something that
is inherent in the poetry itself. The *Elegies* often make use of
abstraction as a means of achieving intensity and compression
of style. As was pointed out before, the concise generalized
concepts often take on a peculiar life of their own. They have
an almost mythical character when they assume autonomous
power in this way. But here in the *Tenth Elegy*, where the power
of the abstractions should be shown at its greatest, they do not
seem to be equal to their task.

II

Some day, emerging at last out of this fell insight,
   may I lift up jubilant praise to assenting Angels!   [1–2]

The two opening lines of the *Elegy* are the beginning of a
fervent prayer or invocation. The poet begs Destiny to permit
him to complete his task and summons his own heart to find
the necessary strength. The prayer is punctuated by the key-
word "may" which occurs four times. Then, after a brief pause
for reflection, the exclamation "Why" (line 8) ushers in the
lament which follows.

The poet asks that he may be allowed "some day" to "lift
up jubilant praise"—i.e. jubilation at the life he has lived and
praise for the fulfilment he has experienced. This final hymn
of praise will also be addressed to the Angels who are the
recipients of all Rilke's deeper pronouncements on life in the
Elegies. Now, however, the Angels will do something which
they never did during life: they will "assent"—confirm that
life's test has been passed and the fulfilment realized.

The word 'Death' is not used. In its place we read "emerging
. . . . . out of this fell insight". The whole of the poet's life is
here considered as an "insight" or vision of what existence

really means. And this vision is terrifying or "fell" because it leaves no detail veiled or obscured and reveals final reality. There is a note of uncompromising commitment running through the whole of this first sentence.

> May not one of the clear-struck keys of the heart
> fail to respond through alighting on slack or doubtful
> or rending strings! [3–5]

There is, however, one danger which threatens the successful completion of the poet's task. This is described in an image which is borrowed from the piano, the keys of which are each linked to a hammer. When a key is struck the hammer hits the appropriate string. Just as the note produced depends on the quality and tension of the string so it is with the heart. And the purpose of this adjuration is to ensure that every awakening feeling, every attitude of mind may strike strings in the poet's heart which are taut, reliable and perfectly in tune.

Again, however, we notice one of those peculiar shifts of style, which Rilke often employs to give his images an added subtlety. The word "clear" refers to the striking of the keys rather than the resounding of the strings: the keys shall be "struck" clearly by fingers which are strong and assured. Furthermore, their striking action shall not be spoilt by the impact of the hammers on strings which are badly tuned or of poor quality. In other words, Death, the last event of all, must be intense and powerful in its finality.

> May a brighter radiance stream from
> my streaming face! May inconspicuous Weeping
> flower! [5–7]

Yet another elusive image. The emphasis here is on *how* the tears are wept and what happens to the person's face as he is weeping. Tears could make his face blind or contorted or perhaps shapeless; *or* the face might attain its maximum expressive power and thus assume a "brighter radiance". It is significant that 'tears' as such are not mentioned but only a face which becomes "streaming". The "inconspicuous Weeping" seems to mean the weeping of ordinary experience which does not belong to the climaxes of life and has therefore no special significance. The poet asks that this weeping may now "flower", that is, take on fresh beauty by revealing its true meaning.

In these introductory lines the elegiac mood develops gradually. Later in the poem it becomes more and more pronounced as we encounter the "Laments", the "Land of Pain", the "Trees of Tears" and the "fields of flowering Sadness".

III

> How dear you will be to me then, you Nights
> of Affliction!   [7–8]

When the poet's prayer for fulfilment has been answered all the sufferings of the past—symbolized here by the "Nights of Affliction"—will be shown in their true meaning.

> Why did I not, inconsolable sisters,
> more kneelingly welcome you, more loosenedly render
> myself to your loosened hair?   [8–10]

The sufferings of life, when viewed from the vantage-point of someone who is steadfast in death, will prove to have been significant and valuable. Awareness of this fact makes the poet realize how little he has turned his sufferings to account. The "inconsolable sisters" here are the same as the "Nights of Affliction", but now personified. This is the first result of that mythologizing process which later produces the clearly personified forms of life's sufferings in the "Laments". They are "sisters" because each night is like the others and together they form a relationship of suffering in time. They are called "inconsolable", not because their suffering is too great for consolation, but because they actually consist of suffering. They do more than simply *express* suffering which has been endured; they *are* themselves embodiments of suffering. They are mythical in character, and therefore in themselves devoid of psychological meaning. They can only assume such a meaning in Man, when he takes them into his life. Each hour of pain signifies the approach of such a being as this. It is then man's task to "welcome" her in a manner befitting a 'mystery', that is, "kneeling" in a posture of prayer.[1] The "loosened hair" of the sisters symbolizes the grief which man accepts.

> We wasters of sorrows!
> How we stare away into sad endurance beyond them,
> trying to foresee their end!　　　　　　　　[10–12]

The mood of repentance becomes still deeper. We men are "wasters of sorrows", for we are blind to the precious possibilities which they contain. We imagine that our sorrows are something unreal and extraneous to life and we hold nothing higher than happiness. So we cast our sorrows away.

We are not prepared to accept the sorrows of life, but "stare away beyond them", looking into the "sad endurance" and estimating how long they will last. But it is this very attitude which makes everything seem so "sad" and miserable. To put the matter more clearly—the sorrows themselves *are* the basic pattern of existence and our very concern about their probable duration is something sad and lamentable. We regard them as entirely negative and therefore approach them with the preconceived purpose of "trying to foresee their end" which we hope will come as soon as possible.

> Whereas they are nothing else
> than our winter foliage, our sombre evergreen, *one*
> of the seasons of our interior year,—not only
> season—they're also place, settlement, camp, soil, dwelling.
> 　　　　　　　　[12–15]

We should recognize that "sorrows" are only the dark side of the reality which man calls the world, the other, brighter side being "joy". And in fact—here the message of the *Tenth Elegy* may be said to begin—"sorrows" are more real than "joy". For the basic stratum, the essential foundation of life, consists of suffering.

In reading these lines our conscience must be on the alert, for if the meaning of suffering is revealed anywhere it is in the Christian religion. Here suffering and sorrow are accepted and lived out to their final conclusion in the very heart of God. But Christianity also says that our normal sufferings are *not* neces-

---

[1] The "inconsolable sisters" seem to owe something to the female figures of ancient cults who represent mourning.

sary and do not form part of the essential ground of existence. There is no such thing as that pain which is later called "Primal", in the sense that it forms the substance of existence. This would make pain an inescapable necessity of life and would deprive it of its ultimate meaning. Suffering is significant as something which exists, but not 'of necessity'. It springs from the action, not from the essence of life. Once it has taken shape, then certainly it penetrates to the very roots. Its significance is thus not unlike that of Death.

But if we look back at the *Elegy* we shall see how a whole series of images expresses this single idea: that suffering is not something which we can get rid of but an essential part of human existence which gives our life its final meaning.

Sorrows are described as "our winter foliage". Joy may be the bloom of life but it only lasts a short time and is therefore unreal. But sorrows, like the leaves of the magnolia or the laurel, last the whole year through on our trees. They are our "sombre evergreen" and represent "one of the seasons of our interior year". This is the inner year of the changes in human life, already referred to in the *Fourth Elegy*, which exists quite apart from the 'external' year with seasons which depend on the sun. The "winter foliage" of our sorrows is a permanent feature in the Summer and Winter of our interior year. In fact it is never 'out of' season.

Finally the image discloses another layer of meaning. The sorrows are "not only season"—not merely a part of the passage of time. They are rather a permanent place where Man must dwell. Here, as often happens in the *Elegies*, there follows a series of words, each of which stands by itself but also serves to heighten the meaning of the word preceding it. The sorrows are called "place, settlement, camp, soil, dwelling". They are the fixed place where the wanderer has settled, the camp where he sleeps, the soil from which fruit grows, and the dwelling where he establishes his life in its lasting shape.

IV

Now we come to the first of a succession of realms or spheres which are described one after another in the *Elegy*. The road which passes through these realms could lead men away from the unreal to the real, but few go this way.

The first realm is one which should by rights remind us of essential values and the deepest truths. In fact, however, it does the exact opposite.

> Strange, though, alas! are the streets of the City of Pain,
> where, in the pseudo-silence of drowned commotion,
> loudly swaggers the casting cast from vacuity's
> mould: the begilded ado, the bursting memorial.   [16–19]

We shall understand the significance of this passage as soon as we realize that it is a description of a graveyard—the place which is concerned with the ultimate sorrow of Death. The "City of Pain" is a necropolis. In order to appreciate the vehemence of the imagery we must bear in mind those burial-places of Southern Europe which really do resemble towns, with their high enclosing walls, their tombs like houses, streets, etc. They make an impression of pomp which seems very strange to anyone coming from the North.

This "City of Pain" is not designed to reconcile men's minds to suffering. It is "strange" and makes no appeal to the heart. It is true that there is a "silence" here, but it is a "pseudo-silence" made of "commotion". It is not the silence of a place where the dead can speak to the living. It is a "drowned commotion"—i.e. the purely negative stillness of a graveyard in contrast to the excessive noise elsewhere; this silence is no more than the *absence* of the uproar and noise of traffic outside—a mere emptiness or vacuity.

Here there "swaggers the casting cast from vacuity's mould". The shape of a casting is always the exact counterpart of an empty shell or mould into which molten metal has been poured. In exactly the same way the false empty "silence" of the church-yard produces a false shape—the "begilded ado" of the "bursting memorial". In reading this description we must visualize the degree of ugliness and tastelessness which gilt allegorical figures and embellishments in graveyards sometimes attain.

> How an Angel would trample it down beyond trace, their market
>   of comfort,
> with the church alongside, bought ready for use: as clean
> and disenchanted and shut as the Post on a Sunday!   [20–22]

The "silence" and the religious figures are intended to have a consoling effect. But this view of Death is cheap and spurious,[1] quite apart from the fact that, according to Rilke, Man should not seek consolation in the face of Death but should rather yield himself up to its power. The whole graveyard therefore appears as a "market of comfort" and the same is true of the "church alongside". The church is "bought ready for use", for its message is not rooted in experience but has been purchased ready-made according to a preconceived plan. It is "clean and disenchanted and shut as the Post on a Sunday"—clean, like everything in the churchyard, but closed so that one cannot go inside. And even if one could enter the church one would find it empty. So it is "disenchanted", which means here 'disenchanting' to the visitor as well—like a post-office on Sunday which is not open for business.

The bitter tone of this description will not come as a surprise if we glance at the letter which Rilke wrote on December 17th 1912 to the Princess of Thurn und Taxis: "Furthermore you must know, Princess, that since Cordoba I have been almost rabidly anti-Christian. I am reading the Koran which in places has a tone in which I am as completely at home as the wind in the organ-pipe. Here you think you are in a Christian country—well, here too that has been overcome a long time ago. It *was* Christian as long as people had enough courage to kill somebody a hundred paces outside the town; so innumerable, unpretentious stone crosses sprang up bearing the simple inscription 'Here died so and so'—that was the version of Christianity here. But now there is a boundless indifference here—empty churches, forgotten churches, chapels that are starving—really one should no longer sit down at this table that has been eaten bare and pretend that the finger-bowls which are still lying around contain food. The fruit is sucked dry and now, speaking crudely, there is nothing more to be done but spit out the rind. And yet the Protestants and American Christians still make a weak infusion with these used tea-leaves which have been drawing for two thousand years. The next to come was in any case Mahomet: like a river through a primeval mountain he breaks his way through to the one God who can

---

[1] We are reminded of Madame Lamort in the *Fifth Elegy* where a false death directs the equally spurious lives of men.

be invoked famously every morning without the aid of the telephone called 'Christ', into which people constantly shout 'Hello' the whole time without getting a reply." This was Rilke's view in December 1912. He expressed himself less vehemently later but his basic position remained unaltered. It finds expression again in his letter to Witold von Huléwicz and in two letters on 'God', the first of which was written to L.H. on November 8th 1915 and the second which he attributed to a "Young Workman".[1]

The same attitude also underlies the above passage of the *Tenth Elegy*. It is no coincidence that Rilke told von Huléwicz that his Angel, who here "tramples it down beyond trace, their market of comfort", was nearer to the Angel of Islam than the Angel of Christianity.

V

Mention has already been made of the different realms through which Man might find his way to reality. The first was that of Death, which assumed the spurious form of the burial-ground. Now we come to the second:

Outside, though, there's always the billowing edge of the fair.

[23]

The "fair" represents the larger life in which modern man exists. Its "edge" is always "billowing" outside, as if it were some shifting incalculable element which always changes its shape—the opposite counterpart of sorrow which is the genuine permanent component of life.

A certain affinity between the images of the *Tenth Elegy* and the *Fifth* has already been pointed out. First there was the "bursting memorial". Now the "billowing edge of the fair" seems to suggest the restless tentacles of town life which can be felt even round the walls of the graveyard.

The things which are on display in this "fair" are part of daily life. The exhibits which absorb people's attention are like ghostly side-shows intended to amuse a public which does not notice that it is being entertained at its own expense.

---

[1] See "The Young Workman's Letter" in Rilke, *Selected Works*, Vol. I, pp. 67–77.

Swings of Freedom! Divers and Jugglers of Zeal!
And the figured shooting-range of bedizened Happiness: targets
tumbling in tinny contortions whenever some better shot
happens to hit one.   [24–27]

"Freedom" here becomes the wild up and down movement of
the fairground "swings". "Zeal"—the seriousness with which
social and business transactions are carried out—is the work
of "divers and jugglers". "Happiness" is like a shooting booth
where the success of every venture depends on hitting or missing
a target. This is a limited bourgeois idea of happiness where
"targets" are always "tumbling" and there are objects to be
shot at everywhere—crocks, wheels studded with clay pipes,
dancing dolls, etc. So everywhere men seek their advantage.
Whenever "some better shot" hits the target it "tumbles in
tinny contortions" and a clown jumps up to ring a bell.

> Cheer-struck, on he goes reeling
> after his luck. For booths that can please
> the most curious tastes are drumming and bawling.   [27–29]

"He" is presumably the "better shot" of the previous line—
unless the pronoun refers to any typical visitor at a fairground.
He has caused a sensation by his success. Stupefied by his good
fortune he now "reels on after his luck". "Cheer-struck" he
wins fresh successes, but these are no more satisfying than the
first. It is all part of a dream through which he staggers on his
way. We are reminded again of the *Fifth Elegy* which describes
another activity which is just as unsubstantial—the restless
mechanical movements of the acrobats. On the surface this
might seem quite different from the reeling marksmen at the
shooting booth since the acrobats had at least mastered the
perfect precision of movement on which their lives depended.
But at bottom both activities are similar. Both are illusory and
empty—driven on by some anonymous power, whether we
call it "Will", "Luck" or "Fortune". The "better shot" and
the "acrobat" are each products of the same depersonalization
which runs through the *Elegies*. The "luck" offered in these
fair-booths which "can please the most curious tastes" consists
of the many opportunities for sensation and success in real life.
And all are spurious—deceptions which "drum and bawl".

One thing in particular is displayed here for admiration—
money and how it is made:

>   Especially
> worth seeing (for adults only): the breeding of Money!
> Anatomy made amusing! Money's organs on view!
> Nothing concealed! Instructive, and guaranteed
> to increase fertility! . . . . . .   [29–33]

The bitter scurrilous character of this image could hardly be
excelled. There are booths in every fair bearing a notice "for
Adults Only", where sex is put on show with a pseudo-scientific
veneer. But the thing that emerges in the image of sex is money.
Money is shown as "Anatomy made amusing . . . . instructive".
The false 'scientific' pretences of the side-show also describe the
equally false seriousness which men apply to the acquisition of
wealth. "Money's organs on view! Nothing concealed! . . . . .
guaranteed to increase fertility!"—perhaps there is also an
allusion here to those institutions where the 'breeding' of
money takes place, namely the stock exchanges. No doubt there
is a real connection between the money and sex which is rooted
in experience. It is not by chance that words which are often
used of money, such as 'passion' or 'lust', also have a sexual
meaning. And it is significant that in the extreme form of
avarice the cold lifeless lure of money replaces the vital human
impulses.

Some perseverance is required to interpret the foregoing
eighteen lines. But the whole of the *Tenth Elegy*, especially if it
is compared with the fresh spontaneity of the *Ninth*, bears the
mark of deliberate exertion. Admittedly, the images themselves
are taken from real life, and that concord between word and
experience, which any image must have, is still apparent. But
I cannot help feeling that these images do not emerge in the
text with that spontaneity which we are accustomed to in
Rilke's poetry. There seems to be more deliberate reflexion
here than is permissible even in poems such as the *Elegies*.

VI

Beyond the fairground lies the third realm which might be described by the words "reality" and "Nature". But first there is a kind of frontier zone to be crossed which provides a transition from the *un*real and *un*natural milieu of the town. This is a suburb which reminds us of the place where the acrobats displayed their arts in the *Fifth Elegy*.

> . . . Oh, but then just outside,
> behind the last hoarding, plastered with placards for "Deathless",
> that bitter beer that tastes quite sweet to its drinkers
> so long as they chew with it plenty of fresh distractions,—
> just at the back of the hoardings, just behind them, it's real!
>
> [34–38]

The fairground is surrounded by a wooden fence on which posters are stuck—"placards for 'Deathless' " advertising a brand of beer. This drink promises to satisfy the fairgoer's craving for an enjoyment undisturbed by death. This is a false deceptive satisfaction, for the beer itself is "bitter" and bad. If we bear in mind the significance that Death had for Rilke it will be clear that the sort of craving described here is a perversion of truth. The drinker, however, finds his beer deliciously "sweet" as long as he chews "with it plenty of fresh distractions". These serve to divert his attention from the bitter taste of the dregs.

It must be admitted that the allegory in this part of the *Elegy* is somewhat heavy and that the abstractions do not come to life. The placards advertising "Deathless" beer still belong to the fair. But "just outside, behind the last hoarding" there is something different. As is repeated more than once, only a single step is needed to take us away from this place into a new realm where "it's *real*". The vain noisy show of the fairground now gives place to a calmer more truthful scene.

> Children are playing, and lovers holding each other,—aside,
> gravely, in pitiful grass, and dogs are following nature. [39–40]

After being informed that 'reality' is now to be disclosed, the reader may be somewhat confused until he realizes that this image is intended to convey something partial and incomplete. This is certainly reality compared to the mere illusion of the fair. Admittedly there is "nature" here, but it is the spoilt nature which skirts the edge of a town, where waste paper and empty tins lie around on the sparse grass.

Here "children are playing"—children of the town's suburbs with pale faces. And lovers are "holding each other—aside, gravely", with a seriousness which springs from poverty. This poverty is heavily underlined in a final sentence which, after the description of the lovers and children, is almost an affront: "dogs are following nature".

VII

Suddenly there is a change of mood:

> The youth is drawn further on;   [41]

After this sudden introduction of "the youth" we gradually become conscious of the new realm which the *Elegy* is approaching. Who the "youth" is we do not learn. Perhaps he is the "better shot", described previously, who went "reeling after his luck" until he was drawn on, beyond the hoardings, to this place. Here there is poverty and distress but also reality and a vestige of nature, even if it is only the nature of dogs. The youth is led on still further—into the realm of true reality. The "reeling" fairground character has turned into a young man who is trusting, confident and filled with high hopes and aspirations. He can feel the relationship between the different realms as he is led from the third into the fourth.

> perhaps he's in love with a youthful
> Lament. . .   [41-42]

This is the explanation of why he is here: the youth is in love. There is a strange contrast between this young man and the wan lovers in the "pitiful grass". For his love is directed towards a "youthful Lament", one of those mythical beings who are composed of sorrow.

The figure of the "Lament" was foreshadowed already by the "inconsolable sisters" of the first stanza. The "Laments" are embodiments of sufferings which have been experienced in the past. There are generations of them, stretching over all periods of time. They inhabit whole regions of territory— strange countries situated in "the other relation". Yet their realm begins in this world, though it is unnoticed by the majority. Anyone who trusts himself to enter it is led further and further on into regions which are increasingly primeval and unearthly.

One of the *Sonnets* puts the figure of the Lament into sharper relief:[1]

> Only Praising's realm may Lamentation
> range in, naiad of the weeping spring;
> watching over our precipitation,
> till our tears are crystals, blazoning
>
> that same rock that bears the gates and altars.
> Round her quiet shoulders, as she broods,
> look, the dawn of an awareness falters
> she's the youngest of the sister-moods.
>
> Triumph *knows*, and Longing is admitting,—
> Lamentation learns still; nightly sitting,
> counts, with maiden-hands, old tribulation.
>
> Then, however inexpertly limned,
> lifts our voice in a constellation
> to the sky her breathing has not dimmed.

Here the "Lamentation" is a nymph—the numen of the spring which rises in the eyes—tears. Really, however, this spring comes from that "rock" or primeval stone which supports the "gates and altars", that is, the fundamental structures of existence. The Lamentation can only walk in "Praising's realm". In other words, grief must be surrounded by affirmation, for sorrow is only one element of life, the other being joy. The *Elegy* says the same thing later when it refers to the "source of Joy" which rises in the "mountains of Primal Pain". The Lamentation is the "youngest of the sister-moods"—the last impulse of the human heart to be awakened, after Triumph and Longing have been mastered. Lamentation is something which has to be learnt, or rather learnt again. For nowadays

---

[1] *Sonnets to Orpheus*, I. viii.

the human heart only knows of negative passive suffering, but is still not acquainted with the other kind of suffering which is positive and affirmative. To the question of whether Christianity accepted the fact of suffering Rilke would probably have replied: certainly Christianity did this, but *without* affirming it as an integral element of earthly life. Christianity did not regard suffering as a part of our existence which is related to joy as Death is to Life or the "ascending" to the "falling".[1]

Among the Laments in the *Elegy* there are young and old. But men have forgotten how to praise suffering affirmatively and must therefore learn this ancient art anew. The "youth" has already begun this task. His heart has discovered pain in all its beauty and depth of meaning. Only the qualifying word "perhaps" prepares us for the later disclosure that he has not understood deeply enough nor loved with sufficient fervour.

> He emerges behind her into the meadows, she says:
> 'A long way. We live out there. . . . .'   [42–43]

The Lament goes on in front of the youth who follows her until they reach the "meadows". This is real nature, open and fragrant. At the same time we must remember that this is part of the same mysterious realm which extends all the way from the town's suburbs to the silent primeval landscape of the "mountain-range" at the end of the *Elegy*.

The youth now catches up with the Lament. Apparently he questions her, for she tells him of the strange country which is her home and which lies "a long way . . . out there". It is clear that these words have no spacial sense but refer to a remoteness of dimension. At first they may seem confusing, for one might expect the appropriate direction in this "other relation" to be 'downwards' or 'inwards'. But we are not intended to confuse the home of the Laments with the depths of the Earth or Hades. Any suggestion of a subterranean realm here would result in a darkening of the horizon—a depreciation of the "other relation" which would be foreign to Rilke's intentions. For him the realm of the dead has nothing to do with the shades of the underworld or Hell. Death does not mean loss or deprivation but essential reality. Indeed it is *more* essential

---

[1] See the conclusion of the *Elegy*.

and more real than our own realm, only it is situated on the 'other side'. It is one of the two 'relations' which make up the 'world' in the true sense of the word. This is why the direction taken by the youth and the Lament is specifically *out*wards, not downwards.

> 'Where?' And the youth
> follows. He's touched by her manner. Her shoulder, her neck,—perhaps
> she comes of a famous stock?   [44–46]

Long experience with Rilke's works teaches us to pay attention to the smallest details. Thus it might be quite significant that the youth's first question, like the second reply of the Lament, is implied but not spoken. The conversation is broken up as if it took place in a strangely rarefied atmosphere, and this serves to bring out the mysterious character of this encounter between youth and Lament. Perhaps it also suggests that he is not sure of himself, that his love is not sufficiently strong and that he is ready to turn back. For the time being, however, he "follows", for he is "touched by her manner". He is moved by the sad intensity of her being. He sees the beauty of her neck and shoulders and respects her noble ancestry.

The plane of action is external and internal at the same time. The beauty of the Lament has awakened the youth's love. And his love now impels him away from the town and the fairground towards the realm of sorrow where the Lament dwells. But here his heart does not respond adequately to the call and it seems that his life will be deprived of sorrow's influence.

> But he leaves her, turns back,
> looks round, nods ... What's the use? She's just a Lament.
>   [46–47]

He now leaves the Lament who was ready to lead him towards reality and turns round. Clearly he is aware that in leaving her he is also losing the key to the value of life. So he "looks round, nods", but then goes back.

Essential reality now appears to be unreal to the youth. It is not worth while, he thinks, to embark on this adventure: "What's the use? She's just a Lament." She is just a creature

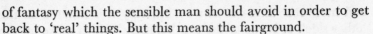

of fantasy which the sensible man should avoid in order to get back to 'real' things. But this means the fairground.

Here again we cannot avoid feeling a certain embarrassment. Sentences like "What's the use? She's just a Lament" do not ring true. The preceding passage, describing the meeting of the Lament with the youth and the whole possibility which it contained, was convincing enough—like a melancholy fairy-tale. But the two last sentences are sober prose.

At last the character of this strange realm is fully revealed:

> Only the youthfully-dead, in their first condition
> of timeless serenity, that of being weaned,
> follow her lovingly.   [48–50]

These words indicate that the youth is still one of the living. He was called away from the fairground and changed from a "reeling man" into a seeker of truth, not by Death, but by one of those encounters which sometimes make a man realize the futility of his life and give him a glimmering of essential reality. Then, however, the everyday world sweeps over him again and the vision disappears.

The passage which follows refers to the dead. But why, we may ask, only to the "youthfully dead"—girls and youths? The *Elegy* might be expected to deal with death in the widest sense. But what is left here of the grimness and hardness of death— those qualities which should not be obscured if the message of the *Elegies* is really as fundamental as it purports to be? Does it not seem that a romantic or aesthetic interest is getting the upper hand? However that may be, we are told that the Lament can only be understood properly by the "youthfully dead". They alone have youth's spirit of surrender which remains effective even in death. The *First Elegy* states that who-ever leaves this life must accustom himself to a new condition. Here we are told that those who have just entered this "con-dition" are receptive to the Lament's teaching: that suffering is positive in character; that suffering is fulfilled in death; and that the state of being dead is fruitful and full of meaning. Indeed, if we take into account the other *Elegies*, death is the only reality.

> Girls
> she awaits and befriends. Gently, she shows them
> what she is wearing. Pearls of Pain and the fine-spun
> Veils of Endurance.—Youths
> she walks with in silence.   [50–54]

The Lament behaves differently towards girls and youths.
She "befriends" the former, appealing to their feminine delight
in clothing and adornment. She "gently shows them what she
is wearing" and her attire proves to be appropriate to her
nature. Her "pearls" are of "Pain", for pearls are traditionally
associated with tears; she wears "fine-spun veils of endurance",
for "endurance", unlike loud complaint, has a silent enshroud-
ing quality. Towards youths the Lament is different. With
them she "walks in silence". Even in this realm where human
desires are out of place her presence fills them with a mysterious, painful love.

VIII

Now the landscape becomes more imposing as another figure
takes over the task of guiding the youth through the land of
the dead.

> But there, where they live, in the valley, one of the elder Laments
> takes to the youth when he questions her:—   [55–56]

This is the landscape of the Beyond, but it extends right back
to the here and now of our world. As we have seen, it was
possible to journey imperceptibly and freely from the fairground
of the town all the way to this valley of the Laments. And, as
becomes increasingly apparent, the landscape of death which
the youth sees after following the young Lament is not unlike
the earthly scene. For here too there are meadows, valleys,
mountains and later we shall encounter new images taken from
that country where Death had particular importance—ancient
Egypt.

The *Sonnets* also tell how the realm of the dead can become
effective in the land of the living. One way—the wrong one—is
through magic. But there is a right way too—that of translating
the Beyond into this world. At the point of transition stands
Orpheus who was granted the privilege of going across to beg

for Eurydice's liberty. He would have succeeded in bringing her back to life if the division between the two worlds had not caused him to doubt and look back.[1] The dead "mix their unused marrow with the clay" of our fields.[2] Into "all that we view" on earth Orpheus brings the "appearance" and the essential quality of the dead.[3] In the Winter the "mysterious turning-in of the earth" takes place, the inward swing of existence to the depths where "around the dead, in the pure withdrawal of the sap, courage is gathered together—the courage of future Springs". The realm of the dead is thus the counterpole in the rhythmic swing of existence, and Winter is the fountain-head of future Springs.[4] Even in human beings dead ancestors can affect the generation of the living so profoundly that the dead father of the *Fourth Elegy* was said to "be afraid" in the fear of the son.

The landscape of the *Elegy* must thus be considered as belonging to this world and to the Hereafter simultaneously. In this world it is the deeper layer of our experience; over there it becomes manifest, indeed predominant, as the realm of the dead. But as soon as Orpheus begins to sing, as soon as the message of the *Elegies* has been rightly understood and the unity of Here and Hereafter is believed in, as soon as sorrow and death have been absorbed into the same inward experience as life and happiness, when "happiness falls" but nevertheless remains happiness[5]—*then* the two realms merge into a 'whole' world of "deep Being".

To return to the text—while the landscape of the Beyond becomes more impressive the young girl leading the youth is replaced by "one of the elder Laments". Perhaps the "valley" which is described by the young Lament as their home is the same as that "gorge" which later leads into the "mountains of Primal Pain" (line 97 ff.) and where the traveller finally disappears at the end of the *Elegy*. The mountains represent the furthest reaches of the realm of death—a place of silent fulfilment.

[1] See "Orpheus, Eurydice, Hermes" in *Selected Works*, II, p. 188.
[2] *Sonnets to Orpheus*, I. xiv.
[3] *Ibid.*, I. vi.
[4] See "O Lacrimosa", *Later Poems*, p. 138.
[5] See the last line of the *Elegy*.

Here, however, we are still in the flat land and the elder
Lament is answering the questions of the youth:

—'We were once,'
she says, 'a great family, we Lamentations.   [56–57]

Here too a specifically elegiac tone is noticeable: sadness at
something great which has passed away—the lost power of the
Lamentations. To appreciate the different layers of meaning
here we must remember the chthonic character of early western
religion. More power was attributed to the darkness and depths
of the earth than to the brightness of the heavens. Hence
worship was focused on the earth's gods. Since the dead had
more reality than the living the whole temper of life was
coloured by an emotional awareness of dark mysteries and the
power of fatality or blood. At that time the Lamentations were
powerful. Then their power declined. We may perhaps general-
ize by saying that the further we go back in history the deeper
man's knowledge of life's tragedy seems to have been and the
greater his capacity to be stirred by the powers of fate and
death. Conversely, the further forward we travel in time the
more self-assured man becomes—the more confident and happy,
but also, according to the *Elegy*, the more superficial and
impious.

And now the effects of these changes are shown. The decline
in man's tragic sense on earth leads to the passing away of its
mythical forms in the Beyond. So the Lament does not merely
say: 'We are a great family but you have forgotten us.' She
says: "We were once a great family", meaning 'you used to keep
us in your minds, but now we are weak and you no longer
know about us.'

Our fathers
worked the mines in that mountain-range: among men
you'll find a lump, now and then, of polished original pain,
or of drossy petrified rage from some old volcano.
Yes, that came from there. We used to be rich.'   [57–61]

The idea of suffering and pain as essential elements of life
now takes on a deeper meaning. Pain becomes the "polished
original" stone of existence contained in the "mountain-range".
Here the Laments, personifications of suffering, used to exploit

the seams, extracting the tragic passions which were fundamental to man's consciousness in earlier times. The implied
meaning of this passage is that since the old workings were
abandoned the ore or stone which came from them has become
rare among men. Or perhaps we might say that since genuine
suffering has become uncommon among men the inhabitants
of the other world can no longer extract it from the mountains.

Only "now and then" do we find among men a "lump of
polished original pain" or "drossy petrified rage from some old
volcano". The passions which filled the legendary figures of old
have become diluted. Only here and there does one man behave
to another in such a way as to remind us of ancient times. Only
occasionally is human destiny as full of suffering as was that
of Oedipus, or one man turns on another with the sort of anger
which raged in the house of Atreus. Apart from these rare
cases the heart of man has become soft and weak.

IX

And lightly she leads him on through the spacious landscape
of Lamentation, shows him the temple columns, the ruins
of towers from which, long ago, Lords of the House of Lament
wisely governed the land.　　　　　　　　　　　　　　[62–65]

The guiding Lament leads the youth "lightly" on. This does
not mean that she does it without effort but describes the 'light'
movements of those who do not belong to the earthly sphere.[1]
She shows him the pillars of the ruined temples which still stand
upright and the "ruins of towers" in which the rulers of this
country, the "Lords of the House of Lament" once dwelt. This
strange landscape is not an autonomous region which exists in
its own right. It is a facsimile or 'double' of the earth. The
kingdom of the dead is continually sustained by the land of
the living, for everything in it was once alive. In the same way
life draws power and depth from death. So when the essential
and significant things of the earthly realm fall into decay and
when man loses his sense of the tragic, these things also decline
in the other realm. Conversely when the power of pain and

---

[1] See the conclusion of the *Fifth Elegy*.

suffering becomes weakened in the "other relation" their influence can no longer reach over here to us.

We must not approach this part of the *Elegy* in too dry and logical a spirit, for it is true that the "other relation" is the real one and that human experience has its roots there, since obviously all the living will some day be dead. The Beyond is the older primordial sphere and the future ultimate sphere at the same time. It is also true that whenever the 'inward' process takes place the Here and the Hereafter are absorbed into a unity of deeper Being. The *Elegy* repeats the same things in several ways and the reader must therefore accept the shifting pattern of its imagery—as indeed is appropriate in a visionary poem of this kind.

Besides the ruined temples and castles of this realm there is also vegetation:

> Shows him the tall
> Tear trees, shows him the fields of flowering Sadness
> (only as tender foliage known to the living);   [65–67]

There is a clear affinity between the "Tear trees" in the land of suffering and the weeping willows of our own world. These trees with their falling branches express a mood of grief or mourning. In the *Elegy* they also appear to be trees of legend with tears actually dropping from their branches. The tree as such is of course a mythical archetype, a primal form which combines roof, pillar and foundation at the same time. It unites the depths of the earth and the heights of heaven. It towers up motionless yet alive, centuries old perhaps but renewing itself each year. Its fruits, ripened by sap from the depths of the earth, symbolize all that is precious and beautiful. Such thoughts as these seem to have prompted Rilke to write his poem called "Lament" in 1914, just before the outbreak of war:[1]

> Now, though, my triumph-tree is breaking,
> breaking in storm is my gradual
> triumph-tree.
> Loveliest in my invisible
> landscape, making me better
> known to invisible angels.

[1] See *Selected Works*, II, p. 306.

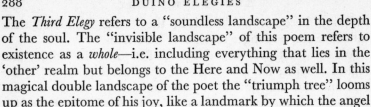

The *Third Elegy* refers to a "soundless landscape" in the depth of the soul. The "invisible landscape" of this poem refers to existence as a *whole*—i.e. including everything that lies in the 'other' realm but belongs to the Here and Now as well. In this magical double landscape of the poet the "triumph tree" looms up as the epitome of his joy, like a landmark by which the angel can recognize him.

There are fields here, too, planted with "flowering Sadness". Whereas the trees express the power of great sorrow, the smaller plants refer to the milder form of grief—sadness. The sentence in parentheses states that the "fields of Sadness" are only known to the living in the form of "tender foliage". This is because "sadness" does not flower into full bloom on earth but only reaches a stage of green unripeness. This is yet another reminder that the two realms overlap. What exists there is known here as well, but only in a less developed form. The sadness which we know here is like "tender foliage" compared to the luxuriant vegetation of the real plant.

> shows him the pasturing herds of Grief,—and, at times,
> a startled bird, flying straight through their field of vision,
> scrawls the far-stretching screed of its lonely cry.—   [68–70]

In this *Elegy* pain or suffering is conceived of as the basic force of life—the stuff of which all existence consists. Hence it may be projected into the most varied phenomena—meadows, valleys, mountains, castles and temples, families and lords, trees and plants. Here it is in the beasts of the field and the birds of the air. To recapitulate, this means that everything that is found on earth in the form of life is also found there—in the form of suffering and death. The same existence runs through both realms but in different ways. Our world only becomes whole when these two ways become one.

Sometimes a "startled bird" flies "straight through their field of vision". It does not rise aloft, but skims over the surface of the earth like a partridge or pheasant. As the herds look up they see the bird and *feel* its flight at the same time through their field of vision. Again we note the familiar intermingling of the objective sphere of Being and the subjective sphere of life. The figure of the bird's flight appears as a fragment of writing—the "far-stretching screed of its lonely cry". This is

a translation of the bird's cry into optical terms. The sight of
the animals is so sensitive that they can 'see' the acoustic shape
in the visual pattern. A similar transposition takes place later
with another bird—the owl—but in the reverse direction. The
whole passage suggests a mysterious alien existence.

Meanwhile the day has advanced and it has become evening
—yet another reminder that everything in our world is also to
be found there, but in a different form.

> At evening she leads him on to the graves of the longest
> lived of the House of Lament, the sibyls and warners. [71–72]

The youth and the Lament now visit the tombs of the great
ones of the realm. These are now dead—and this means 'dead'
in a double sense, for in one way everything in this realm is
already in a state of "being dead".[1] But the great ones are dead
in another way—like fallen temples compared to those which
are undamaged, or like a ruined castle compared to those which
are still occupied by their lords. The theme of the *Elegy* is the
same as before: the decline in value of suffering and pain while
'happiness' is in the ascendant, though it is a superficial
"bedizened" happiness produced by success at the fairground.
A new life is taking shape in which everything is practical,
efficient and hygienic but lacking destiny and high purpose.
It is the same form of life which the *Ninth Elegy* describes as an
"imageless act".

The great ones lie in their graves, doubly dead. Their very
deathly power has died—death within death. These were the
mythical lords of the land—the "longest lived of the House of
Lament", including "sibyls" and "warners"—figures like Old
Testament prophets who exposed the guilt of their contem-
poraries and warned them of the disaster which would ensue.

> But, night approaching, they move more gently, and soon
> moon-like emerges the all-
> guarding sepulchral stone. Twin-brother to that on the Nile,
> the lofty Sphinx, the taciturn chamber's gaze.   [73–76]

Night falls and the steps of the two travellers become appropriately quiet, awe-struck and expectant. Before long they are
confronted by something new and impressive. It is that strange

---

[1] See *First Elegy*, line 77.

statue or structure which does not fall properly into any
aesthetic category, but which is the most powerful expression
of death's presence among the living that we know. This is the
Sphinx—a "sepulchral stone" which 'guards all things'. It has
the countenance of a "taciturn chamber" for it contains a
hidden room where the king is at rest. The mysterious inaccessibility of this inner tomb is reflected in the immobile face
on the lion's body.

This Sphinx in the world of the dead is called the "twin-
brother to that on the Nile". This seems to mean that it is
different from the Sphinx on earth though closely related to
it. In his letter to von Huléwicz Rilke wrote that the "Land
of Lamentation, through which the elder Lament leads the
dead youth, is not to be *identified* with Egypt . . . but is, as it
were, a reflection of the land of the Nile in the desert clarity
of the dead person's consciousness".[1] Thus the Sphinx of Egypt
has objective reality. In the Land of Lamentation it is part of
the consciousness of the dead youth. The next three lines
describe how impressed the dead are by the "regal head", so
we are probably justified in regarding both Rilke's Sphinx and
the whole of the other realm as projections of human consciousness in death. There is indeed a close connection between the
description of the Land of Lamentation and the 'inward' sphere
where things are transformed by the human heart. What the
dead see—this whole landscape with its trees and animals and
mountains—really belongs to the "deep Being" of the world.
In the *Elegy* these things are 'externalized' anew so that they
can be viewed clearly from without.

If we consider the passage from Rilke's letter together with
the *Elegy's* 'graphic' description of the bird's cry—and later the
'tonal' shape of the owl's flight—we shall see the difference
between Rilke's view of the hereafter and that of the ancients.
In the *Seventh Elegy* the poet was overcome by the glory of the
stars in the summer sky and cried out, "Oh, to be dead at last
and endlessly know them". Being dead thus means more than
being alive. Death offers access to the inexhaustible fund of

[1] Magda von Hattingberg reproduces in her memoirs part of a letter which
Rilke wrote from Egypt, giving an account of the experience which underlay this
passage in the *Elegy*. The same vision of the Sphinx recurs in the letter, down to
the very details of feelings, description and style. It is significant that he writes
there too of the owl's flight and its translation into acoustic terms.

"deep Being" where the whole abundance of the world has become 'inward'. After death we shall appreciate this with all our senses in a way which would be inconceivable on earth. The relation between this view and that of Christianity will be dealt with at the end of our interpretation.

> And they start at the regal head that has silently poised,
> for ever, the human face
> on the scale of the stars. [77–79]

The light of the sun differentiates objects on the earth equally from one another, but the moonlight throws the Sphinx into sharp relief and accentuates the grandeur of its stone structure. The spectacle is so impressive that both the Lament and the youth "start at the regal head". They stand and stare in wonder, overwhelmed by the sight of this crowned head resting on a lion's body which has "silently poised, *for ever*, the human face on the scale of the stars". Here the Sphinx is comparable to the constellations of Andromeda or Orion in the sky, for it embodies something transient and earthly in cosmic and eternal form. It exalts the human face to the same level as the stars.

> His sight, still dizzy with early death,
> can't take it in. [80–81]

Unlike the Lament, the youth is not equal to the sight of the Sphinx, for he has just left the land of the living. His strength fails him until he gradually adjusts himself to his new condition and the powers which confront him in the "other relation". We are reminded of what was said in the *First Elegy* about the dead: "It's hard, being dead, and full of retrieving before one begins to perceive a little eternity."

Nevertheless, even at this stage, the youth's vision is mysteriously heightened. Whereas on earth the faculty of sight is always deflected, blurred or merely a passive mirroring of the object, over there it becomes a *power*. The eye's action is twofold: it 'takes in' what it sees outside and it also reveals what lies within a person. This is why we use the same word to describe how we 'look at' someone and also how we 'look to' other people. It is through the eye that we receive the visual impression of what we observe and it is also through the eye that we transmit the power of our inner being to the other person's

T*

heart. So the eye is a focal point and a source of light at the same time. In the realm of the dead this positive 'transmitting' action of the sight is particularly strong.

> But her gaze
> frightens an owl from behind the pschent. And the bird,
> brushing, in slow down-skimming, along the cheek,
> the one with the ripest curve,
> faintly inscribes on the new
> death-born hearing, as though on the double
> page of an opened book, the indescribable outline. [81–87]

"Pschent" is the name of the crown of the Egyptian royal house, symbolizing the unity of the Northern and Southern kingdoms. This is the double crown on the Sphinx's head behind which the owl sits until it is frightened from its nest by the powerful 'ray of sight'. What follows is perhaps the most striking image of the whole *Elegy*. Flying down from its eyrie "in slow down-skimming", the owl skirts "along the cheek, the one with the ripest curve", i.e. the cheek of the Sphinx which embodies the human face in its "ripest" or most expressive form. We recall here the earlier reference to a bird's flight in which the creature's cry changed into an optical impression. Here the reverse takes place as the owl "faintly inscribes" the "indescribable outline" (of the cheek) onto the hearing. The "new death-born hearing" is so sensitive that it can detect both the silent beating of the owl's wings and the line of its flight— or an acoustic equivalent—as it passes along the Sphinx's cheek. The audibility of the owl's line of flight, like the visibility of the bird's cry described above, suggests an acute sensitivity of eye and ear which transcends all the normal limitations of the senses. This illustrates the larger thesis of the *Elegies* that the world can only be fully experienced in the realm of the dead.

The stanza concludes with a purely optical image: the outline is inscribed "on the double page of an opened book". It is perhaps not too fanciful to interpret the two pages of the open book as the ears which hear the course of the owl's flight. The outline is called "indescribable" because it cannot be conveyed in visual terms. It can only be heard by the "death-born hearing". Like the "untellable things" in the *Ninth Elegy* and the "indescribable carpet" at the end of the *Fifth*, so here the "indescribable outline" is intended to convey the transcendental nature of this realm of death where sense impressions have ceased to be limited and fallible.[1]

> And, higher, the stars. New ones. Stars of the Land of Pain.
> Slowly she names them: "There,
> look: the *Rider*, the *Staff*, and that fuller constellation
> they call *Fruitgarland*. Then, further, towards the Pole:
> *Cradle, Way, The Burning Book, Doll, Window.*
> But up in the southern sky, pure as within the palm
> of a consecrated hand, the clearly-resplendent *M*,
> standing for Mothers. . . . . "   [88–95]

Above the lofty figure of the Sphinx stand the stars—"new ones", unknown to us on earth. The Lament "slowly" gives their names as she points them out to the youth. These names may have a peculiar relevance to the realm of the dead or perhaps they simply stand for a number of forms taken from real life which are full of symbolical meaning.[2] Particular emphasis is laid on one star—the "clearly-resplendent *M*" which stands in the "southern sky" and is described as "pure as within the palm of a consecrated hand". If we look at the lines on the palm of our left hand and join the second line to the third with an upward stroke we shall see the clear shape of a letter M. This shape, according to the *Elegy*, stands for "Mothers".

X

Finally the companionship of this journey comes to an end:

> But the dead must go on, and, in silence, the elder Lament
> brings him as far as the gorge
> where it gleams in the moonlight,—
> there, the source of Joy.   [96–99]

"The dead must go on", for they are driven on, not by any external compulsion, but by the logic of their condition. The Lament feels this necessity and points out his way to the youth. She is silent, for words would serve no purpose. She leads him

---

[1] Compare the essay "Primal Sound" in Rilke, *Selected Works*, I, pp. 51–56.
[2] The constellation of the rider or horseman also occurs in the *Sonnets to Orpheus* (I. xi): "Look at the sky. Is no 'Horse-man' reckoned there in starry outline?"

into the heart of the country—"as far as the gorge" which leads into the mountains. Here the "source of Joy" has its beginnings, "gleaming in the moonlight". This brook which springs in the mountains of Pain symbolizes real "Joy", not mere pleasure or good cheer, just as real "Pain" is different from annoyance, irritation or torment. The two are closely related, for the deepest joy springs from pain or suffering which has been accepted, endured and overcome. True Joy is also capable of absorbing pain into itself. In Rilke's view of life these two realms belong essentially together, like day and night, Summer and Winter or Life and Death. And since for him the centre of gravity lies in the Land of Pain this is where Joy has its source. It is perhaps typical of the elegiac form to link the two in this way, as Friedrich Hölderlin does in his beautiful poem "Menon's Laments for Diotima": "I smile in amazement, Finding such feelings of bliss here in the centre of grief".[1]

The *Elegy* continues:

> With awe
> she names it, says 'Among men
> it's a carrying stream'.   [99–101]

The spring of Joy which rises here only flows abundantly "among men"—in the other 'relation' of daylight. It is only on earth, under the light of the sun, that Joy can become a "carrying stream".[2] There, if the order of things permits, Joy may become capable of "carrying" or supporting life. But its fountain-head lies in the beyond.

The next two lines are full of deep sadness:

> They stand at the foot of the range.
> And there she embraces him, weeping.   [102–103]

The Lament loves the youth, but only in the way that a mythical being can love—without hope, since there can be no personal communion between her and a human being. She is

---

[1] See Hölderlin, *Selected Poems*, p. 85.
[2] We must not demand of poetry the consistency of philosophy, otherwise we might well ask whether Rilke's 'other' realm, where *everything* is supposed to exist in its internalized form, does not also contain a sun. In fact, since we are told that evening and night are approaching, it must be presumed that the day preceded them. But it is significant that the sun is not mentioned. The moon, however, casts its magic light on everything and the constellations stand out clearly in the sky.

a personification rather than a person, and the youth's relation
to her is rather like that of a brave fighter to the idea of courage.
The Lament is a mythical character whose natural element is
Being. But Man, by contrast, possesses a heart in which he feels
the abundance of possibilities which lie open to him; he also
has the power to make decisions and a capacity for repentance.
This is why all the relationships between human beings and
creatures of the other world, as described in legends and fairy-
tales, are tragic. The above lines contain something of this
tragedy, unless the "weeping" is merely the natural response
of a being who belongs wholly to this "Land of Pain" like the
"Tear trees" and the "pasturing herds of Grief".

The "Lament" is the youth's guide through a specific area
of the other realm. The dead youth must now pass beyond this
to his final goal.

> Lone he ascends to the mountains of Primal Pain.
> And never once does his step sound from the soundless fate.
>
> [104–105]

What the youth finds in these furthest reaches of the other
realm is not stated in the *Elegy*, but presumably it is the fulfilment of his deathly state. Previously the youth's road still lay
in front of him and he had to accustom himself gradually to
his new condition. In the mountains of Primal Pain he at last
becomes one of the "endlessly dead" (line 106) and "endlessly
knows . . . all the stars".[1] Beyond this nothing more can be
said about his condition or its implications, for this is a "soundless fate"—a state of Being without words. He is in a place
where not even the sound of a footstep can be heard and the
Lament herself falls silent.

The ninth and tenth stanzas contain only two lines each,
whereas each of the two concluding stanzas contain four. This
arrangement of the lines in the original manuscript, although
it is not found in the standard edition of Rilke's collected works,
gives the conclusion of the *Elegy* its proper weight. The last
words of this poem are like a final seal which has been set on
the whole cycle of *Duino Elegies*.

[1] See *Seventh Elegy*, line 28.

Before the last lines are examined, however, something must be said about one peculiar feature which is apparent through Rilke's whole description of the land of the dead—the infinite loneliness. When we read in line 96 of the *Elegy* that "the dead", i.e. in this case the youth, "must go on", we cannot help wondering exactly where all the dead *are*—the countless other beings who have passed over into the realm beyond. We may recall the hosts of dead shades in the *Odyssey*, in the sixth canto of Vergil's *Aeneid* or on the shore of Dante's Acheron, where the description makes us feel that the dead must be countless in number. Rilke's purpose is, however, not to depict masses of people or souls. In this *Elegy* he seeks to suggest the other world through the single experience of an individual, for in matters of existential importance the position of one person is more revealing than a thousand people together in a mass. There is yet another difference which strikes us if we compare Rilke's description of the land of the dead with others from eastern or mediaeval western literature, and especially the work of Dante. Rilke does not try to build up a cosmology of the other world which would reflect certain scales of value and show the fulfilment of history. There is nothing here which might suggest a system. The reader simply follows the journey of an anonymous individual through a landscape which, in the strangest possible way, derives from the landscape of the earth itself.

The *Tenth Elegy* belongs to the same category as other poems which depict the world of the dead in the form of a journey. But it also displays peculiar features of its own. It describes first the transition of a *living* human being out of this world—out of the "reeling" state in which the youth first found himself—and this transition seems to take place almost by accident or chance. Then, with abrupt suddenness, we read of the *dead* youth finding his way towards *death's* perfect fulfilment.

Anything which might be associated with moral or religious responsibility, or with judgment or punishment, is absent. Dying appears as a process which takes place within the totality of our world. Death becomes the counterpart of life, or rather, it becomes life's true reality. All this is expressed in the *Elegy's* prevailing mood of deep loneliness. One youth, accompanied by one mythical creature, wanders through a strange country which becomes increasingly remote and silent until neither sound nor information can reach us.

The ideas which recur again and again in the *Elegy* are those of *suffering*, *death* and *grief*. Indeed the feelings or conditions which are represented by the Laments in their Land of Pain have such a positive character that they seem more real than happiness, pleasure and life.

XI

The poet now pronounces his concluding words which round off this *Elegy* and the whole cycle:

> And yet, were they waking a symbol within us, the endlessly dead,
> look, they'd be pointing, perhaps, to the catkins, hanging
> from empty hazels, or else
> to the rain downfalling on dark soil-bed in early Spring.—
> [106–109]

The "endlessly dead" are those who have gone the whole way and who attain the ultimate limits of the other world. They are remote and inaccessible. They know the final meaning of existence, but there is no word to express this meaning, for their fate is "soundless". If, however, we could question them and the dead could "wake a symbol within us", then they would perhaps point to the "catkins, hanging from empty hazels". The hazel bush blooms in the early part of the year when it is still "empty" of leaves. Its blossom—the male—does not rise but hangs down. And though this 'hanging down' is like a gesture of grief it also germinates the fruit which is to come. The second symbol is that of the "rain downfalling on dark soil-bed in early Spring". This too is a downward movement into darkness, but from it springs the seed of the future.[1]

> And we, who think of *ascending*
> happiness, then would feel
> the emotion that almost startles
> when happiness *falls*.
> [110–113]

[1] Compare the lines from a poem by Rilke already quoted:
"Those intimate evenings! We rained,
earth and I, softly and Aprilly, into the womb."
See above, p. 85.

What could we learn from these "symbols"? We normally
associate happiness with the idea of rising, with success or with
flowering in complete freedom. But if we understood the above
images correctly we should be aware of the contrary sense of
happiness. "Almost startled", we would feel the mystery of that
happiness which "falls": when joy turns into grief but still
remains joy; when life dies but accepts death because in
'falling' it brings forth new life. Both the rise and the fall are
merged in the larger all-embracing Whole of existence.

XII

We have tried in the foregoing to define Rilke's view of
Death as it is expressed in the *Elegies*. The question still to be
answered is what relation this has to the Christian view. To
distinguish between the two is clearly a duty which is all the
more urgent amid the conceptual chaos of our time. Apart
from this, such a distinction will assist our understanding of
Rilke's own thoughts, for he came from a Catholic background
and this fact has never been given due importance. For although
he declared in his letter to von Huléwicz that he was "withdrawing himself more and more passionately" from Christianity,
even if we take these words literally, there still remain traces
and echoes of the Christian message everywhere in his work—
quite apart from the fact that any repudiation always depends
on the thing repudiated and can only be properly understood
from it.

The poetic images of the *Elegies* are impressive and full of
affirmative power—but they deprive Death of its real seriousness.[1] For one essential feature of Death is that man is incapable
of affirming or approving of it—Death *as such*. Any affirmation
of that kind inevitably lacks conviction.

We may leave aside here the oversimplifications of materialism. There remains something paradoxical about the way in
which men come to terms with Death in the light of their
knowledge and experience. On the one hand we know that
Death is quite inevitable, but on the other we cannot help

---

[1] There is no need to emphasize that we are not questioning Rilke's *personal*
seriousness here—in the way that he envisaged and experienced his own death.

protesting against this very thing that cannot be averted. This does not mean simply the impulse of self-preservation, but a deep-rooted consciousness that death has no proper place in a meaningful pattern of existence. Nor does this protest imply a refusal to endure death. Willingness to face death is a part of the moral life, like a readiness to risk one's life for an idea or the people one loves. In such a case as this a man might argue with himself as follows: It is quite in order for me to endure my approaching death bravely, or even for me to accept death voluntarily for the sake of something greater than myself. It is the whole fact of my *having* to die which is unacceptable. This may seem fantastic in the light of modern science. But it is only when the above paradox has been accepted that death shows its true character. Despite all the poems and wise words of writers and philosophers any man who is mentally alive cannot help feeling that death brings not only destruction but also humiliation. To be a person at all implies *personality*—that is, self-possession and responsibility for one's actions in a unity of mind and body. The destruction of this unity in death means ontological disgrace.

Repeated attempts have been made to get rid of this feeling. Philosophical naturalism in all its forms dismisses it as a delusion, in so far as it is concerned with this subtle phenomenon at all. According to it the individual is a biological creature whose death is taken for granted like the death of any other animal. But in fact man differs from the animal in his whole structure and behaviour so that death too means something altogether different for him. The 'spiritualist' philosophers on the other hand maintain that the essential part of man is his spirit, which, they say, is indestructible and does not enter into the fullness of existence until after death. The only problem then is how the spirit ever became imprisoned in the body in this way and how its liberation should be achieved. In fact, of course, the real human being does not consist of pure spirit at all. He is made up of a body and a spirit joined together. And the human personality is not merely the spiritual part of this unity but that whole independent body-soul entity which is achieved through the spirit.

The contradictions which are inherent in Man's condition cannot be resolved within the closed circle of our normal

human experience. The only satisfactory answer is the one
provided by divine revelation which states that God created
the world and also guides the course of history.[1] By exalting
Man and setting him apart, God made him a person and placed
him in the context of a destiny which has its roots, not in Nature,
but in Freedom. God raised Man up to a state which he would
never have attained alone and which also satisfied his innermost
longing—that of not having to die. This is dealt with in the
early chapters of *Genesis*. But *Genesis* also says that this state
of life was made dependent on Man's obedience. The account
of the Tree of Knowledge sums up Man's freedom to obey or
disobey and to choose Good or Evil.

This is not the place to explore the Biblical story with its
many and profound layers of meaning. As was stated in an
earlier chapter, there is a modern misapprehension that Adam
in his original innocence represents primitive natural Man, and
that he emerged into a state of maturity in eating the forbidden
fruit. From this point of view the freedom from death which
was promised to him appears to be part of a fairy-tale or mere
childish fantasy. In fact Man was intended to assert his dominion
over the forces of life, but in a correct relationship to God. He
was not forbidden to seek knowledge but was commanded to
acquire it by obediently recognizing God's supremacy. The
prospect of freedom from death was dependent on the preservation of a harmonious relationship with the absolute. Of course
Man's life was destined to end, for it has a shape of its own,
and every shape reaches fulfilment at its conclusion. But the
end of his life was not meant to be Death as we understand
it today, nor in that form which determines our modern attitude
to life. Exactly how his life was meant to be completed cannot
of course be said, since the original possibility was not realized.

The condition of Man today is not 'natural'. But the reason
for his 'unnatural' state is not that he is essentially 'spiritual'
rather than physical and organic. The reason is that his existence is historically determined—i.e. it is determined by free

---

[1] *Genesis* i–iii. It may be objected that the problems of earthly existence should
not be treated from a point of view which is *itself* for many people 'problematical'.
Yet even if we regard the belief in revelation simply as a phenomenon in the
history of thought it still discloses a vast fund of human experience. Hence we
should be able to take the content of revelation as a working hypothesis and discover how much light it throws on man's attitude to death.

decisions, the first of which was the choice of Evil made at the very beginning of human history.

This is the root of the paradox which makes our attitude to death such a puzzle. We know that Death *is*—and yet should *not be*. It is unavoidable, but for us it has not the natural inevitability which it has for the animal. It is rather the historical consequence of human action. And this provides the foundation on which a right attitude to Death can be built. Mindful of his first God-given mission, Man still affirms his protest against Death; but he also accepts it as an expiation in the knowledge that it gives a new meaning to life.

The way in which Christianity defines the nature of immortality is as follows. Immortality is promised for eternity, in the form of *human*, not merely spiritual existence. Immortality is more than a consequence of our indestructible spiritual core, for it springs from that process which, in religious terms, is called the Resurrection—the assumption of a new corporeal state which transcends the earthly form. This resurrection will take place at the end of history, just as the offence against God took place at the beginning. Between the two, however, lies the grace of redemption which alone gives us a right view of Death and enables us to overcome it.

All this formed a body of living knowledge in the Middle Ages. But modern Man is trying to destroy it. The radical protest against Death is now being displaced by a variety of techniques for postponing Death. Or else, unable to avert Death, Man tries to repudiate Death in the forms of his burial customs, memorials, etc. Attempts are also made to make Death acceptable, either as a natural necessity, or as an occasion for heroism or as part of a dionysian absorption into the Universe.

The most recent form which acceptance of Death has assumed can only be called a capitulation. To a large extent Man has renounced his protest against Death because he is no longer equal to the conflict which it imposes on him. He has thus surrendered an essential part of his ontological dignity— an event which is closely bound up with the influence of biology and the social sciences on our view of existence.

As far as Rilke's own views are concerned, he himself called his doctrine of Death, together with his doctrine of Love, the principal message of the *Elegies*. He conforms to modern trends of thought to the extent that he renounces the Christian protest against Death, rejects the idea of Death as an atonement and also makes Death into a necessary element of human existence as a whole. But Rilke goes beyond the modern view by considering the realm of the dead as real and important for our world—by attributing to this realm a special meaning of its own within the universe. His conception of the dead and their existence has a peculiar intensity which brings it close to the ideas found in mythical religions. But his view is clearly coloured by occult experiences as well.

There is a close connection between Rilke's doctrine of Death and his doctrine of Love. Both are tenable only if we ignore human personality. For nobody can call Death the "friendly inspiration of the Earth" if he knows the meaning of the word 'person'—any more than he can believe that the climax of love is attained when both the subject and the object have been excluded.

POSTSCRIPT

THIS book is the result of a preoccupation with the *Duino Elegies* which has lasted many years. Despite the pressure of much other work Rilke's poetry has continued to engage my interest for a variety of reasons. There was the beauty of the poems themselves and there was the pleasure of interpretation as such, which in the case of the *Elegies* was particularly rewarding. But the chief reason for my interest was philosophical. For 'poetry', no matter how we may define the word, always serves to make an experience or a thing—or perhaps human destiny— more meaningful and more clear. In poetry those things in our existence which seem confused or obscure are drawn together into patterns which make them alive in such a way as, to quote the *Ninth Elegy*, "never the things themselves hoped so intensely to be". Real poetry is an affirmation, not simply of what the poet feels or thinks, but also of what *is*.

This is the assumption made by a philosopher before he turns to a poetic work in search of answers to his questions. In ancient times and in the Middle Ages men were convinced—just as the more sensitive minds of today are convinced—that the words of a poet reveal greater depths of truth than could be seen through our own observation. It follows as a matter of course that we must not only ask the poet what he wants to say about life, but also whether what he says is true. This is the conviction which has been my guide in the foregoing interpretation and I hope that my quest has not been altogether unrewarded.

There is one feature running through all the *Elegies* which should be emphasized here in conclusion. This is the dangerous tendency to deny the value of the human person. In this matter Rilke does not speak for himself alone. He is the spokesman of our time. Although he himself was not necessarily conscious of it, his poetry reveals something which has been going on since the end of the First World War—the loss of our sense of personality. The signs of the times have indicated, not just now

303

and again but repeatedly and consistently, with all the spontaneity of a genuine symptom, that the human personality is in danger. This is of great significance, particularly today.

As his whole life shows, Rilke was one of the most thoroughgoing individualists of modern times. He could never bring himself to accept any ties or bonds finally and wholeheartedly. He always made reservations or left alternatives open to himself. His life was a long journey from place to place. His relations with people were numerous but never wholly committed him.

Although his poetry owed something to the past and gave something to the future, there remains something singular about his poetic language. Any attempt to take his style as a model is doomed to failure. It is only in Rilke's own work that we tolerate his peculiar treatment of grammar and syntax, his practice of divorcing words from their normal usage and giving them new associations. And even in Rilke we only accept these things under protest. For although his use of language has opened up new possibilities of expression it has also had a destructive effect. The new frequencies which he sets in motion and the light which he throws on hidden places are to a large extent the product of sacrificial fires which devoured something intrinsic in the structure—one is tempted to say the *dignity*—of language. This is why any would-be poet in search of a teacher may find one in Mörike or Goethe, but must be warned against Rilke.

This most consistent of all individualists—and here we approach the central problem of this very problematical poet—tends to deprive the individual personality of its meaning. He calls into question the integrating centre of life, the fountain-head of all judgments and decisions, the very foundation of everything we call character and integration. He was such an individualist that he objectivized his own personality and finally regarded it as a disturbing factor. The *Fourth Elegy* makes the monstrous statement that we spoil the pure relation of life "by our mere existence".

What is the significance of this tendency at a time when the world is so much under the sway of impersonal forces? We must remember that every process requires a pole and a counterpole. There can be no assertion of the mass-will at the expense of the individual, unless the individual is prepared to surrender himself. The totality or mass can only triumph—as it is doing at this hour of history—if the individual wants to be relieved of his self, if the distinction between *I* and *It* or *I* and *We* is obscured, and if human dignity, responsibility and freedom are all felt to be simply troublesome and perplexing.

Modern man has asserted his autonomy in all realms of life. His attitudes and his actions depend more and more on himself alone. Nietzsche carried this tendency to its logical conclusion by proclaiming that man was now mature enough to take over all those decisions and responsibilities which, in his former stage of tutelage, he had vested in a deity. But in future man would be his own final authority, with the power and the obligation of finding and fixing his own norms and values.

This was untruth—existential untruth pure and simple—as was shown by the destructive strain which his autonomy imposed on man in practice. The strain did not result from the *degree* of freedom which he now enjoyed but was inherent in his new position. For with his autonomy man assumed rights which were not his and responsibilities which he could not bear. As a result his position proved untenable and laid itself open to perversion. Between the two World Wars it became clear that presumptuous demands and exaggerated responsibility readily turn into their opposites. After proclaiming that he was master of his self and hence lord of existence, man began to weary of his own claims. But instead of reverting to his own true character he then adopted an attitude of surrender. Having rejected the rule of God and the authority divinely appointed on earth, he abandoned himself to totalitarianism.

The latter is utterly different from *authority*. Real authority, despite its excessive zeal in individual cases, depends on freedom and makes claims on the conscience. But totalitarianism repudiates freedom and asserts itself by violence. Revolution and dictatorship spring from the same roots and both deny the value of the human person. They are the evil parallels of that genuine antithesis, freedom and authority, both of which take the person as a starting-point.

The over-burdening of modern 'autonomous' man creates

an empty space which is soon filled by totalitarian forces. More than that—the empty space *attracts* these forces, for life, like Nature, is quick to fill the vacuum which it abhors. The same gaping void is revealed in the poetry of Rilke, a man to whom any kind of dictatorship would have been anathema.